The Emerald Covenant

By
Michael E. Morgan

Dawn Trader Books, LLC, Scottsdale, AZ

First Edition: Copyright © 1996 by Michael E. Morgan
Second Edition: Copyright © 2007 by Michael E. Morgan

All rights reserved, including the right to reproduce this work in any form whatsoever, without permission in writing from the author, except for brief passages in connection with a review.

For information write:
DawnTrader Books, LLC
34522 N Scottsdale Rd.
Scottsdale, Arizona 85266

If you are unable to order this book from your local bookseller, you may order directly from Amazon.com or the publisher. Quantity discounts for organizations are available.

ISBN 978-1-7322981-5-6 (paper)

10 9 8 7 6 5 4 3 2 1

DawnTrader Books, LLC

DawnTrader Books, LLC serves to facilitate the spreading of spiritual truths and wisdom in books for all of the people in the world at a time when little of what would be called wisdom still exists. The world has grown harsh, crass and bent on materialistic pursuits. With saber rattling and actual military conflicts raging, the instability of financial and political systems threatens life as we know it. There is little for anyone to count on in the way of real support and the all but forgotten sense of the real meaning of life as well as, the heart felt values that were once held in high esteem. DawnTrader Books, LLC seeks after the lost and buried treasures that still exist in the world. We serve to refresh the public mind of what is worth seeking after, true adventures and the exaltation of the spirit through that which is written down in books which, offers hope for a better life here on Earth.

Contents

Author's Preface..Page 8
Prologue..Page 10
Chapter 1, Shattered illusions..Page 15
Chapter 2, The High Road..Page 30
Chapter 3, Loose Ends..Page 45
Chapter 4, Low Road...Page 50
Chapter 5, Wake Up Call...Page 60
Chapter 6, Up In Smoke..Page 70
Chapter 7, Proving Grounds...Page 79
Chapter 8, Master of Fire..Page 107
Chapter 9, Serving Two Masters.....................................Page 118
Chapter 10, Pilgrimage to the Sun..................................Page 132
Chapter 11, The Trial..Page 153
Chapter 12, Grand Canal of Light...................................Page 173
Chapter 13, Long Labors End..Page 194
Chapter 14, The Darkness Passes..................................Page 210
Chapter 15, The Pilgrimage to the Moon........................Page 230
Chapter 16, Ascent on Delphi..Page 254
Chapter 17, Beyond the Ring of Fire...............................Page 269
Chapter 18, Fire and Ice...Page 284
Chapter 19, The Cornerstone Revealed.........................Page 303
Epilogue..Page 312
Glossary..Page 326

Author's Preface

This book's story isn't over yet. It's just beginning and is still going on. I've stopped the action long enough to tell you about what's happening, somewhat like a live action news report.

The people you'll read about are ordinary people like you and me but in extraordinary circumstances. I've changed some of their names to offer the participants some measure of privacy despite this exposure.

I am the author of this adventure, and yet I am a participant as well. I am probably one of the least gullible people you'll ever meet. My engineering background has not made me rigid, but it has trained me to be logical and discerning. Although I like to think of myself as reasonable and sensible, much of what you will read will hardly seem reasonable or sensible. I would scarcely believe it myself, if I hadn't experienced it firsthand! The story is absolutely true and describes how ordinary people decided to shift from their normal experience of life to extraordinary adventure.

There is so much self-help information out there from which to choose, and much of it can be contradictory. It reminds me of going to a new restaurant in New York. When the menu is large, the decisions can be agonizing, especially if you're not sure what you want or need to eat. If you're like I am, your arms go into the air and you ultimately rely on a friend's good recommendation.

I think choosing paths in Life is like that, too. We spend so much time trying to figure out which is the best way to live that we lose precious living time, holding back our enthusiastic energy, not investing, not experiencing life to the fullest!

One of the most important things I have learned from my teacher Yokar is:

"The danger is not in choosing the wrong path in life but not choosing at all. Any path is as good as another! It is better that you go down the wrong path, and so discovering it, you have learned more, rather than to enter onto the right path and not know anything for sure!"

This book will probably surprise you because my story will stretch your belief envelope and it could change your perspectives on life if you allow it. It will perhaps disconcert you and undoubtedly it will make you scoff and you'll have a hearty laugh on me.

If after you've read this book cover to cover you're still not sure, go back and read it again. Savor the parts that upset you. Highlight the parts that amaze you. These are the important parts to consider. Rest assured that my intention is not to put you to sleep with a fantasy, but to awaken you to the magical reality of the rest of your life.

Michael E. Morgan

Prologue

My story begins in the fall of 1972, early one morning...

It was now 7 a.m. and my shift was almost over. The night had been unusually busy in the studio, and my body was beginning to ache. The day crew was beginning to straggle in, and the hush of night was giving way to the hustle and bustle of the day shift madness.

I had one more adjustment to make on the editing recorder before the early news break. Often the smoothness of a show depended on many of these unseen tasks. Then I suddenly remembered that the tool I needed, my adjusting screwdriver, was still in the shop located on the opposite side of the lobby from the editing room. I stood in silence for a moment, angry at myself for being absent-minded. I figured that my efficiency had reduced to about twenty percent.

Time was running out. The opportunity to make my adjustment was almost gone. I needed my screwdriver and fast! To get to the other side of the building and back in time, I needed to rush. Within moments, I was running through the hallway and down the ramp toward the main lobby. By the time I reached the lobby area, I was at full gallop.

With added momentum, I flew up the second ramp and into the shop, grabbed the screwdriver, and was back to the lobby in a heartbeat.

My mission was halted abruptly. There were urgent warnings coming from the people standing nearby. "Stop!"

I came just short of lurching headlong onto an empty wet floor. Some of the day crew, as well as the remaining night crew, were staring at me. I struggled to regain my balance.

"What's up?" I asked.

"Take a look at the floor," someone responded.

The floor had been recently mopped. I could see that my tracks had obviously marred the handiwork. I shifted my focus around the circle of onlookers until I found the night porter standing, mop in hand. "Sorry, Karl," I said sheepishly.

Now there was only silence, as the bewildered faces waited for me to discover what they already knew. All eyes were fixed upon the floor. Then I looked again.

My Nike running shoes had defined a stylized trail across the wet black tiles. Next to them was another set of tracks, larger and more spread out: bare feet with a view of all the toes. I strained to see. Daylight and artificial light had mixed together, making my view of the lobby floor difficult. The additional prints were wide and giant-like, suggesting someone very tall, weighing several hundred pounds.

This isn't possible! I thought. Then I vented my disbelief. "Okay. Who's fooling around . . . playing Bigfoot? Come on, I want to see the rubber booties."

Joel's expression turned fearful. His voice carried a suspicious tone. "Hey, Morgan, who's your friend?"

Everyone's eyes turned upon me with equal suspicion as I began to squirm. "This is ridiculous!" I protested.

The mounting tension shattered when the night guard, Scotty, cracked a joke about the Jolly Green Giant being a personal friend of mine. Everyone laughed nervously. Then Joel, the sound man, stepped cautiously onto the wet floor. He stretched out his legs alongside the strange footprints to measure the distance between them. Even with best efforts, his feet couldn't match the distance. Joel had become spread-eagled on the floor.

"Damn it, man!" he said, astonished. "This dude is big!"

The atmosphere again seriously chilled, but the tension was cut short by the sound of the front door opening. The chief engineer had entered the building, bringing with him his usual air of impatience. Everyone turned away as if to ignore what had happened. No one had the courage to mention this piece of news to him. He strolled over to the site with an easy gait, completely unaware of the prints or their significance. I leaned against the wall and observed the enigma fade slowly from view as the moisture evaporated.

When I glanced at my watch, my attention shifted back to my work duties. I hurried on to make my last-minute adjustment. Soon, all was back to normal. Later, in quiet reflection, I decided there was probably some simple explanation. It just wasn't obvious to me at the time. Other pressing matters demanded my atention. There was still a meal and some much-needed sleep to be had. I made no further attempts to pursue the events of that day. For the present, it would remain strangely inexplicable.

Five years later . . .

In the summer of 1978, I picked up an ad about a medium who was coming to New York. The young woman allegedly could go into trance and at the same time produce a measurable physical phenomenon. The ad went on to say that the phenomenon had been documented by experts in the field of parapsychology at Duke University. I became very excited at this information. It was unusual for this kind of thing to be studied under the scrutiny of academic research professionals. It suggested authenticity.

The story aroused my curiosity and I had a hunch this event would be fun. I called my girlfriend's attention to it. She also seemed excited about the prospect of meeting this medium. She enjoyed anything that involved the psychic or paranormal, so I made arrangements.

The event took place in a posh loft apartment, on the Upper West Side of New York. Since the loft was quite close, we were able to walk there after some light dinner. We walked up three flights, I rang the doorbell and a smiling young girl answered the door. She motioned for us to enter.

The lights in the living room had been dimmed and augmented by candlelight. The apartment was all white, decorated in Art Deco fashion. There were no chairs in the living room. A lush white carpet sprawled throughout, contouring over steps leading into a conversation pit. Soft pink and blue silk pillows were sprinkled strategically, inviting us to sit and to relax.

There were about forty or fifty people in attendance. The atmosphere appeared dreamy, but everyone's mood was electrically tense. I suspected that many did not know what to expect. To my girlfriend's surprise, the loft belonged to a friend, so we easily mingled with the crowd.

There was no large seance table. People were sitting around in concentric semicircles, holding hands. Olivia, the medium, asked that everyone join in a gospel hymn as she entered into the trance. It was just an hour beyond dusk, and the room was already dark except for a few well-placed candles. After we sang a few verses, Olivia began to speak in a rather husky voice. The voice had the distinct intonation of an elderly male person, one Doctor Malone. I watched in awe, struggling to match the male voice with the female body.

"Good evening," he (she) said. We seemed to be transported magically to another place and time. We learned that the good Doctor Malone, allegedly, was alive on the Earth during the 15th century and functioned then as a bone doctor. We listened for hours to the antics of an old bard weaving tales of mystery and wonder. The crowd was miraculously transformed into a group of eager children lapping up every word of this aged pied piper. I listened with amusement while Doctor Malone issued friendly jibes and comical anecdotes that kept everyone laughing.

People began to ask personal questions about their relationships, troubles with work, and financial difficulties. I found some of his answers to be quite moving. For instance, one man couldn't get along with his boss and wanted to quit his job. Doctor Malone suggested that the man was actually competing with his boss as though his boss were his father. The man began to cry and admitted that he always wanted his father to recognize him for his own worth.

Often the seriousness would be interrupted by trivial and comical questions. One man wanted Doctor Malone to suggest a way for his mother-in-law not to visit so often. During one of these lighthearted moments, my girlfriend was inspired to poke me sharply in the ribs.

"Ask about the footprints," she whispered loudly. "Well . . . go on!"

At first, I felt foolish and flushed with embarrassment. I thought the evening was enjoyable, but I wasn't ready to offer my own personal questions. I just wanted to observe quietly. She wouldn't let up. Finally, my fear of getting involved was dismissed.

Oh, well . . . okay! I thought. What the hell.

"Hello, Doctor Malone," I said, smiling. "So, tell me about those footprints?" I looked over to my girlfriend and winked. I left out certain details to test the true psychic ability of the entity.

"Well, Michael," he said. "These footprints were made by your spirit friend. His name is Yokar, an Atlantean, I believe . . . a good friend of yours, too. I think you'll be seeing him a lot more later on."

Astounded at the answer, I was stone-silent, although I held onto my smile. Moments later, I recaptured my composure enough to thank the entity. I turned to my girlfriend and offered a shrug of my shoulders.

"Well, what do you make of that?"

Her eyes twinkled the brightest blue as she smiled proudly at me. "It's exciting, don't you think?"

"Yeah, I guess . . . if you can believe in this sort of thing!"

I felt vulnerable and tried hard not to reveal my fear. My smug reaction didn't work with her or myself. I retreated behind a thin veneer of calmness that I quickly molded over my face. My belief system sagged under the strain of this new information. The problem was, it seemed to make some sense! The memory of that odd experience involving the strange footprints flashed before me over and over, like still frames from an old movie projector. Somehow, I couldn't remain the same.

SHATTERED ILLUSIONS

This all started when I wanted to meet and talk with God. Sounds crazy, doesn't it? But it's true! For a boy my age, ten years old, it wasn't crazy. I sat patiently listening to the stories in Bible class about Abraham, Moses, Jesus, Elijah and the other prophets. The stories amazed me.

I began to wonder how it was then. Why was it so different now? I wondered why they were able to see and speak to God and we don't now. In my innocence, I asked if my Bible teachers spoke to God. They smiled and said no. They were quick to add that they did pray to God every day. I asked them if they had heard Him answer. They declined to give me a straight answer.

Before long I began to realize that no one spoke to God anymore . . . not like it was in the old stories. I was disappointed. Something had changed. All that remained of God were the stories!

I wondered, where's God now? Had He taken a long vacation and forgotten we were here? I questioned my Bible teachers about this issue. They said that my faith was more important; it would be enough. Then the preacher told me I didn't need to actually see or speak directly to God if I had faith. He scolded me, adding that it was prideful and ambitious of me to want more. He promised that on the great day of resurrection, the faithful would see God. So when would that be, I asked. The preacher said when the world comes to an end!

I considered this for a time and returned later to ask why didn't the spiritual leaders in the past have to wait until resurrection to speak to God? I think my teachers were thunderstruck by my question. They didn't answer. Before long, the deacons of the church surprised my parents with talk about grooming me to become a minister of the church. I wasn't interested!

I actually felt guilty for asking such questions, but, deep inside, I wasn't satisfied with their answers. There were other burning questions that I never had a chance to ask. Why did God appear to the men of the ancient past as a wrathful, vengeful God and then to Jesus as benevolent, kind, and forgiving? Had the God of our fathers changed so much? I was taught that God was unchanging and perfect. I concluded that what they taught me had something missing or was wrong. I was going to find out for myself what it was.

I often thought of my grandfather. He died when I was ten years old. I had good memories of him. There were stories to tell, real adventures, like some of the stories from the Bible. No, my grandfather didn't part the Red Sea or lead thousands of people out of slavery, but he was my hero and I can still remember the adventure I felt with him.

I learned how to call birds with a leaf whistle and how to amaze my friends by balancing a leather belt from the tip of my finger with a piece of wood he cleverly carved for me.

He once told me about meeting the James brothers on the trail one night. Even though his life was in mortal danger while he was with them, he offered Jesse and Frank a hot cup of coffee. Yeah, my grandfather was a cool customer. The James brothers declined, but that's another story.

I remembered and missed our talks together. Later, I compared those memories to the stories of the Bible. I wondered if my grandfather's impact on my life would've been the same had another relative simply told me stories about him, instead of my experiencing him for myself. Perhaps it's not a fair question . . . or is it? I concluded that, as in my experiences with my grandfather, we should all have our own stories about direct experiences with God!

I remained obedient, a "faithful follower" until my teens. By then, my rebellion had taken root and I was more outspoken. I was fed up with all the fake religious morality and blind faith rhetoric. I could see hypocritical behavior in all the people around my family and me too. Why didn't everyone else feel the way I did? Maybe they just wouldn't or couldn't admit such feelings, even to themselves.

It was okay to be unloving and unforgiving during the week but on Sunday, a sacred day, all imperfections were wiped out or appeared to be.

Like many others', my innocence was shattered by a series of unfortunate experiences. I discovered that double standards existed everywhere—for example, my parents' attitude toward race.

At the age of eleven, I met an old black janitor at my father's place of business. He worked at the store every day, was well known and liked by everyone. Soon, we became quick friends, but it was an ill-fated friendship from the beginning.

One day, he had taken his coffee break time to show me some drawing techniques. I wanted to learn more. We agreed that I would continue my lessons over hamburgers, my treat, during his lunch break at the dinette next door.

I learned quickly, from my mother, that he was not a fit luncheon companion for me. I asked why. Then, I was informed that I was white and shouldn't be seen eating with a black man in public! I couldn't understand what our color had to do with it. The whole thing seemed stupid to me, and I protested her outrageous inconsistency. I quickly directed attention to the black family who came to our home for dinner every weekend. The adults sat around and swapped stories or watched the TV, while I played games with the other children. Sunday dinner was always a great event and a regular feast. I easily accepted them into my life. My mother became angry with me and declared there was a difference. I pressed her for an explanation, but she could not tell me why.

I was forced to tell the janitor I couldn't eat with him and broke off our friendship. He told me not to worry myself about it, but I couldn't shake my feelings of anger, disgust, and shame. I stopped my drawings in protest.

Every day I grew less tolerant of the corruption around me. I imagined myself above and beyond the Earth in a kind of spiritual utopia. There, all people said what they meant and kept their bargains without hurting or deceiving others. It was a noble fantasy but, deep within my heart, I felt despair. I knew my life on Earth could never be anything like my fantasy!

My church was a branch of protestant fundamentalism that

taught that every male member needed to be circumcised and that mixed bathing, dancing, and unchaperoned dating outside of church socials was forbidden.

I felt restless. It all seemed boring, a lifeless tedium that offered only restriction without meaningful cause. I never met anybody who truly wanted to embrace all that idealized moral structure. It was supposed to be satisfying, but this kind of spirituality had become just words to me, old worn words that had all the feelings sucked dry from them. Maybe, I thought, it was like eating flour paste soup with greater expectations.

A good friend, whose family raised him in the Lutheran tradition, was as curious about my church rituals as I was about his. One day, we decided to attend each other's Sunday religious services to see and understand the differences.

I went first. There was much more pomp and circumstance in his services. It seemed similar in fashion to a Catholic service. I liked it and took communion along with the rest of the congregation. I felt very comfortable with the universality of communion ritual. The following Sunday, my friend joined me at my church services. Afterwards, one of the deacons approached me to inquire about my absence. I proudly told him about my visit to my friend's church, expounding on the similarities and differences. He stopped me in mid-thought.

"Michael, we are happy that you shared fellowship with your friend, but it was not wise to miss your communion here."

I quickly asserted, "Oh. I didn't miss anything. I took communion with my friend during their services!"

After a moment of silence, the deacon went on.

"Michael. That was not a good idea! You have sinned against your baptismal vows to this church!"

Now I was silent. Disturbed by his comment, my mind turned to thoughts of Jesus and the Last Supper, the event on which this ceremony had been based. A provocative thought struck me. I couldn't wait to speak my mind.

My head cocked to one side, as I sized up my new adversary.

Then I let him have both barrels! "So how do you account for the fact that it was a rabbi that was offering the last supper to Jews in the first place?"

This time the deacon was silent. I knew that I had struck a sensitive and vulnerable target. There was no turning back. I was on a roll and couldn't hold myself back from attacking this poor man. The break for me from the church had begun as surely as the walls of Jericho had tumbled down. I continued to rub his nose in his pious morality.

"Now I'll tell you one more thing, preacher. Picture this! It is a Sunday or any other fine morning. I am in the gutter with another man and we have only saltines and a bit of Ripple wine to share between us. If we share that bounty with love and respect for the grace from God, then that is Holy Communion as far as I am concerned!"

I walked out and never returned. To this day, my preferences still lean toward Jesus' teachings, although one could not call me a devout Christian in practice.

By the age of sixteen, I was struggling to stay in school while I watched my parents sink deeper into self-destructive alcoholism. My personal life was in shambles. My sense of self-esteem was crumbling, and I desperately needed something or someone to cling to. I considered Western religion bankrupt and defrocked. I decided to thrust myself into Eastern religious mysticism.

I fell in love with Egyptian history. I had been religiously tutored about the negative interactions between the Jews and the Egyptians. Now I wanted the Egyptian version of the story. The Egyptian mystery schools fascinated me, especially since I already knew that Moses trained to be a high priest in one of these schools as a favored son of the pharaoh's household, before he was cast out of Egypt. Then it occurred to me that he also ended up speaking directly to a burning bush that was never consumed--viz., God!

Maybe there's a connection, I thought.

By chance, I met an old friend of the family shopping for some music at my father's store. He was a well-known and respected pillar of the church community. John and I talked in private about my parents and their difficulties. He was mostly interested in their impact on me. He offered to come and see my parents at my home and give some friendly spiritual comfort. Although I agreed, I expressed serious doubts about the significance of his gesture, certainly about the outcome.

Meanwhile, in my spare time during my passion for Egyptology, I had been sculpting large replicas of the Egyptian gods out of paper maché and mounting them in my bedroom. Curiously, I found a certain solace in their presence.

On the eve of John's arrival at our home, it soon became apparent that John's efforts to bring my parents around to a resolution about their drinking problems were fruitless. I decided to invite John to see the marvels I had constructed in my bedroom. He was very surprised by what I had done. He seemed suddenly nervous and acted strangely, asking me questions about my interest in Egypt. My curiosity was piqued by his behavior.

As he departed, he took me aside and told me we needed to discuss Egypt again. "We need to talk more privately about some of these things very soon," he said with an urgent tone to his voice.

I agreed with some enthusiasm.

Weeks later we met again. Our next meeting was on a Sunday at his house, after church services. He took me to his cellar, where he revealed to me a secret "sanctuary." This time it was my turn to be surprised. As it turned out, the church had disenchanted John many years before. Now he directed all of his enthusiasm to the mystical spiritual path. He was a Rosicrucian!

I learned that the Rosicrucian brotherhood was an ancient fraternal order dedicated to the principles allegedly taught in the original mystery schools of Egypt under the directorship of Amenhotep IV. According to John, the Rosicrucian order claimed lineage that could be traced directly to the temples of Karnak and Thebes. The bells went off in my head. I knew that these were the same temples that had supposedly taught the mysteries to Moses. Now I wanted to know more . . . much more!

Our meetings continued in secret as he introduced some of the Rosicrucian teachings. John revealed that he had learned to travel astrally, or what he called "controlled Soul travel." I was excited to know more about this out-of-body work and to learn the techniques as well. As he began to teach the basic principles, I couldn't help feeling that I was putting one over on the Church. The clandestine nature of the whole experience was great!

Soon I discovered that the practice wasn't so easy to accomplish. My ability to focus and concentrate was weak, and my patience was short. John concluded that I needed to begin the study from the beginning and develop my ability slowly, as he had done years ago with the order.

He sponsored my entry into the order, and I began to receive monthly training material by mail. The thrust of the training centered on a philosophy that life was a wonderful mystery. Further, that the lack of understanding of the mystery was not a drawback but could actually be enjoyed. The lessons seemed to be more or less a set of moral attitudes directed from a mystical and fraternal point of view. There wasn't much in the way of uncommon psychic experiences within the material that John was talking about.

The next shock came when I learned that John was gay and many of his mystical inclinations were a backdrop for his sexual interludes with young boys in his secret sanctuary. That revelation, along with a subsequent play for my sexual favor, ended our friendship. I continued the Rosicrucian training for two more years, looking for any signs of extraordinary psychic develop-ment. I learned nothing significant from them.

Later, I had to conclude that John was just a frustrated believer who had become attracted to a spiritual tradition of ancient legends about magic. More stories! This path also failed to offer any direct experience of the holy of holies. So I believe he sought, in its place, the short-term gratification of his sexual fantasies. I continued to seek, hoping to find the missing keys to communicating with God.

The crisis around my parents' drinking finally exploded into a massive legal confrontation with my father at the age of 17. I moved out to live with my aunt and her family. I knew they kept apart from my parents, and I felt assured I would not have any contact either.

My aunt's husband, Henry, was a dynamic and often charismatic individual. He was a handyman by trade, a self-made philosopher, and a "mad inventor" of sorts, a skill he developed while serving in the Army. He controlled his family with an iron will and sometimes by an iron fist, his temper matched only by his cruelty. Henrys' volatile disposition was often crested by a touch of genius and genuine psychic ability. I found him at once fascinating and terrifying. Living with him was an emotional roller coaster ride. Sometimes, he was forced to enter hospitals to restore his psychic and emotional stability. These mental health episodes caused tremendous financial difficulties for his family. This added to the general stress.

I lived with my aunt for a year, until I finished high school. During that time, I learned about the power of my mind through painful and emotionally trying experiences under the brutal tutelage of Henry.

One notable instance occurred when a chronic nervous affliction flared just before I entered my last year of high school. My hands would break into a condition called palm pox. The skin condition presented a series of small red blisters covering my fingers and palms. Eventually, the blisters would break, spreading a drying fluid that destroyed the first layer of skin. After the dead skin peeled, the symptoms would repeat their cycle until bleeding resulted, and did so throughout the school year. It was itchy, painful, and generally debilitating.

I believed that the impetus for this affliction was the stress of performance and competition I often felt while in school, as the condition arose only around the beginning of school.

When Henry first discovered my condition, I was doing my chemistry homework at the kitchen table. He noticed that I was having difficulty holding my pencil without some pain. He grabbed my hands forcefully, seizing upon me with the fierceness of an angry tiger.

"What are you doing to your hands?" He suddenly bellowed with a heart-stopping scowl.

Henry strongly believed that nothing was an accident. Any illness, in his opinion, was always psychosomatic. His meaning was that I self-generated my condition by intention, regardless of the circumstances.

"It's a problem with my nerves I've had since I was small. My brother has it, too," I reported anxiously. I had a fleeting hope that a condition shared by another family member would lessen the terrible confrontation that was on the rise.

As his grip tightened, I knew I was not off the hook.

He hammered at me verbally, as his eyes blazed with disapproval. "Why are you doing this to your hands?"

Tears flooded my eyes but I tried to hold them back. I knew Henry well enough by now to know that tears would have no effect on my case. I was in for the worst of it. Fear began to rise within me as my heart readied my body for a fight. A small shiver traveled quietly along my spine.

"I don't know exactly!" I said sobbing.

"You know how I feel about this sort of thing, don't you?"

"Yes, sir," I said.

"You are responsible for this carnage! I want you to stop it right now! Do you understand?"

"Yes but . . ."

Now my tears began to flow uncontrollably down my cheeks as my voice shook under the strain of my fear. "I don't know how to stop it!"

"You must find the reason for doing it in the first place," Henry demanded. Then he went on. "That will be a good place to start. You've got just one hour to tell me the reason. Otherwise, you're out of here and back home by tomorrow!" His words left the air still and cold. The silence lingered for a moment. "I will not tolerate this kind of behavior in my house, around my family . . . you understand?"

"Perfectly," I said.

Henry left the kitchen with such energy that I could almost feel the vacuum follow close behind, taking the wind from my lungs. I thought I would never breath again. I knew I was alone. My aunt could not come to my defense or she would certainly suffer also from his terrible rage.

I sat in my room quietly picking through my feelings, desperately trying to find the reason I would or could harm myself in such a way.

I never questioned the validity of Henrys' charges. He was too intimidating. I would not risk re-entering my parents' home, not since I had had to humiliate my father in front of a judge to break free of that horrible environment.

Henry was scary enough, but my father was crazy and proven dangerous. I quickly concluded that the alternative was too awful to think about. I would find an answer to Henrys' liking. And I would do it quickly!

My time was nearly over and I was crazed with fear. Then, in a sudden rush of insight, a reasonable cause for my problem unfolded like a flower before me. I wasn't sure if it was the right reason, but it was close enough.

My feelings revealed that I was angry with myself for not being the kind of son my father wanted me to be. I couldn't do physical things with the same finesse as my brother. I was awkward at everything. The most terrible string of words I ever heard my father say to me was "you're as worthless as tits on a boar hog." I hated that. I couldn't do anything well, so I attacked my useless hands! I was sure it was close to the truth.

After I recounted my explanation to Henry, he seemed stunned by my answer. I must've hit the mark. He was satisfied. He then proceeded to work on my feelings.

He explained that I had to release my anger and begin to forgive myself for not meeting my father's expectations. I had to apologize to my hands and forgive myself. It was to become a mantra of sorts, which I spent the rest of the night uttering to myself until I fell asleep.

By morning, I noticed that the redness and swelling had reduced and there were remarkable signs of recovery. By the end of the week, the blisters were all but gone and I was amazed. I began to believe in Henrys' ideas and enjoyed more confidence in myself.

My training with Henry and his mind-control techniques didn't stop with personally afflicted illnesses, but extended to any negative ideas that could adversely affect the body.

The whole family would go on outings every Sunday. The only

thing planned about these trips was that everyone—my aunt, my nephew Brian, and I—got into the car early in the morning with Henry the designated driver. After that, no one knew where we were going or when we would return.

One day, we ended up in a field of high grasses stretching over some lazy green hills in which an old abandoned farmhouse nestled. This was one of Henrys' favorite pastimes: exploring abandoned farmhouses. During our exploration, I discovered my young nephew Brian standing knee-deep in a patch of poison ivy.

I called desperately to him to get out right away. Henry looked back over his shoulder to catch Brian's attention. I noticed some subtle communications and a recognition that passed between them.

"You know what to do, son," Henry said firmly.

"Yeah, I know what to do," Brian responded obediently.

Brian reached down to seize hold of the ivy all around him with both hands. He pulled at the vines until he had a large number of leaves filling both hands. I watched in horror as he began to rub the oily leaves all over his skin, all the while smiling at me. I turned, staring at Henry. I wondered how he might have mesmerized his son to do such a terrible thing.

Henry looked confident. He looked upon his son quietly and proudly as he coached on. "Tell your Uncle Michael about the truth of the ivy, Brian."

Brian responded, rubbing the leaves more vigorously over other patches of exposed skin. "You see, Uncle Mike," Brian declared matter-of-factly, "the ivy isn't poison, the poison is in your mind!"

He proceeded to hand me the vine and gestured that I should repeat his performance with verbal affirmations: "The ivy isn't poison, it's just another plant" and "I am removing the poison from my mind as I make this plant my friend."

I gulped as I received the ivy from my nephew. I rolled up my sleeves in preparation for this terrible initiation; while my mind remembered the many times I had experienced the vicious sting of this "friendly" plant. Then I suddenly remembered my palm pox, and doubt began to fade. My fear gave way to a thrill, which rushed through my belly. My newfound enthusiasm displayed itself with some vigorous vine scrubbing on my exposed skin.

"Yeah. It's just a plant!" I said defiantly.

The postscript to this story is that poison ivy had not affected me afterward.

I stayed with my aunt's family until my graduation. My harsh training with Henry continued. I had many other intense experiences that helped to permanently mold my willpower and self-confidence. I left their rural lifestyle to pursue college. That endeavor lasted for two semesters, until the Vietnam War pressed me to enter the military service.

In the years that followed in the military, I learned to separate the positive aspects of Henrys' mind-control concepts from the brutality and cruelty he inflicted upon me. Although he caused much suffering from his unbridled fury, I realized that I also have that hideous strength. As he awakened that strength in me, I realized that my unwanted rage was buried along with it. Because of his example, I knew it had to be closely monitored. Someday, I thought, it will be possible that my fury will be transformed into something useful and trustworthy.

While my friends wanted desperately to escape military duty, I believed that going in early would narrow my odds of getting caught in the conflict. I was only partially correct. Although I went into the Air Force to minimize the risk, I still ended up in Asia and eventually became part of a support team for a tactical fighter squadron that fought in Vietnam.

I won't bother to describe my own sense of the 'Nam' experience here. Suffice it to say, it was a terrible and debilitating experience personally and for the country. I think the country's wounds from this conflict have not healed and will not heal for many years to come.

The stresses of mere survival in the military were immense, and I felt desperate. So I returned to organized religious services for solace and comfort. The music would be nice sometimes. Once in a while, there would be a moment, a brief moment when I thought I felt something, but the feeling didn't seem to be attached to anything

I was doing or saying. No matter how hard I tried, I couldn't consciously bring that special feeling back.

While in 'Nam', I questioned others, the faithful soldiers around me, about the lack of experience I felt in religious practice. They were compassionate and consoling.

"Keep going, it'll come to you some day," they told me. "You got to have faith," they said.

I asked the smart ones, the driven ones, the pastors and chaplains in the field of fire, to tell me about the truth. I wanted them to tell me if they had had any personal experiences.

I was told that the deal was in the waiting. "You don't have enough faith, soldier!" Expectation was enough for the faithful.

I didn't believe, couldn't believe in all the rhetoric. I needed more! I told them of my desire to meet and talk with God. The chaplains all felt that I thought too much of myself. Why should God talk to me? They asked. I couldn't answer that question. But I did retort with, why not?

They have to be mistaken, I thought. It must be possible to have a direct, more personal relationship with the Creator God. Somehow, I was determined to find a way. I continued to explore other religions, but it was all the same. It was just more tedium, mindless adoring and genuflecting. I was puzzled as to how I could make use of my newfound willpower and inner strength within any of these spiritual rituals.

I was tired of tiptoeing around the holy records of the Supreme Being and all His advocates. I needed something that I could actually do for myself. What I wanted was to have a heart-to-heart with the Supreme Being. I wanted God, in whatever form, to express himself as all-powerful, all wise and omniscient right to my face. Not history. Not secondhand!

Then, one day, I found a great book by Arthur Koestler at the base library. It was called The Lotus and the Robot. It was my first introduction to the practice of all levels of yoga. It seemed to answer the basic question about the preparation to meet God, about what I could or should do to get ready. The body and mind needed to be perfected and trained made clean and purified before the supreme altar of the divine. I could relate to that. So, I set my mind and will to master this practice.

I learned that there are many paths of yoga, but in simple terms, there are really only two. The first is perfection of the body through Hatha practice, the physical discipline of postures and fasting that most people associate with yoga. The other path is a complicated series of practices geared to accessing and stimulating endocrine secretions to flow in certain ways around the body, especially inside the head. It is all done with a set of bizarre breathing techniques, esoteric meditations, and specially uttered sounds or chants called mantras. These practices seemed to be from a master named Patanjali.

I have since learned that there are many yogis around the world. All of these yogis enjoy a range of skills that mainly control autonomic functions of the body. The autonomic nervous system governs such vital functions as heart rate, blood pressure, and respiration. There are some old legends about great yogis who had psychic powers resulting from their practice, including the ability to talk to or control wild animals, levitate, and walk on fire. I found this all very interesting and seemed to relate back to the magical powers attributed to the priesthood in Egypt. But I still couldn't see that there was any modern evidence of anyone who could reach or speak with the Creator God!

After a while, all these practices seemed pointless, beyond enjoying good physical health and a reasonably long life. I decided that yoga was a good tool for cleansing and purification and a strengthening for the mindfulness toward awakening one's consciousness, but that was all. Since I could find no one who was "awake" in the present day, I concluded that yoga must also be a system of knowledge that was incomplete!

Even with this disappointment, I still believed that all people, if they really put their minds to it, could meet the All and Everything. I've read and listened to lots of stories and legends about such meetings. Perhaps you're thinking that these stories are just the fantasies of people who suffer delusions of grandeur. I believe some stories are from sick people—people who feel unimportant and want desperately to be acknowledged or people who suffer from psychotic delusions. I know that some of the "true" stories are grossly exaggerated, weaving myths and truths like a fisherman's rope.

I didn't care about that. Even though I felt alone in my endeavors, I knew deep within my heart I was right. Supposing less than one percent of the stories are real stories, maybe less—I didn't care about the odds! I was interested only in one fact; some of the truth could and would emerge somewhere. I also knew in my bones that I'd recognize the truth when it came to me.

I've questioned my motives plenty of times. My fear and dread of walking my own path provided plenty of visions of lightning striking me down or the Earth opening up to swallow me. Because of this fear, I waited for a long time for something terrible to happen, but nothing happened!

I finally realized the whole fear-thing was wrong! I became angry at all the Bible thumpers I've known or heard, the fire-and-brimstone evangelists that are determined to save other souls, even when they don't want to be saved! I became angry with myself for having believed in them. They have meant well for the most part, but they need to be more flexible and compassionate.

I couldn't accept a loving Creator God who could remain silent and not communicate with His flock, especially in my case. The Creator couldn't ignore an honest and forthright desire for something more substantial than a historical flash in the pan!

I mustered my courage and set out seriously to find my truth. I never thought for one second that I was doing something silly or blasphemous. And I believed with all my heart that what I was asking was fair! I was prepared to meet the truth, whatever the outcome.

High Road

Nausea churned violently in my stomach while my heart started to pump furiously. Anxiety filled my body with a paralyzing numbness. Brilliant flashes of white light momentarily blinded me. My mind screamed, what the hell is happening to me? Immediately, I was aware of an awful discovery: the yoga practice, fasting, and meditations weren't enough. I wasn't ready. My mind felt squeezed as the pressure and pain kept increasing at my crown. I imagined my scalp being torn apart by hawk's talons. A singular fear emerged: was this only the beginning?

Like it or not, I was in New York. It was 1972 and I had been caught off guard by a raging altered state of consciousness. This wasn't my plan, you understand. According to what I have read, spiritual journeys are supposed to begin beyond the city, in the wild, where life supports the soul on a journey. I wanted to be aligned with that wisdom, out there in the wilderness, in control of my faculties. In this place of stone, steel, and hollow people, I felt raw, vulnerable, and out of control.

Maybe, I thought, my first lesson has begun; spiritual development always begins where the mind ends.

My abdomen was now beginning to ache from the convulsive quaking rippling through my solar plexus. The waves of nausea interrupted my concentration, causing momentary lapses of cogent thought. My body trembled all over. I thought, I must look like one of those drug addicts in rehabilitation with the DTs. I felt wet all over, too.

I kept checking my brow, trying to wipe off the excess sweat. Funny thing was, my brow was only slightly damp. The wetness must've been an illusion of some sort.

There was also a strange taste in my mouth. It seemed distinctly metallic. A faint related memory emerged from my childhood. A particular favorite pastime was to suck on the mixing spoon my mother used for stirring chocolate cake batter. The chocolate flavor seemed to intensify the metal aftertaste of the spoon.

The fear that I held at the periphery of my consciousness deepened to a sense of paranoia. The urgency tore me from my reminiscence and encouraged me to hide. I could feel what seemed like many eyes staring at me. I was not convinced that it was people looking! It seemed like more, something else. This fear is ungrounded, I assured myself. Park Avenue is always teeming with people, but no one was gawking at me. My body was weak, but if I could walk for a while and dump the excess energy, I knew I would feel better.

I gripped the metal railing that encircled the waterfall and pond, which decorated the front of the Park Avenue office building near where I had been sitting. With all my willpower, I braced my suffering body for a long stroll. My intention was to reach Central Park. It was an early spring evening, just a little after five. Hordes of restless people scurried past me for the nearest public transportation home. My difficulties were clearly unimportant to them. I was another stranger, perhaps from their point of view one more of the many stumbling homeless wandering through their territory.

The violent shaking began to convert to a series of softer thrills shuddering silently through my muscles and connective tissues. The nausea shifted between voracious hunger and no appetite at all. The brilliant flashes of blinding light that heralded the onslaught of this mind-bending episode finally stopped. All that remained from the torrent of brain-slamming throbs was a burning glow existing somewhere up behind the inside of my eyelids. I finally came to accept it as a strange sort of backlighting in my field of view.

Then my body suddenly stopped. It seemed to take stock of some new impending danger. There was a strong sense that all of reality was about to mutiny. I picked a convenient nearby port, an old city fire hydrant, to weather this new storm. No sooner had I plunked down on that metal toadstool than everything melted. The street, buildings, cars, people, and sounds all collided together as if they were being thrown into some giant vegetable blender. It all became a meaningless collage of light, color, and noise. There was no structure anywhere to relate to or from. I couldn't derive any bearings.

I remained there, sitting on the hydrant, until it all passed. Even though I couldn't see the hydrant under me, I was convinced that its essence would remain a close and present friend, not betraying my trust. It would continue to provide me a fine shelter.

I felt strangely calm. The meaningless mass swirled in front of me while I sat totally helpless, trusting that it would be fine eventually. Like a sudden summer thunderstorm, it did finally pass.

I stood up and took a deep breath and let out a long sigh of relief. The energy was calm again. There was a deep sense of well being all over. I think I actually felt happy, more confident in myself after that.

I had been walking for several minutes when I approached a small park of trees with quaint wrought iron benches encircling them. It looked like Fifth Avenue near Central Park. It was attractive and seemed to call to me. An old feeling awakened deep inside. I was filled with awe and wonder. I felt an urge to communicate with everything around me. People were strangely absent from this place too, but that didn't bother me so much. Anyway, I was looking for something different.

A curious and wonderful light blue energy current weaved like a mist through the air and trees nearby. I didn't recall ever seeing anything quite like it before. The odd mist appeared soft and silky as it moved. It was very appealing, and I wanted to make contact with it. It seemed to be conscious of my intent and drew closer to me. Weaving around my body like a cat wanting attention, it sang a strange song as it rubbed against me. My skin was ravished by the thrill of its touch. There was some intelligence in its melodious message. I thought for a moment that I could almost understand the song it was singing. My rational thought reminded me that this was nuts, but I couldn't resist extending my hand to touch it.

The mist responded instantly to my urges for more contact. It met and ran through my fingers with a gentle lover's caress. It was warm and wet, like water gently pouring. The strain to understand this new friend was overwhelming and quickly exhausted my strength. My body cried out to rest.

I eagerly sat down on one of the benches. Everything looked normal. But then there was the mist. I couldn't explain that. This moment offered me a chance to consider how I could've arrived in this new place. More importantly, rational thoughts had turned to how I might get back to my own surroundings. Everything was different and yet seemed oddly the same.

Even the iron bench wasn't what I expected. To my surprise, it wasn't hard and cold. On the contrary, it was soft and warm, not like iron at all. I jumped up for a moment, feeling startled. What the hell? Nothing is what it seems around here. I reached out to touch the iron again, this time letting my fingers run slowly along the edge of the metal. My attention followed the texture and contour. It was as though I was meeting iron for the first time, a new kind of iron. It was nothing like the metal I was familiar with. It was black alright, and shiny too, and its line was sharp and appeared hard. But it was soft and spongy like rubber.

Ah, it must be rubber and not iron, I said to myself confidently.

On a hunch, I reached into my pocket and pulled out some change. A quarter will do, I thought. Pounding on the blackness, I listened for the sound of metal against rubber. A good scientist would do so to confirm his hypothesis. To my utter amazement, it clanked like metal! I can't believe this. It is metal! My mind felt troubled with this incongruity. Things that are soft as rubber don't clank like something hard! Perhaps it was then that I realized, once and for all, that I had drifted apart from the world I knew. Maybe back there, when everything melted into chaos, that's how I had lost the world. How will I find that doorway back? I wondered. A cold chill ran down my back. Then I began to feel lonely.

I sat back down. This time, I accepted the softness of the "iron" with graciousness. It belonged to another world I didn't know. I closed my eyes to catch my mind's breath for a moment, wishing that this were all a dream and it would soon go away. I tried to think of the swirling pool of chaos, but it made me dizzy. Then the memory of it snapped out of my sight with a pop. All was black. Then the blackness gave way to depth . . . I was in some sort of room. The bench and park were gone. I was standing . . . alone.

Out of the fading depth emerged several tall beings dressed in dark robes. Cloaks that drooped over their heads hid their faces. They surrounded me and looked very ominous. I looked around defensively and counted them. There were nine altogether. As I contemplated being mugged or torn apart, my thoughts of annihilation were interrupted. One of them moved closer. I moved back as he began to speak.

"You are in the sacred corridor, in the midst of the inner sanctum. The One is near."

I looked around, trying to grasp what he was talking about. I could feel a presence, an unusual light nearby. But it was elusive, like that burning glow behind my eyelids; I couldn't seem to focus my attention on it. Then the apparent leader spoke again.

"If your desire is to be with the One, you will have to make a sacrifice."

"Sacrifice, what kind of sacrifice?"

I was surprised by my presumed assailant's offer of a choice. The dimly lit features of the room became more sharply defined as I considered my options. Again it seemed oddly familiar. It was a rectangular room. The walls seemed distorted, becoming narrower as they vaulted high into the darkness above. Stairs ascended endlessly behind the one who was talking. It seemed as though I belonged here. It felt like my home.

Before I could answer, I noticed that my body was trembling again. The anxiety returned. Then, out of the corner of my eye, I saw it. Along the edges of the walls where the ceiling and the floor joined, wide cracks were exposed. Behind the cracks I could see the churning chaos oozing through. Terror abruptly interrupted my heartbeat. I didn't have much time. I felt I was going to lose my mind. The one who addressed me moved closer and urgently spoke to me again.

"You have to choose now! You have to sacrifice your life! Or you cannot enter the inner sanctum. What will it be?"

I stared hard into the blackness of his drooping cloak, trying to see his face. There was nothing. He had no face, no hands or feet. There was only the void. There was nothing there but the demand of his voice. I knew instantly that the black robes were just empty shells draped to suggest someone present. I shivered.

"Who are you?" I asked.

"We are the Council of Nine." His tone was authoritative. "You haven't much time. What will be your decision?"

"Listen," I pleaded. "I need just five minutes here. I need to think this out. And uh . . . what do you mean by sacrifice my life?"

"You must give up all that you are and enter with purity. You must sacrifice your life."

Even though he explained my choice a little further, the ominous quality wasn't very appealing. On the other hand, the oozing cracks in the floor were widening. My consciousness couldn't hold back the chaos forever. He and I both knew that soon I wouldn't have a mind left to choose with. Stepping away quickly, I turned my back on him and the others for a moment. I weighed the possibilities.

On the one hand, I thought to myself, if I don't give it up, I would have gone this far for nothing. On the other hand, if I go on, it sounds like I'm definitely not coming back and I'll be stuck out here knowing the truth and not being able to share it with anyone. What am I doing here in the first place? I argued adjacently. It's for my own sake, right? Hang the others. They can find out for themselves. Well, that's it then, I concluded. Let's do it!

Then I spun around, facing the ringleader, and declared with a gulp, "Okay. I've decided. I've already lost most of my mind anyway . . . It's not like I'm throwing away much at this point. Let's do it. I surrender Michael Morgan and all that he is, that he stands for and believes in, all and everything."

"So be it!" He said with finality.

The Council of Nine vanished. The vision of the vaulting room disappeared into the night. The remaining walls of my mind finally collapsed. The last vestige of my known self disappeared as the raging river of chaos rushed in with a roar to consume the rest of me.

I began to sense acceleration. I felt myself rising, faster and faster like a rocket-powered elevator, straight up. Everything faded behind me, far down below. The higher I went, the brighter it became. The light was overpowering and blinding like the sun. It was strangely similar to those blinding flashes that started all this. There was no quaking now, no nausea. The hawk clawing at my scalp was gone. Even the throbbing headache was gone. The top of my head was wide open . . . free . . . to look at the whole damn universe.

There was something else, warmth, and a presence. It loomed larger and closer. It seemed to be in the light all around me. Then I realized it was the light. My consciousness was struggling to grasp it. Some part of my consciousness was saying; Are you . . . Is this . . . Can this be . . . Oh my God, you are . . . God!

The brilliant radiance was streaming through and around me. Pink and violet flames with emerald green and golden streamers shooting out like some fantastic fireworks display. The colors were unique. Not like anything I'd ever seen on Earth before. Every fiber of my being was laughing and crying at the same time. The energy extended all around me, holding me up the way a mother and father would hold their baby for the first time as a great smiling, a great love shown through their eyes of flaming light. I felt nothing but love pouring from the energy, a divine love, unquestioning, undefined, unlimited; a supreme love, all directed at me. This divine presence didn't care about anything except me. I was its only focus.

I began to feel ashamed. I felt undeserving of these gifts, of this magnificent celebration. I began to shy away from the light, thinking, I have challenged you and your existence. I have not loved you many times. I have not respected what you created. I have turned away from you, denied you and even used your name in vain. How can you love me without question?

But the light did not speak. It just continued to smile at me and continued the pouring out of love, surrounding, supporting, and nurturing me. My words were hollow, without meaning. My frustration and resistance continued until the presence finally spoke deeply within my being.

Why do you mourn your ignorance? None of that you speak has any importance. You did what I required of you. You loved me so much that you were willing to sacrifice your life, everything you cared about, just for one glimpse of me. For that, all that I am and all that is . . . is yours to behold. It is your sacrifice that makes you pure and worthy to be with me.

I felt a sudden change of heart. The logic was perfect. I couldn't find a worthy dispute against it. And I began to consider the implications as I replied in my heart. God, if You can love me like this, despite all that I've done and said on Earth, then there is no reason why I shouldn't love me completely too! Right?

God said nothing. But in Its radiance there shone a new glimmer of happiness. It could see that I was about to accept its love into my heart, into my soul, and that made its joy with me complete. With that, I started to cry and laugh again. Then I wrapped around myself and squeezed with a deeply loving and forgiving embrace. We began to laugh together. It was wonderful.

While I was holding myself with love, God surrounded me again. This time, as I looked into the radiance, I could see another pattern emerging deep within the light. It appeared to be a kind of flower with petals, but not like a plant. It was fleshy like and red in color with many woven layers all undulating in a rhythmical opening and closing. It seemed very sexual, but not polarized male or female; it seemed to be both at once. It was shocking and at the same time exhilarating. My whole being became filled with the excitement.

I thought, so this is why people keep God separate. They're afraid of this joining! But I wasn't afraid. I wanted to join and I returned my sexual nature back to it. I was consumed and we were one together in the bosom of the Most High God.

During the exchange, I experienced a unique scent coming from God. It was sweet and delicate. Mixed with this delightful odor was a sprinkle of golden light. I could see that it was all over me. I believed that I belonged to God now. He had marked me. It was quite clear. When I thought of trying to explain this . . . well, I just dismissed it as a ridiculous idea. It didn't matter anymore anyway. I was in spirit. My understanding seemed complete and needed no explanation.

We began many dialogues together. I asked about the creation and what it was all about. God withheld nothing from me. The intention was that one half of reality would watch while the other half experienced. Then the whole thing would switch like a giant oscillating pendulum. It made perfect sense to me at this time. But using mere words really couldn't begin to touch the concept.

As we continued to enjoy reality together, another wrinkle appeared in my emotional fabric. The impact of it seemed to weigh heavy on my heart. I began to feel a new love growing. I felt my love for my brothers and sisters on the Earth. I began to explore their agony and their loneliness. I marveled at their ignorance. I turned to God and said, *you know, it's amazing to me, that nobody knows you down there. I can't think of anyone in my life there, who has the slightest idea of what you are all about.*

A few have known me. But it always brings difficulty. That's why I send teachers once in a while, to remind them. We don't want them to get too far away. So tell me what you have growing in your heart.

Well, I've been feeling the need to share with them what you're all about. Their finding out the truth about you is more important to me than being with you.

I gulped. My statement was serious and caught me by surprise. Suddenly I knew everything was going to change between us.

I love You completely and that will never change, I said. But they don't know You like I do and that has to change!

The boldness of my declarations made me a little nervous. I could feel God considering my feelings with the greatest care and concern. After several eternal moments, God spoke to me again. This time there was a very serious tone to his radiance.

What you are asking for is a serious step. You want to serve as a teacher from the highest realm. It will change our relationship forever. It will mean a deeper responsibility for you. The path you

are now choosing is a thorny path. There are others who will teach. You don't have to worry about them on Earth. They will come around eventually.

What you ask will threaten the very essence of our connection. It will mean that you have to become physical again. The Earth is not like this place. It will be easy to forget what you have learned here. If you go back now, you will suffer again. You will become unconscious again. You will even deny me again.

I spontaneously fell to my knees.

Oh King of the Universe, Maker of the Light, my Love, let me do this thing I ask. I want to be a gatekeeper, a watcher for you at the edge of the darkness. I want to look out for those who, by their actions, define a readiness to embrace the truth about you. With this act, I will feel that I can give back to You, something of what You have so graciously given to me . . . please, Lord.

You don't have to do anything for me, just remain with me, that is enough.

You're wrong about me. I will never forget you, let alone deny you. Trust me, Lord. Let me carry your light to the edge of the darkness.

I felt God fold into great deliberation about my request. He loved me so much He couldn't bear to see me suffer. Then, with a heavy heart, He relinquished and expressed a lover's sigh.

So, you will leave me then, for the sake of the ignorant?

We won't be apart, Lord. I will keep you in my heart at all times. In my heart, you will guide me.

I was excited. I was on my first mission for the sake of God and all my family. But I was just a child, really. And I was so naive.

You still don't understand, do you? This realm is far from the physical worl,. worlds upon worlds, descending into darkness. Your odds are slim indeed, but you are just like the others. Your love for your brothers and sisters is commendable and for that, I will reward you. Go now.

Almost immediately, I could feel my essence changing, a distinct sense of reduction, a descending. God faded from view and the light began to dwindle quickly. I had the sense of swirling again, the chaos surrounding me again. I thought I could see the stars, big red ones and little blue white dwarfs shining off in the distance, hanging like ornaments through great tufts of gossamer clouds glowing with mauve and eerie green tones. All became a blur, roaring through my consciousness like a huge tornado, whisking me away, far far away.

Another sense began to intrude. I felt heavy and tired and sad all at the same time. I wanted to see. I tried to peer ahead but all was dark and cold. Then my eyes opened. I felt disoriented. I was in a park but not where I last left off. It was different. I could smell salt in the air. I was lost. I cried out, "God?"

He wasn't with me like before, but His presence was very near, just beyond me. It was darkness all around. I was in the corridor outside of the inner sanctum of God, where I first met the Council of Nine. I couldn't see God, but I could still communicate with Him mentally. I called out nervously again. God, can you hear me? Then God responded.

Well. This is what you wanted. We are separate again and it will grow worse. I will stay with you for as long as it is possible, until the vibration dissolves.

The roar of the chaos faded, and I was back on the Earth. On the ground before me were spread many small white pebbles. The area was covered with fine gravel. I followed the stretch of rocks until it dissolved into grass leading to some trees beyond. The sight was breathtaking. Everything sparkled like diamonds. I could see the blue energy current swaying and dancing with everything—the grass, the rocks, and the trees. Then I looked up to see the stars. They didn't twinkle as expected. They were large and dangled, motionless, in the deep black sky. They showed forth their multi-colored lights like uncut jewels. The sky seemed warm and exciting. Everything was beautiful.

The energy current was swimming around me, carrying my feelings and thoughts to the rocks, grass, and trees. The trees seemed to be drinking from the rocks and the grass through this same current. It was marvelous. I greeted them with the love current I had learned from God. It was a total sexual experience. I knew them and they knew me. We trusted each other now, together knowing the truth of my joining.

I commented to God. So this is how you see the Earth . . . fantastic.

God didn't answer. But it didn't matter. I knew in my heart He could hear me.

Suddenly, I remembered a favorite story I had read many years before, a fictional story called Stranger in a Strange Land, about a man who had been raised in a different culture, a Martian culture. A Martian expression, "grok," was used in that story to define a complete and profound understanding of things. That expression has greater meaning to me now. "I grok this life in fullness." Now I'm convinced that Robert Heinlein, the author, must have touched God somewhere in his fantasies.

Urgency broke through my lingering thoughts. I must hurry. There's not a moment to lose. I need to find a way home. Mary, my wife, will be terribly worried. It must have been several hours since my leaving.

As it turned out, I had been gone for days. Three days to be exact. My wife believed me to be dead in a ditch somewhere and set out with a police search. During my spiritual journey, my body had been mysteriously transported from New York City to Montauk, the tip of Long Island. I hadn't a clue as to how my body got there. I don't recall having climbed aboard any transportation. Getting back home from there was no easy task, either. Trains were scarce and, unless I wanted to wait until morning, I had to get a taxi. It was three hours by car to my house in Suffolk County.

When I arrived, Mary burst into tears, but her anger surfaced soon after.

"Where the hell have you been? Do you realize I've had the police looking all over for you?"

I stared out of the kitchen window, looking into the back yard. Nothing had any meaning to me. Where I was, and her questions all seemed unimportant. I was on the Earth again—that part was real enough. I pondered her question. It was going to be difficult to answer. You see, Mary was an atheist. She believed in the grass and the trees and the animals and our three beautiful little girls. But to ask her to believe in a supreme being was going too far. There was a gentle reminder that God was still within mental reach as I looked down at myself. I could still see the golden splatters of light sprinkled over me like fairy dust. The delicious sweet odor of His scent still marked my being. I turned to look at her, expecting her to notice. She apparently couldn't see or smell any of it. Was she that blind? It was hard to believe she could not sense what was so clear to me. This was going to be tougher than I thought. I took her hand and we sat down in the den as I began slowly.

"Look into my eyes and tell me what you see."

She blurted out with more tears, "Is this another one of the games you play? This is hardly the time for games!"

"No! Mary.. really. Just take a good long look and tell me what you see." As she began to look me over, I mentally connected to God, my divine lover. I could still feel God's loving energy coursing through my body. I felt confident. Patiently, I waited for her to respond. She stopped spewing anger. Her eyes became teary again, and she began to laugh between sobs. Then she spoke again, more softly.

"What happened to you?" she said with wonder in her voice.

Now we're getting somewhere, I thought. You see, Lord. This isn't going to be so hard. I mounted my courage like a fine white stallion and marched right into her consciousness, holding nothing back.

"What you see, my love is the result of being with God. That's where I've been for the last three days. Only for me, it's been only a few hours." She was silent. But her reaction was predictable. As an atheist, she couldn't accept what I said. She had no prior ecstatic religious experience that would allow her to relate to what I was saying. Under normal circumstances, I probably would've felt the same way. But these were hardly normal circumstances. She said nothing more.

Later, I joined her in bed; but after she fell asleep, I got up several times through the night. I felt restless. Something was wrong. I was exhausted and yet I couldn't sleep. The energy was intense and prevented me from relaxing. I didn't know what to do with it. Rapidly, I was feeling out of place here on the Earth. I was definitely losing my grip on this reality.

By morning light, the mental contact with God was completely gone. I missed Him and I mourned our disconnection for the rest of the day. The feeling of discomfort continued. The intense energy was mostly gone, but I felt out of sorts. I was unable to cope either physically or emotionally with anything. It all seemed too difficult to handle. I felt like an emotional cripple. I was an alien being hosted by a human body. I hadn't the slightest idea what to do about it!

The feeling of discomfort grew and began to frustrate me. I went into the bathroom several times throughout the day, defecating large amounts of waste each time. With each experience, I felt more and more disgusted with my body. It felt dirty, unclean. I wanted out of it badly.

I went into the shower, trying to wash off the uncleanness. Then the awful reality finally settled in. I was a divine creature locked inside an animal body with no escape! I stared at the hair on my arms and legs. Then I screamed at the top of my lungs in utter horror. "No . . . No . . . No . . . Ahhh!" As I sobbed with complete defeat, I saw that the hair on my body had grown almost an inch within seconds. It was the final insult. I looked like some helpless ape! I cried out, "Oh, God, help me! I think I'm losing my mind!"

I lay across the bed thinking that I wasn't going to make it. I was weak and God was right. Then an idea hit me. I would clean the house one room at a time. Somehow I felt, in this way, I could put my own internal house in order. I dragged out the vacuum sweeper, the mops and brooms. After three days, I had cleaned the entire house from top to bottom. Mary was delighted. She hated cleaning.

In the meantime, my mental faculties were rearranged and my ego was put back in place. I had sacrificed something else in the process. My experience with God was hanging in the balance. Slowly losing ground, the substantialness of the experience seemed less and less. Without contact, I began to question the whole thing as a grand hallucination of monumental proportions. The result of family stress and pressure at work, I conceded.

A painful source of family stress was Mary's and my unhappy marriage. Our relationship had deteriorated long before. Any good feelings we had enjoyed in the beginning were lost in bitterness. Now we had become mutually unconscious and destructive. My anger was growing steadily and I feared that I might lose control.

A dim memory of my conversations with God returned one day while I was mowing the lawn. I started to laugh. He was right all along, I thought. Well, I guess that's why He's number one! He pegged me pretty good. Here I am, just like He said, denying the whole thing.

Now the perspective was clear. In a shot, I gleaned from this insight another insight. I was wrong about needing Him to be there all the time. I was feeling sorry for myself and realized another spiritual truth: I needed to claim the experience without the support of His presence. Besides, I thought, this is far more fitting if I am gonna be a strong spiritual teacher and guide for others. I also saw the need to choose whether or not it was real for me, from this perspective, this Earth! I needed to bring God down to Earth, into my life, not the other way around.

I knew that my life would have to change drastically, that my wife of eight years wouldn't be with me. I knew I had to leave. I needed to find a way to support my new insight, and I knew it wouldn't be here with her. I prepared myself emotionally to leave my family.

LOOSE ENDS

One spring afternoon in 1975 . . .

I mustered the courage to go home from work early. My plan was to catch Mary at home with the children still at school. I declared my resolve to separate. I won't minimize the pain and agony it caused. Mary was at first very hurt and then angry. Later, my children were stunned and confused.

Now, my old life was over. I knew in my heart that, with time, Mary would recover. She was a survivor. I wasn't so sure about my children. I had three beautiful little girls whom I loved very much. Their agony would become my nemesis for many years to come. As I put on the "black hat," I had to trust that one day my children would come to understand the true meaning of my actions. I felt very alone with my decision. My doubt about the price of my new spiritual purpose reached new heights as the struggle toward a divorce proceeded slowly.

Six months later . . .

My life seemed to proceed forward by the snail's inch. I just tried to get through each day without greater expectations. Emotionally, I was a wreck. When there was time to think, I ate compulsively to numb the dreadful feelings. I knew what I wanted, but I didn't know how to accomplish it. My positive feelings about God seemed so far away. When I was with God, I felt enthusiastic and everything seemed so easy. Now it was different. I felt lost and depressed. Then, one day, something happened.

I met a woman at work, the new make-up artist hired for the studio. Her name was Dianne. She was a blue-eyed blond, quite pretty, and she seemed strangely familiar to me. When Ira, the stage manager, formally introduced us our bodies jumped back automatically. Ira couldn't help but comment, "Do you two know each other?"

We shook our heads in the negative. For the next six months, we would often sit in the lobby of the studio and talk during breaks and lunches. We talked about everything from gurus to Earth shoes. I liked her, but I thought she was pretty ditsy, a real space cadet! She would always stare above my head as we talked. I wondered what she was looking at.

Sometimes, I felt she made no sense whatever. At times I exchanged funny stories about her behavior with Scotty, the night guard. We both agreed she was very sweet, but we would enjoy a good chuckle over her from time to time.

In time, however, I grew fonder of her and less critical of her "Holly go-lightly" manner, a reference to a similar character from one of my favorite movies, Breakfast at Tiffany's.

Eventually, I wanted to hang around the make-up room more and more. One night I finally asked her out. Initially, she refused. But after I was very persistent, she finally agreed to share drinks. At the local pub and with a second wine, she declared honestly that I was interesting to talk with but definitely not her type! She was into health food and spiritual pursuits, while I was into greasy hamburgers, fries, and a cold cola to slosh them down.

Although I professed to a sincere interest in her spiritual pursuits (I had not revealed my experience with God just yet), she was not convinced! I had to admit that my diet and outward behavior didn't match those interests. It didn't take a rocket scientist to realize my appearance was not terrific! At the time, I looked pretty dumpy. I was a needy 235-pound near-sighted knight in tarnished polyester armor, sporting gold-rimmed glasses. She would've preferred a longhaired hippie type in bluejeans from the sixties.

One afternoon, I stopped by her apartment to join her for lunch with some other friends. She was still doing her make-up and called out to me from the bathroom.

"If you're hungry and can't wait, you'll find something in the frig."

"Sure. No problem," I said.

I opened the refrigerator door to help myself. All I could see was a fifty-pound bag of organic carrots squatting on the bottom shelf!

"What the hell is this?" I remarked sarcastically. "Are you some kind of friend of Harvey, the rabbit?"

She didn't catch my reference. It didn't really matter. Clearly, our tastes were very far apart. While I dreamed of Twinkies and Coca-Cola, she asked if I wanted fresh carrot juice . . . I had to politely decline.

"Uh, I'll pass if it's all the same to you . . . okay?"

But despite all of our differences, we became closer. It was obvious that our bodies had recognized and remembered a deep inner truth from childhood to which we were catching up. Certain coincidences astonished both of us. In quiet moments together, we could remember dreams that we shared which occurred in our childhood.

On occasion, we could remember similar details of a special place. When we were young children, we had joined in astral flight to a far away place, on an unknown island. Once there, we spent the entire night flying through the trees, falling in love. After we parted in the dream, I wept at breakfast over the loss of her. I was only nine at the time!

It had been a long time since I had trusted a woman. I no longer felt alone. Dianne eventually became a good friend and companion; I concluded God had sent her so that we could help each other.

We had both changed a lot since childhood. Our view of each other had come only from our meeting in our dreams; however, the practical circumstances between us now were difficult, and the chances for our joining again were slim. She had hardened herself about men due to several painful relationships, and I was still married and with children. The problems were great enough that we couldn't bring ourselves to believe there was any hope. Despite all of these obstacles, we still joined emotionally and supported each other. Together, we tried to believe again in our dreams.

By the second year of my separation, an amicable divorce was clearly not in the cards. Child support expenses and rising lawyer fees drove me to find another job promising a better salary. Dianne sometimes brought me to her house for dinner because I didn't have enough money to buy my own food. Times were hard, and I grew more dependent upon her.

Months later, things began to turn for the better. My relationship with the management of the new production company became strong and my salary suddenly jumped, promising a brighter future. My financial reliance upon Dianne lessened, creating hope that life with her could become more permanent. The divorce still progressed slowly, but I was more confident. One night after dinner, I asked Dianne to live with me. I argued that we were strong together and that it would be good for both of us. She was sympathetic but didn't agree right away. She was still involved in a relationship. He still played a prominent part in her life and she wasn't sure. Despite my insistence, she wanted to wait to resolve that situation.

Weeks later, I called to take her out to dinner. She declined my offer. She already had dinner plans with her boyfriend. I was devastated. All my doubts rolled over and flattened me like a steamroller.

A thunderstorm had gathered over New York City, and it was raining hard. I left the studio in a daze, wandering the streets in the downpour. I couldn't believe this was happening! I felt my friend was pulling away. Eventually, I found a stoop of a building not far from where Dianne lived. I sat soaked, growing cold, but I didn't care. I wanted the storm to wash away my pain. The hours passed slowly. By morning I was numb and stiff. I couldn't wait to telephone Dianne to talk. She invited me in for breakfast.

While I consumed a hot cup of tea, Dianne explained that she had needed the time to clear up old business with her boyfriend; and then she declared that the relationship between them was over. For me, the storm had finally ended. Now I felt we had a chance to begin our relationship.

In the fall of 1976, we began to live together in a large apartment on the Upper West Side, close to where we both worked.

One day, as I prepared to go to work, there was an unexpected visitor. While I was in the shower, I thought I could smell something. I paused to analyze the scent. It was very distinctive and familiar to me. It was an odor that I had almost learned to forget. The memory of that special scent suddenly flooded my mind and an immediate smile broke across my face.

Sprinkles of golden light began to appear everywhere inside the shower stall. I could feel that loving presence again. I started to laugh uncontrollably as chills went down my spine. I was so happy. I had not lost my mind . . . after all!

It's You! I cried out, "My sweet Lord, it's you."

Are you with me? He whispered softly inside my heart.

I blurted out, sobbing, "Are you kidding? Anytime, anywhere! You name it, Lord, I will always belong to you!"

You will need help to accomplish your desire on Earth. Expect it soon.

"Thank you, Lord . . . thank you."

Low Road

The journey had seemed obvious at first. Since I had made up my mind that my marriage wasn't going to work, my decision was clear. Leaving, I discovered, was only the first step in my awakening process. As time went by, my journey became more mysterious and perhaps more haphazard. I began to flounder. I needed to find some sort of guidance.

With the approaching winter solstice in 1976, I began to focus inwardly on many unresolved emotional issues. My feelings were confused and complicated, and I wanted answers. I needed to resolve my anger about what happened in my marriage and with my parents, and I wanted clarity about my spiritual path.

I was especially torn over the fate of my three small children, suffering in the aftermath of the separation. Many hidden feelings erupted within me, including a fear of failure and an old lack of self-esteem. I discovered that I had many hostilities toward women and a deep fear of men.

This continued turmoil created serious emotional blocks. My career and my relationship with Dianne wobbled. I began to seriously question my search for an inner spiritual path. I felt worse instead of getting stronger! This road to consciousness seemed rocky and dangerous to me! Insecurity, guilt, and terror filled me while I questioned my original decision to leave my family. Many times I wanted to give up my search, but Dianne encouraged me. She insisted that I keep going no matter what I found inside myself. Fortunately, I trusted her instincts.

I felt desperate for solutions. I turned to an ancient Chinese book of wisdom called The I Ching. The I Ching was an oracle that became a constant source of advice and solace for me. Ironically, The I Ching did not offer any quick solutions, but seeking its advice was like talking to the grandfather that I had lost.

This time it said, "Your friends lie to the West, your enemies to the East and your council will come from the North."

How odd! I thought.

I continued to work patiently in New York while I waited for something to come from the North. A week later, I received a telephone call from Bearsville, a small town near Woodstock, New York. The studio manager for Bearsville Records requested my help with some technical problems with a studio belonging to one of their artists. It was the only call from the North, so I took the job!

The following weekend, Dianne paid me a visit.

"How is it going? Did you learn anything yet?"

"No! I haven't got the slightest idea what I'm doing here, other than my regular job. It's been a week and there's been nothing so far."

"Well, I'm sure something will turn up," she said confidently.

During one of the recording sessions, Dianne was introduced to the studio manager. Afterwards, she came back to report with some excitement. "Michael, you must find out more about what the manager is doing. She has very shiny eyes! I just know she must be doing something really unique."

I frowned at her. My hands rested on my hips in disapproval. I just couldn't believe she could think that way. I couldn't hold back my sarcasm and feelings of judgment.

"Shiny eyes, eh? Boy I've heard some cornball impulses in my time. Shiny eyes? Dianne, give me a break!"

In the name of peace between us, I made some discrete inquiries. Nothing turned up. Then one of the studio secretaries met me one evening at a popular restaurant pub in Woodstock. After dinner, she handed me some lectures.

"Here," she said. "You might find these interesting. But don't forget where you got them. They're mine and I want them back, okay?"

"Sure, no problem," I said reassuringly.

I perused the lectures over coffee. They seemed genuine and sincere. I was particularly impressed with some of the spiritual concepts. The lectures consisted of inspirational material from a woman named Eva Pierrokos. I learned later she was a medium living in the mountains near the town of Phoenicia.

The secretary proudly went on about the "body work" being practiced by the community she represented. Now, I was really intrigued. So I asked to see the place for myself. The secretary seems to flinch at my request. She seemed strangely violated. She silently considered my request. Then she declared, "It will require an appointment for an interview."

"An interview? What for?" I retorted indignantly.

"It's the only way you can get in. Okay?"

"Yeah . . . sure, okay."

Later, I learned that the studio manager was also a member of this strange community in the Catskill Mountains.

Strange, I thought. Maybe Dianne's instincts are better than I thought.

A woman named Judith met me for my interview by the main meeting hall and offered me a tour of the Center. Afterwards, we sat casually on a wooden bench overlooking the grounds.

The place was beautiful. Many grand fir trees towered over quaint buildings that overlooked the valley. I could easily imagine the snow-crested mountains of Tibet in the background. With an air of serenity all around, the experience strongly suggested a sense of Shangri-La.

We talked of my background and my domestic problems. I explained that I was seeking advice and counsel. I told her I felt drawn to the spiritual principles outlined in the lectures.

The whole time we were together, talking with Judith reminded me of rare talks I enjoyed with my mother, when she wasn't drunk. A bit of gray hair gracefully swept along her temples, and her Austrian accent suggested charming austerity and an aristocratic quality. Although I didn't know her, I found myself admiring her. As she stared across the grounds, a slight squint of her eyes suggested some unimaginable wisdom. She turned abruptly toward me. Then she spoke with a startling tone of authority. "I think Bill will be the one for you to work with first."

This declaration was the first indication that my application to be a Center candidate had been accepted. I accepted her choice without question. Not knowing what to say, I simply responded, "If you think so."

Days later, Bill examined me physically, to understand my "body type." Understanding the shape of my body would enable a therapist to discern where I was holding emotional energy. This understanding would determine what approach to take in my physical/emotional work.

I learned that Bill would not become my personal therapist, but he did lead my confrontational group in the city. In addition, I acquired two helpers, as they were called—a Dutchman, Niels, and a young woman from Michigan by the name of Mariah. They worked personally with me at the Center in Phoenicia and in the city.

Once I had experienced a "Saturday night group" at the Center in Phoenicia, I spoke enthusiastically about the work to Dianne. My excitement convinced her to join me in this new adventure. We entrenched ourselves in the community and all its activities. Every other weekend we came to the Phoenicia Center to study the lectures of the Guide, an embodiment of psychological knowledge from a spiritual entity channeled by Eva.

The information contained a spiritual perspective on the problem of blocked emotional energy. Eva's husband John was a successful psychotherapist and a member of the community. His psychic insight into the human energy field and the bodywork he helped develop along with Alexander Lowen provided a rich physical component to the psychological and spiritual insight.

The community consisted of about thirty members living at the center and four hundred transient members coming from all walks of life, mostly living in New York. The members would gather together in Phoenicia on alternate weekends, since there were accommodations for only two hundred or so at the Center at one time. The thirty residents made up the staff and faculty. Their efforts provided the necessities of food, housekeeping, office supervision, and land management in addition to the ongoing counseling and teaching work.

The total concept envisioned by the leaders was a university of teacher/counselors helping the membership with the rudiments of understanding of their own complex psyches. Those who wanted to could study to become helpers themselves.

Everyone who came to the Center was deeply involved on the path. The term "path" came from the Guide entity, in his description of the work. Later, it came to be known as the Pathwork.

Eva would channel once a month to provide further detailed explanations of complex psychological insight, while John continued to provide the staff with his insight on the energy aspects of bodywork, stemming from what he called Bioenergetics. Later, John added the spiritual component and called it Core-energetics.

Personal emotional confrontations proceeded in private sessions, in groups, and openly in social situations. The helpers assisted each member to reach, and if possible resolve, deep emotional traumas. The basic concept of John's work emerged from Wilhelm Reich's theories. The basic theory stated that traumas emerging from an individual's life experience serve to block the creative energies in the body by freezing or suspending the healthy flow of emotional energy within the physical tissue.

John had a burning vision of this form of therapy, the Guide's insight combined with modified Bioenergetic work, as a superior system. He believed this practice often yielded greater success in accessing deep-seated emotional issues very quickly. Otherwise, these issues would remain untouched by other standard therapy models for longer periods, prolonging the agony of the patient.

After years of watching people struggle with their demons on the path, and observing my own work, I was convinced that John was right. The Pathwork did seem to be superior to anything known at the time. But it wasn't easy. It required the utmost in personal courage to do the work. You needed to be brutally honest with yourself and with others at all times. In the beginning, I was very enthusiastic about the work. I wanted to plunge into it with everything I had.

It became my whole life. All my friends, including Dianne, were on the path. I studied hard to become a good helper. I belonged to several dynamic groups in the city, my own encounter group, a couples group, my training class at the Center, and of course the community Saturday night groups—to name just a few. Additionally,

I had my own Core bodywork with a Core helper and sessions with my two conceptual helpers.

I was also involved with numerous committees at the Center from time to time. I was involved with the planning of building sites and the caretaking of the Center grounds while on the Planning board, and I helped to tackle Future Science issues in the Science committee. The consumption of my time and energy was monumental. I scarcely had any time to do anything else.

The Center wasn't just a vision of personal emotional freedom for me. It was a total movement model for humanity. I believed that the Center work would become the underpinning for the emotional rehabilitation of the world. When other international communities, such as Findhorn and Lindesfarn, began to interact, I was even more convinced. The impact was intoxicating and commanding simultaneously.

At the same time, the Center had become something else. It had become the family I always wanted. I think, in retrospect that was true for every member at that time. I also believe that unfolding archetypes of individual family images became inextricably intertwined with the community. These images eventually caused greater upheaval in the community, and the community underwent many drastic changes, which caused many to finally leave the Center. The Pathwork could make deep changes in people. The results were often astounding while sometimes surprising and unpredictable.

The turning point for me was something called an intensive. It involved a weeklong experience of personally styled physical and conceptual therapy geared for my particular emotional problem set. There was a team of helpers working with me several times a day.

Dianne, concerned about separation in our work together, had also decided to take an individual intensive at the same time. The personal changes we made during that week was dramatic, and in the end, her worst fears were realized when we could no longer relate to each other in the same way as before. This separation actually threatened the original basis of our relationship. Later, the consideration that we might split up prompted a joint session. The session was used to effectively smooth the differences in our new personality structures. It was quite a struggle, but ultimately successful.

Something dramatic happened toward the end of my personal work that week. During my last physical exercise, I had to go around to all of my team helpers and shake them violently about the shoulders with my arms and hands. When I finished one round, I had to continue around again and again. While I was shaking them, I kept yelling at them, "Look at me! See me!"

Then something unexpected happened. An incredible energy suddenly surged inside of me, causing my body to shake violently. I fell to the floor convulsing and entered into a fetal position. I was almost catatonic with tetne, a form of paralysis caused by hyperventilation. But I wasn't hyperventilating! The team members stood around me in a circle, trying their best to support me. They could all feel the amazing energy pouring out from my body from almost six feet away. I remember that one of the team members actually proclaimed, "My God, he could be a healer!"

After the energy calmed, I returned to my room, feeling terribly shaken, cold, exhausted, and stunned speechless. What was this energy? I had never experienced anything like it before.

Later, in my private sessions, I explored this energy with one of my helpers. To my utter amazement, he was helpless to provide any insight into managing it!

Here was a remarkable physiological phenomenon: an unknown energetic reaction, presumed to be of spiritual origin, was predicted to exist inside my body and now I had experienced it! At first, I could hardly believe it. Then I felt worse, because I wanted to understand this energy beyond theory, to further my development.

In time, I became very troubled and disillusioned. I felt that the function of the Center was to find a way to stimulate and encourage this fantastic energy. I believe this should have been the real purpose of all the intense emotional work. In my opinion, there was insufficient experience at the Center to further develop this end of the work. The Pathwork was very good at reaching and culling negative emotional issues, but it seemed to be caught up in an endless trail of negative emotional debris. I couldn't see a plan for the eventual release and utilization of transformed spiritual energy.

I believed that I needed to find someone outside the Center who knew about this kind of energy and, more importantly, could teach me how to develop and manage it.

Meanwhile, I was trying to reconcile the impact of this energy and at the same time deal with the impact of certain serious decisions from my past: first, my choice to leave my first wife Mary and my three young children after eight years of marriage to pursue my own truth; second, my decision to put my own healing and self-worth before the needs of my children.

I kept asking myself over and over, How could I reconcile putting the healing of myself before the care my children? My helpers did not have any answers. Actually, no one did! The problem seemed unresolvable. I had planned for a long time to ask Eva's spirit Guide about my dilemma of worthiness and the children.

A new and shocking development reared its head at the Center. There were rumors that Eva was seriously ill. Questions about her survival were running rampant. I felt worried. If Eva is very sick, I thought, perhaps she will not be able to enter full trance anymore. Or even worse, she might pass away altogether!

I knew her demise would be devastating to the community and to me. My own selfish concerns and needs were running high. I was sure that others would feel the same way. Dianne learned that Eva was still dictating the Guide's messages, in conscious trance, to someone else. She still answered personal questions for a few. This would be my last chance. Keeping my fingers crossed, I sent my questions to the Guide, addressed to Eva.

A community group was held on Wednesday nights once a month in the New York City Center. This particular night would turn out to be Eva's last lecture from the Guide. Ann, an old member of the community, was chosen to read it to everyone.

The lecture was amazing, as always, but I believed that I could hear a fond farewell enclosed within the words of the Guide. Astonished, I mentioned it to everyone around me. My perception was quickly dismissed by everyone as my misunderstanding. More importantly, the long-awaited answer to my question about my children dangled at the end of the lecture like early morning dew.

The Guide Entity said, "In the case of the man who divides himself from his wife and children, be aware that much darkness comes out of this joining. And out of this negative activity, it often requires a more negative act to break the bonds that bind the man to such negativity. How can the man, who is himself distressed, be of any comfort to the others in distress around him? If care is taken to consciously mend the feelings and misconceptions in the man, then the man will be ready to help the children later, when they will need his help the most."

I sat stunned among the three hundred people present. At first, I was red with embarrassment. Then I looked around and found everyone transfixed, paying no attention to the words meant for me. It was as though I alone heard those words! As it should be, I thought.

With the new guidance and inner resolve, I pushed ahead with my personal work to complete the divorce from my first wife. It was two years before I saw my children again, due to legal advice that evolved from the awful struggle to agree to terms with Mary and her lawyers. It was painful and perhaps the most difficult thing I've ever done.

Then one day, after the terms of the agreement were settled, I returned to greet my children. I finally shared in their pain. It was even more difficult than I had imagined. Their agony and confusion was so great that they could not reach out to me. I was not terribly surprised. I cried with them, as I tried to reassure them it would get better. I knew it was really up to me.

My path suddenly seemed lonely again. While I was with them, I felt like a man talking to himself. Minutes after I had left their home, I entered the main highway leading back to the city. I blinked and rubbed the flowing tears from my eyes. I could see faint bursts of light exploding like fireworks in many colors, superimposed on the clouds in the sky. I was surprised. Then I expressed my thoughts openly to Heaven. So, you think it's time to celebrate, eh? In my own view, I could only anticipate a long and painful road to recovery with my children.

Several weeks passed . . .

With the resolution of my divorce and marriage to Dianne, I could now focus on another unresolved issue in my life. I was now ready to break with the Pathwork community.

One Saturday evening, I stood up in the meeting hall and declared that my studies for helpership had come to an end. My heart was heavy as I tried to explain my feelings to the members of the community. I stated that I had to go elsewhere for the answers I wanted. The mood was solemn. Disappointment filled the air. I could feel disapproval from the leaders present. Many among the membership, who loved me very much, felt abandoned and betrayed by my decisions. In the face of this reaction, I proclaimed my love for the work and vowed to continue my personal sessions with my helpers. But I knew, beyond any doubt, that my commitment to the community had reached an end.

For a time, this decision put great stress on my relationship with Dianne. She supported my decisions but remained a strong member of the community. Meanwhile, she continued her studies to completion and extended her work for three more years of special Core training. I was proud of her, completely supporting her achievements.

I did honor my commitments to personal sessions in the years that followed. Even though Dianne eventually let go her desire to see me return to the community, certain members of the community believed me to be in darkness and continued to pull at me through her. But I remained firm and determined to find the answers I needed from other sources. I knew I had to find another teacher!

WAKE-UP CALL

New York's city parking rules are always inconvenient. Every other day, vehicles have to be shifted from one side of the street to the other as in a game of musical chairs. The rules are in effect in the early morning hours, supposedly to accommodate the street sweepers. There are too many cars in the City and few parking spots. Everyone avoids prowling for spaces in the morning by moving their cars the night before. Every time Dianne and I would flip a coin for who would draw the chore, I would always lose the toss. One particular night, I had set out to face the grim chore alone. The night's drizzle was an unfriendly companion. I stiffened to brace myself against the wetness, as I quietly jibed myself, Damn, I didn't bring an umbrella.

By the time I reached my little blue Toyota, I was drenched and cold. The rain made it an easy night for thoughts. They drifted in and out, forming lingering pictures. The windshield wipers squeaked back and forth, struggling to cut through layers of city oil and sludge. My view was blurry. A soaked cold-to-the-bone reality settled in as I pulled the car slowly into traffic on West 75th street. The rearview mirror revealed that no parking spots had magically appeared behind me. No luck. I was in for the long haul.

The music from the radio slipped quietly into the background. My thoughts turned angry. I just wanted to be in bed! The drizzle of water droplets splashing on the windshield mesmerized me as they randomly picked up the colors of the changing traffic signals. Everything appeared surreal and mystical. For a moment I was lost.

The next traffic signal change was irritatingly overdue. My impatience nagged at me. I clenched my teeth against the conspiracy to delay me. I silently declared, Even this light is determined to keep me out all night!

When the light shifted, I was Mario Andretti jockeying for a better position. Now the problem was the guy in front of me. I began to ask rhetorical questions to myself. What was he doing . . . why wasn't he moving? Perhaps something was wrong . . . maybe he suffered a heart attack?

As my door was about to open, his car inched forward slowly. I entered the intersection behind him and paused to consider a left or right turn. The wrong decision now might condemn me to another thirty minutes out on this miserable night. My intuition suffered against the weight of my reason. It will be a left turn, I thought.

When I began to turn the wheel, a bright light flashed into my eyes. Disoriented and blinded, I shut my eyes instinctively. For a moment, I thought the sun had fallen from the sky. There was a loud bang. All was dark and quiet.

It was difficult to determine how much time had passed. I was aware of an unusual calm and a distinct sensation of floating. A mist appeared to hang around my body.

It's a dream, I proclaimed. My face feels wet. Shit! . . . I must've left the window open . . . the rain . . . it's in my face.

The mist gradually cleared, revealing the street below me. I was floating all right! I seemed to be about ten feet above the street . . . There's my car! The windshield was shattered and much of the car seemed irregular, or mangled. There was blood everywhere . . . it was mine!

The quietness became disturbing. The scene set my mind on a rampage. A single thought collapsed on me: Maybe this is not a dream! Then I . . . I must be . . . can't be dead! Oh, God!

I scrambled for alternative ideas, but there was nothing. I couldn't explain why my body looked so relaxed in that terrible situation. It was an awful inescapable conclusion. A feeling of regret covered over me like a cold wet blanket.

I felt sadness in my thoughts.

Yet, I wasn't afraid.

I should be scared out of my wits.

I was amazed that I had no fear. There was a deep calm despite my sense of regret. Then another thought occurred to me.

Hey, maybe someone's coming to get me?

Someone spoke softly behind me. "You're not dead, just apart."

At first I was startled and afraid to look. Then, slowly, I turned to respond. I stared at the sky above for an eternal moment and saw nothing.

"You guys don't waste any time!"

"Don't be afraid," the voice comforted. "We haven't come for you in that way. We do want you to come with us. We have some things to show you."

A shape began to emerge from the darkness. It was a large man dressed in heavy purple robes. He had long white hair and appeared to be very old. I noticed his expression seemed kind as he smiled at me. He stretched out, gesturing to join him.

A strong feeling of loyalty for my body surfaced. If I left with him, it would be permanent. I hesitated and feared I would never see my body again. That option did not appeal to me! I began to make some feeble excuses.

"Uh . . . shouldn't I sort of stick around? That is, leaving may not be such a great idea right now . . . you know! Maybe somebody needs my help down there, or something."

The old man didn't answer. He just smiled at me again and offered a gentle nudge, encouraging me to move away. The concern for my body was still very strong. It was like leaving a friend behind.

"Listen," I asserted, "I feel weird about leaving my body down there. Are you sure I'm not dead?"

"You have not transitioned, but you are apart and it is an excellent opportunity to introduce you to other things."

"How long are we going for, anyway?"

"Do not be concerned," the old man counseled. "No time, as you understand it, will have passed."

"Really?" I blurted with surprise.

Cautiously, I relinquished control. The scene below began to fade. The mist surrounded me and carried me along like a soft chariot.

"By the way, you didn't bother to mention where we were going."

"We're not going anywhere really," the old man answered calmly.

"It is more that your vibration is increasing; that is to say, we are changing your state of being."

The sense of movement stopped and the mist cleared. I was standing on a stone verandah. The hardness of the stone felt real beneath my feet. The new environment seemed quite substantial. The view in front was a rolling landscape of dark olive-green hills dotted by clumps of trees. Some of the trees were tall and cylindrical like poplars. Every part of the lower sky glowed with a pale yellow moonlight. The night sky directly above was a deep mauve dissolving into blackness. In the deeper blackness, stars appeared but didn't seem to twinkle. My fascination with the new surroundings lessened my fear and concern for my body.

The elderly stranger now appeared before me on the verandah. He studied me for a moment before he began to speak again.

"We thought it best to prepare you for what is to come. You've had quite a jolt, created to re-establish a firm foundation between your soul and the spiritual realm. You were about to make some serious decisions that would have created terrible obstacles for the work you have chosen here. When you wanted to start your own enterprise in engineering counseling, your intent was to gather a great deal of currency. Correct?"

Thrown back by the old man's knowledge of my innermost desires, I answered defensively. "Yeah! So what's wrong with that?"

"You have also committed yourself to serve the Most High God. We understand that you wanted to be a 'spiritual bridge' for others. Correct?"

Now I was really curious. This stranger knew an awful lot about me! "Yeah . . . maybe. Who are you?" I demanded.

The stranger ignored my demand for the moment and went on. "We have halted you temporarily. This will give you another opportunity to reconsider your present direction. Of course, we cannot stop you. Ultimately, we cannot violate your free will. However, we can offer you other views of your choices."

I began to study this old man more closely. He was very tall, towering above eight feet. A long mane of white hair surrounded his bald crown. On the right there was a separated lock of hair bound half way down by a metallic ring. His bushy eyebrows, mustache, and beard were all purest white. His beard and draped mustache almost hid his mouth. A large band of multi-colored stones bound into a rope-like sling hung diagonally over his robes. It seemed strangely important.

His complexion was dark, perhaps red. I couldn't tell because of the dimness of the light. His eyes radiated icy blue like sparkling gemstones. A small gold ring clung to his left ear. He reminded me of the image of the cleanser man, Mr. Clean. I began to chuckle at this thought.

Determined to know to whom I was speaking, I repeated my inquiry. "Who are you . . . really? What is this all about?"

He smiled slightly and answered, "I am Yokar, manifesting from the wisdom of the Most High. You needed assistance in your endeavors."

"So, you don't want me to be an engineer. Is that it?"

"We want you to consider your desire to amass large amounts of currency, for the sake of your illusions. This violates the laws of the Life Force."

I felt indignant.

"And what's wrong with having lots of money to realize my dreams? You can be spiritual with money. It's not like I'm going to hurt people with it! I will put it to good use, not just to help myself. Others can be helped if I am prosperous! Right?"

"Michael, it's not about that. It's dangerous for you to build up a lot of energy without having a good foundation. The currency is just another form of energy. You must possess a strong out-flowing quality before you gather a greater influx. There must be a balance in all things. The Life Force eliminates massive imbalances, because of the danger of stagnation. Stagnation brings putrefaction in the living universe."

"Does that mean the Life Force you're talking about is trying to redistribute the wealth to others? Am I taking away from somebody else who needs it more?"

"No. That's not it either," Yokar confirmed. "You see, my son," he continued, "you want to amass large quantities of currency so you can feel safer. Correct?"

"Yeah. I suppose so."

"All this is based on fear. You can't or won't trust life to support you at every turn. You want to sit on considerable wealth to protect you. The problem is you will grow to trust the currency more than yourself. The Life Force won't allow that. Do you see? If you don't trust yourself, how will you help others to trust themselves? If you truly want to help others, you must reach for greater levels of energy flow, from a sense of confidence, not fear. Do you understand?"

"Yeah, I guess so."

"That's only part of what we want to tell you. We are here to help you accomplish what you deeply want in your life. To help you become a 'bridge' to your brothers and sisters on the Earth. For this, you will need training. When you are ready, we will guide you toward that training. You will benefit from it and help others at the same time. There is much work to do to prepare you for this. The time has come for you to meet your chosen destiny. We want to remind you that the Most High loves you and wants you to flourish.

"There are many wonders already in the Earth that will be useful to you along the way of your chosen task. You will need to learn how to access them and take the best possible advantage of their properties. For now, you will need to return to Earth and complete the reconstitution that has already begun. It's time to return. We'll talk again about this and many other things later. This is the beginning of your deeper training."

His form began to dissolve from view. I concluded to myself, So this was the Atlantean spirit Dr. Malone was talking about.

I called after the fading image. "So, Yokar. Are you the Atlantean . . . from God? He has sent you to help me?"

With his image almost gone, his voice responded. "Yes . . . let us say for now, that it is in your best interest that we continue together with your development. We are from the Most High realm and will guide you with your life . . . as you have requested. All things that are asked for . . . are given. . . ." His voice trailed off.

"Requested! What do mean requested?" I yelled after him but

there was no answer.

Then the mist swept around me again as a disappointment filled me. Now it was too late. He was gone. The fascinating landscape that had captivated my attention before fell away and only his words remained.

While the mist swept me away, my ears buzzed and tickled as if some insect were flying around my head. I tried to focus on the buzz and make it go away but it was not continuous. The sound kept breaking up at odd intervals. I tried to listen with more effort because it felt important. After a while, I realized the buzzing was the sound of a voice, but far away. My ears strained to separate the words.

"Are you all right?" The police officer said.

The floating feeling was replaced by other unpleasant sensations. The sensations grew stronger. They gathered into recognizable pain that was increasing. I tried to speak, but all I could do was groan. My facial muscles moved a little, but no other sounds came out. Words were difficult to form. Finally, my mouth worked. "What did you say?"

"I said . . . are you all right?" The officer repeated patiently.

"I think so. I don't know."

Images came into focus as the mist trailed off behind me. The new surroundings were odd and disorienting. Broken bits of glass sprinkled over my lap as twisted metal entangled me. I couldn't move. The metal completely encased me.

The officer pressed on for a report. "What happened?"

I couldn't put two words together or make any sense of it.

"You were in an accident . . . do you understand?" He coached.

"I've been hit?" I mumbled with surprise.

"Yeah . . . just stay put, buddy. Don't worry."

Real and imaginary images dissolved back and forth and I wanted to move. Then I mumbled again. "I can't move."

My words sounded funny or drunk, although I didn't remember drinking. My head started to spin. My ears were ringing. It occurred to me, the police would definitely think I am drunk! I rambled on incoherently.

"What about Dianne? Oh God . . . Dianne!"

The officer looked puzzled. "There's no one else in here, buddy!

Who's Dianne?"

I didn't answer.

"Look," he commanded softly. "Stay put. I'll be right back."

Then he left to talk with the other officer already engaging the other driver, a tow truck operator. I could just overhear them talking.

"Pete, I think this other guy had a pretty good whack on the head. He's delirious."

My body seemed numb or asleep. When I tried to move my arms and legs from the wreckage, everything screamed in pain. Thoughts rolled around like loose marbles. I felt suddenly claustrophobic and my thoughts turned desperate.

Ahh . . . oh my God, I can't stay like this . . . I have to get out. Gasoline! I can smell it. Explosions! My body will be burned. I have to get out.

With overwhelming will, I ignored all the pain and exited quickly. The car became my crutch. The claustrophobic feelings started to fade as I leaned over the fender. All I could do was try to stand. My thoughts were muddy. I wasn't even sure if the policeman was real. Speaking was like pulling weeds. I felt exhausted and remembered that I should've been in bed.

I wondered, Why aren't I in bed?

The officer returned, surprised to see me out of the car.

"You okay?" he said.

With my head in a fierce spin, words sounded drawn and slow. His words were slow too and easier to understand now. I smiled at him while I still leaned on my car.

"Your head is bleeding!" He went on. "You should sit down."

He offered help to lower my body to the curbside. I had to admit, it felt good to sit. My left arm was beginning to throb and both legs were aching and a little shaky.

"Are you sure you're all right? We can call an ambulance for you. It's no problem."

The officer seemed reluctant to believe that I was really okay. But I was very persistent. I kept reassuring him that all the blood was due to my tendency to bleed easily, even with slight wounds. "I'm okay, I think. I'm just a little banged up. I've got to get to a phone," I declared. "Gotta reach my wife, Dianne . . . she's nearby . . . probably worried too!"

The officer listened carefully and began to act less concerned about me. My considerations for Dianne had probably made me seem more coherent. Now he began to explain certain details about the other driver.

"Well, we thought you oughta know, this guy doesn't have any license and his insurance card is not up to date! We gave him a summons. We've also alerted the city towing service to take your car to a pound. Here's the number to call. Okay?"

"Yeah. Thanks," I said softly as I shoved the paper into my pocket.

Minutes later, the patrol car sped into the night with the tow truck close behind. The vision of the accident scene faded into blackness.

I don't know how I got back to my apartment. The next thing I remember is standing in front of the door to my apartment, fumbling to find the correct key to put into the lock. Suddenly, Dianne opened the door. When she saw all the blood on my face, she gasped. She thought that I had been attacked on the street! She began to clean me up as I explained what I could about the accident.

A few days later . . .

In the doctor's office, Dianne was beside me as I went through all the tests. The impact of my nightmare was upon me. I was still numb on my left side, my vision still blurred, and I couldn't put two words together to make any sense. My speech hadn't improved much, either.

The neurologist seemed like an average man. His manner was comforting, something like that of a country practitioner. Specialists usually act pompous and arrogant. He took the time to explain everything, and I was impressed by his obvious expertise. He carefully stared for moment into my droopy eyes. With a measure of kindness, he began to speak. "Young man, you've had a serious head injury and it will take some time to heal. We'll need to do a C.T. scan to confirm my prognosis.

"Uh . . . how long will it take?"

"Well, it's hard to estimate. The scan will take about thirty minutes to complete. I would say your injury would take at least a year, perhaps two, to heal."

I was silent. Dianne stiffened, rising to meet this news with protest.

"Are you sure about that, Doctor? Could you be mistaken?" She challenged. "Isn't there something more you can do?"

I watched helplessly, as they went on about me.

"Look, I realize how you must feel, Mrs. Morgan. It's very clear!" he said with finality. "Michael has suffered a serious concussion. It's just going to take some time to heal!"

I could tell Dianne was holding back tears. I wanted to defend or console her. Then she took on warrior-like qualities. She turned, smiled gently in my direction and flashed her soft blue eyes with resolute defiance. She bowed her head and made a solemn vow. "Don't worry, honey. We'll find someone. There must be another way." Then her eyes seemed to burn with greater intensity. "I'm going to find you a healer!"

Weeks later, I met with the lawyer. Through the ringing in my ears and numbness that continued to persist in my body, I strained to listen as he explained the problem of my case: It was simple; there was a problem because of "no-fault." No-fault in New York means you can't sue unless there's evidence of permanent injury or broken bones. I had no broken bones. The lawyer told me not to worry. They'd work on it. Meanwhile, the concussion had impaired my ability to perform my engineering work. Fears of permanent brain damage began to creep in. Doubts about my business's success began to rise.

I was left with my broken head, no answers from the doctors, and no answers from the lawyers. I had only one place to turn: Dianne and her search for a metaphysical solution to my crisis. The conventional world was not helping. I had no other choice.

Up in Smoke

Dianne hailed a cab, with the confidence of a trader. She wanted to get me to a healer quickly before I changed my mind. Although I was not in any shape to give her any resistance, I did have some strong doubts about the success of "laying on hands."

I felt my injuries were serious, not the kind a faith healer could cure. Faith healers belonged in a carnival tent! I imagined a barker shouting, "Come one! Come all! See the amazing Lazardo perform healing miracles in front of your very eyes!" Maybe my doubt existed because I was aware of their tricks. Before the accident, a team of wild horses couldn't have forced me to a healer's table.

It was a short ride to the healer's apartment. When I opened the door, a puff of cigarette smoke curled out to sting my nose. "Oh, boy," I groaned. My eyes rolled in disapproval. There was a small nudge from Dianne urging me on. In a whisper I asked, "So what do you know about this healer anyway?"

"Well, my friend Charlotte knew Bianca for a long time and she comes highly recommended!"

"Yeah? Well, she's going to have to be pretty good to fix me up!" I retorted with a grimace.

Dianne grabbed me by the arm with a glare of disapproval. "Listen," she whispered sternly, as she ushered me into the apartment, "I want you to give this a fair chance, okay?"

"Okay. Okay."

"If you have another idea . . . let's hear it!" she continued stoutly.

Before I could answer, she interrupted. "Oh hi, Bianca!"

Dianne rushed before me into the smoky room to greet a small thin woman sitting on an antique couch. The room was filled with people. I followed, trying not to trip over a small mop of a dog that was desperately trying to chew off my toes. The woman's raspy voice suddenly rose above the cackling chatter.

"Chips! Now you get over here!"

She peered over her clasped hands that held a smoldering cigarette and extended a casual smile toward Dianne.

The woman's hair was drawn back, exposing milk-colored, baby-smooth skin. Her small round dark brown eyes folded into soft, almost unnoticeable wrinkles. I couldn't determine her age. She sat upon a couch that had been upholstered very much like my grandmother's. In front of her was a coffee table covered with papers, a bit of unopened mail, and some books hidden under old magazines. The whole thing was stacked so high; it had to have been collecting since the turn of the century.

Dianne giggled. "Well, it took a lot. But I finally got him to come." Everyone laughed. She sat upon the opposite couch and joined the landscape of odd people that draped around Bianca. All of her visitors seemed to nest on cushy pillows like hens in a house. There were other indescribable odds and ends that loosely decorated the view. The room seemed full. There was nowhere to sit. I felt awkward. Everyone looked on, chatting quietly. They all smiled kindly at me. I couldn't figure out whether they were about to be treated, had already been treated, or were just gawkers. I kept staring as I wondered, Are they sick or injured? More importantly, have they survived Bianca's treatment?

My wife introduced me.

"Bianca, this is my husband Michael."

She didn't get up. I peered down at her and noticed that her eyes weren't brown but jet-black, like crow's eyes. She smiled and motioned for me to sit. Amazingly, an opening appeared on the couch near where Dianne was sitting.

I waited patiently for my wife to look in my direction. Once I had attracted her attention, I mouthed discreetly, "Interesting." I then punctuated with a small cough. Dianne ignored my obvious critique.

Bianca leaned over the table. In the only uncovered space sat a giant ashtray, which almost overflowed with cigarette butts. With a quick survey of the group, Bianca put out her cigarette in the rising pile.

My contemptuous feelings continued to mount. Yet I found this woman eccentric but rather charming. It disturbed me that she was a heavy smoker. When I was a child, my entire family smoked and I barely survived it. Now, I was expected to let this "dragon" cure my ailing head. I thought, If she fixes my head, then she'd be able to remove any lung cancer I develop here!

Then I wondered if she could sense any of my judgments. I dropped my gaze to the floor, trying to deflect my thoughts away from her. I glanced up momentarily to check her reactions. She indicated nothing.

She seemed perfectly ordinary. I couldn't find any signs of her special ability. When I studied her more closely, I noticed that the palms of her hands were a bright cherry-red color.

"What happened to your hands?" I asked.

"Oh, that comes with the work," she said nonchalantly. "It's the energy, you see? My hands have been that color since the beginning of the work. I've gotten used to it by now, you know?"

Ceremoniously, she poured hand lotion into her palms and vigorously rubbed them together. After she made absolutely sure that her skin was thoroughly covered, Bianca pointed toward the table. She stood up and signaled for me to get on.

"Well, Michael, let's see what's wrong with you."

Dianne added, "He had a terrible accident. The doctor says it's a concussion!" Bianca said nothing. Then Dianne began to sob. It was then that I realized how scared she was.

"Please remove your shoes and the stuff from your pockets and your belt," Bianca requested.

I raised my eyebrows indignantly about emptying my pockets.

Then she added, "All that stuff really hurts my hands, you know?"

She began to tap lightly on my head and neck as I thought, Hey, I'm gonna get a massage. So this won't be a total loss!

Again in that gravely voice, she asked me to turn over. She passed her hands over my head and body, tapping gently on my skin. It was as if my skin were a piano and she the master musician. She returned to my forehead and stopped.

Then she groaned, "Michael, your brains are really scrambled!"

I agreed, laughing nervously. "I know! I know. That's why I'm here. Can you do anything about it?"

She paused in her tapping to consider my query. "My doctors can do just about anything," she stated frankly. "But they don't tell me much. I really don't know much about the healing I do. I just let the energy pass through me and they do all of the work."

Although I appreciated her honesty, I didn't find this declaration particularly reassuring. Her tapping continued up and down my spine and along my legs and arms. Her pattern worked in a kind of rhythmical fashion. Each hand tapped a different beat with the sound in syncopated rhythm. I never felt anything quite like it before.

I noticed a chill beginning to penetrate my body. I still felt compelled to fill the silence with conversation about what Bianca was doing.

"You know," I said, "I really have a hard time with this sort of thing."

She retorted, "Oh, it doesn't matter. It won't affect the work! Actually, most of my clients do their best when they don't believe in what's going on." She proceeded to tap upon my brow quite vigorously. It became quite painful. Just as I was about to complain, she stopped. The cold chill now completely filled my body and I began to tremble. I was so absorbed with the physical effects that I was completely unaware that she had finished.

As I began to get up, my head started throbbing. Dianne sensed my weakened condition and inquired, "How are you doing, honey?"

I couldn't answer. I managed to sit up to let my legs and feet dangle. I watched them lazily swing to and fro. I imagined I was sitting on a dock staring at the water with a hot sun over me, making my brain stupid. I felt strange and I couldn't hide it. I looked up to see all of the strangers' faces still smiling. They all seemed to know something I was still trying to figure out. I turned my attention back to the floor. It seemed less obtrusive to me, somehow. I wanted to run out of there right then. My focus came back to Bianca, now sipping on a martini. All my images of a healer had been blown. At least I wouldn't get a sermon on the glory of God today. I was relieved! Through the smoke, alcohol, and lack of pretense, this "down-to-

Earth Witch Doctor" was very appealing.

The evening conversation revealed that Bianca's doctors weren't physical people. Even as she explained that the doctors were spirit guides who passed energy through her, she casually remarked that her background was scientific. She complained of constant pain in her body as "they" adjusted her nervous system to accommodate more energy flow.

Once again, I was disarmed by her practical assessment of an absurd situation. As I listened, my views began to blur between the real and surreal. The line of sanity no longer seemed clear to me. This scientist had taken a walk on the wild side and never returned! My engineering background always provided me with a staple against the "lunatic fringe." Now, I found myself considering the gray areas. Frankly, I was disturbed. It frightened me a little that her scientific training could be undone by a world of unmeasurable, unprovable psychic phenomena. Yet Bianca had obviously adjusted to her reality.

I continued to see Bianca almost daily. The treatments repeatedly produced a drowsiness and strong sensations of cold. Only the faces of gawkers would change from one session to the next.

One day, she began working on my back. When I turned over, she straightened up and yelped in pain. I was alarmed. She held both ears, grimacing in pain.

"Bianca! What's the matter?" I asked.

"That sound, it's going right through me!"

"What sound? I don't hear anything!"

"It's an awful high-pitched squeal . . . " She paused to contain a very strong pain. I didn't know what to do.

Then she exclaimed, "There's somebody here, and he's not one of mine!"

I glanced around the room but couldn't see anyone. I wondered cautiously if this was some ploy to reel in my disbelief.

"What are you talking about?" I exclaimed.

Her face revealed her alarm to be quite genuine. "I don't know . . . but it's really huge and very near!"

Again I looked around but saw nothing. I tried to engage her analytical self, hoping to reduce her fear. "Huge, you say—can you be more specific?"

My doubts were rising. Maybe she has totally lost it, I thought.

Not knowing where this was going, I continued to encourage her description of the experience in more detail. At least it would take her mind off of the pain. She described a humanoid creature, tall in stature, about eight or nine feet in height.

Then I remembered the footprints. Eight or nine feet? I tried to recall the details of that day at work. I had managed to avoid that experience for all those years. But now I couldn't shake the awful feeling. Those prints seemed to match the size of the creature Bianca was describing. There was something else, another feeling. The sound, the presence and size all seemed familiar.

"I wouldn't worry. I have a feeling I know who it is!" I said boldly.

She was surprised and somehow relieved. "Is he friendly?"

I shrugged. "Actually, I can't really say, but I haven't known this thing to hurt anyone yet." I couldn't believe what I was saying. I didn't have the slightest idea what I was talking about, yet I felt perfectly fine in telling her this. I knew it wasn't much for her to go on, but it was the best I could do. She seemed satisfied by my comments and calmed down. She went on working, trying to tolerate the new energy that was present.

"Well, are you going to tell me about your friend?"

"There's not much to tell," I said.

I did not remember any of the conversations I had with Yokar in the accident, but I went on to recount the incident of the strange footprints appearing at work years before. Then I told Bianca what the medium had told me years later. "The medium said my guide was called Yokar and that allegedly he's an Atlantean spirit here to help me."

Several minutes passed. Neither one of us spoke. Suddenly, she straightened up again and seemed to listen. Now she expressed herself differently and with some authority. "Your friend, Yokar, has asked the doctors to rewire you so that you can hear him speak to you."

"What?" I exclaimed, choking.

She calmly repeated herself. I laughed out loud.

"But they need your permission!" she said.

I laughed harder. Then Dianne blurted out from across the room, "Oh, rewire me! Rewire me!" This was too much. I was laughing so hard I was crying. Even Bianca started to laugh.

Moments later, Bianca continued to hound me. "Well, are you willing to do it?"

I just stared at her, smiling. "You're serious, aren't you?"

She looked into my face with the cool demeanor of that scientist hidden inside. Her eyes twinkled as her lips turned up slightly in a wry grin. "I never joke about what the doctors have to say!"

I looked over at Dianne. I knew it was her heart's desire to have some kind of direct contact with a spirit. I let go of any remaining incredulity.

"Okay." I declared. "Wire me up. After all, what have I got to lose, my brains? I lost those already! Sure, go ahead. Why not."

She went back to work. This time, it was very different. It wasn't so much how she tapped, but where. She went all around my head, up my neck and around my ears on both sides. I felt dizzy. She seemed to be mumbling under her breath the whole time. I couldn't make it out. I knew better than to ask, as she probably didn't know what she was saying anyway.

It was another week before she finally announced, "Okay, Michael, that's all I can do for you."

I seemed to have better control over my speech, the blurred vision had cleared up, and the numbness was also gone. But I wanted to be sure, so I went back to see the neurologist.

I was ushered into his office by the receptionist. He looked up at me inquisitively. "What can I do for you, Michael?"

"Well, Doc, I'm here to get another work-up."

"Michael . . . " he paused, looking to phrase his words patiently. "You know what the outcome will be. These things don't change overnight, no matter how much you might want it to go away. Look! You can see here for yourself. " He directed my attention to the stack of medical reports he held in his hand. "You have a full concussion! I'm really sorry . . . it's just going to take time to heal."

I listened patiently. I knew he would not consider my proposal if I didn't allow him this sort of practical discouragement.

"Doctor Kaplan, I need you to do the tests again. I believe something has changed. You'll have to trust me on this. Will you run the tests again?"

"Michael, I can't justify another battery of tests just because you feel different. These shifts are momentary, believe me. I'm your doctor."

"Yes I know, but this is different. My speech is better and my numbness is gone."

I pleaded with as much feeling as I could muster.

"Even my eyesight is improving!"

He looked at me for a few minutes. I could tell he was sympathetic, but his traditional experience was also speaking to him. He leaned forward, bringing his chair fully upright again. "Well . . . you realize the insurance isn't going to cover this. It's going to be your quarter!"

He was hoping that the element of the cost would finally persuade me. Granted, it was persuasive, but I had to know if the whole thing with Bianca and Yokar had worked. I told him I wanted the tests.

"Okay," he said, "but don't get your hopes up."

Later that afternoon, I sat in his office, waiting patiently for the results. He swung boldly past me with swift assurance. He sat down behind his desk and opened a manila folder. He thumbed through the pile of medical reports with careful deliberation. At first he said nothing. From time to time, he looked up at me and smiled slightly. He began to rap upon the papers with a freshly sharpened pencil. Once again, he looked at me, but this time he looked perturbed.

"I just can't make this out."

"What do you mean?"

"Your new tests indicate a complete reversion. But only three weeks ago your record shows a full concussion."

"You mean I'm cured?"

"To be quite frank, I don't know what it means. Did you do something between your last checkup and now that I should know about?"

"Yes, that's what I wanted to confirm."

"Well," he said, waiting, "tell me about it."

"I don't think you're going to like it, but I went to a healer."

His expression turned. "You're right! I don't care for the answer." He paused before he spoke again. "But your condition has changed drastically in a very short time. That warrants an entry into my journal."

I bid him farewell, but then he stopped to say that my lawyer had been in touch. To develop my case, my lawyer had requested long-term disability and therapy records. Given my "new" condition, he was puzzled about what to do. I declared I had decided to let go of the lawsuit. I preferred my health!

He warmly supported my decision and said, "In my experience of cases involving lawsuits, those who go for the claims end up with some permanent disabilities of one kind or another, physical or otherwise!"

I had been reborn.

Proving Grounds

I was alone in our New York apartment. Dianne had gone to work, leaving me in the quietness to focus on some unfinished business still lingering since the time of the accident.

The novelty of my recovery from the head injury had ceased to be a topic. I was worried and wanted my consulting business back on track. My severance pay rapidly dwindled and the bills continued to pour in. When the future looked dim, the accident would replay in my mind. Each time, my body would shudder. The faint experience of Yokar faded and I wanted the accident experience to slip quietly out of my life, like a bad dream.

I pushed hard against that memory. I tried to shove it into the background along with the rest of my worries. Like a mantra, my thought repeated everyday. I want to forget it . . . want to forget.

Then today my mantra was interrupted.

"You're not supposed to forget!" Yokar suddenly declared, his voice booming behind me. "Your calamity served to halt you temporarily from the self-serving direction you were taking, a position far from your desire to help others! Don't you remember?"

"What are you talking about?" I asked.

I turned around, startled. That voice was unmistakable. I expected to see that friendly old giant. There was only empty space. Oh, great! I thought. Torture! I'm losing my mind!

"No. Not torture," Yokar continued. "It's just a reminder of your purpose."

Tension seized my body. My breath was suspended between heartbeats. I realized I was still alone, talking to thin air! His voice stopped, and a warm current ran down my back. I smiled. Giddy feelings rumbled inside my chest. My smile turned to a chuckle. For a crazy minute, all this seemed normal!

Shit. I'm losing it! I confirmed quietly to myself.

I waited for more . . . but the experience was gone. I told myself, Hey look! This is just my subconscious trying to vocalize my trauma.

I settled back uneasily into my chair. Reluctantly, I began again. I needed to work out a new strategy for re-launching my business. I needed to communicate about my skills to the people I knew. The approach needed to be simple, something that didn't cost a lot and that I could handle easily. This time I was going to make a modest living and give myself more time to enjoy life.

As I reviewed my old business plan, it revealed I had a lot more going on before my accident than confidence. The words were strangely unfamiliar. I had written bold statements, such as: "Within one year a 30% market share will be realized. As franchised service bureaus are established regionally across the U.S., and with superior management strategies made available, each bureau will become a profit center within 3 months."

I had written this document, yet a totally different person was speaking. I seemed all puffed up, ready to bring the world to its knees!

Man! Oh man! I thought to myself. Listen to me . . . I was really cocky! Looking down on the world as my oyster . . . what pride I had.

The idea of making all that money still felt alluring. I believed that having all that money would make me safe. I still believed that nothing could stop me.

Then Yokar spoke again. "Nothing but a large truck rushing out of the darkness!"

There was another blinding flash in my head . . . a loud Bang! There it was again . . . another rerun dancing in my head. My body shivered to see its image slumped over in the mangled car. Confusion and doubt rushed in to fill me up. I pondered the aftermath of my pride and arrogance and lamented.

"Maybe this is the way it's always going to be."

Yokar said softly, "It will soon pass."

My jumbled thoughts dangled uncompleted. Broken conversations, disturbing images, and unresolved feelings interfered with my ability to concentrate on my business plan. Everything merged together into a wailing drone. Sleep settled over me like a warm breeze. I awakened later to find the room electrified. I looked around and the room was staring back at me.

"Michael!" Yokar called.

I looked up. The quality of his voice was familiar, but I was disoriented. My heart beat strongly in my throat. My mouth opened to respond, but there was only dryness with the throbbing.

"Do not be alarmed!" he continued. "It is Yokar."

I felt alone and afraid with him. I called out for Dianne, but she wasn't home. There was only the silent space to comfort me! The temperature seemed to increase as I flushed with fear.

"We are very near and can assure you, you are not in any danger!" It was the first time I could really focus on Yokar's voice. It sounded older, warm and quiet, with a slight guttural accent. I couldn't determine the origin. It mimicked many European dialects at once.

Everything was silent again. My heart pounded loudly inside my ears. All my thoughts raced into the final lap round the track of madness. I wondered, how can someone determine when he has totally lost it? One thing seemed sure—I was absolutely wide-awake and conscious. My body shook violently all over. Then I saw a tall form begin to materialize out of the air.

"Don't you remember?" He cajoled. "You agreed to this connection."

My eyes widened at the sight of his apparition. "I did?"

The events of the healing began to creep in like small waves breaking onto the shore of my mind. The memory suddenly unfolded.

"Oh, you mean the 'rewiring' job at Bianca's?" I answered, chuckling nervously. "Listen, I didn't take that too seriously, you know."

My words dangled alone in the air. I began to giggle again. More fear settled over me like frost. I couldn't move. My mouth was dry. Sweat began to bead at my hairline. I didn't want to wipe at it and be so obvious. To do so, I thought, would be a sign of my weakness and vulnerability.

"Why don't you dry yourself?" Yokar said with a broad smile. "No reason to be uncomfortable!"

He can hear my thoughts! I exclaimed silently.

"Your thoughts, feelings . . . everything is available to us."

This was definitely not my subconscious or my inner voice. This was coming from outside of me . . . I think!

"So who are you—really?" I challenged.

"I am Yokar, your guide . . . your spiritual instructor. Your instruction will occur from within from now on."

"Where did you come from?" I persisted.

"A plane of existence beyond the first cause or causal. Our realm is the form aspect of the Most High God, that which we call Stellar Mind."

"A psychic woman told me once that you are Atlantean. Is that true?" "The soul experience you speak of was the last sojourn on the Earth in a region called Atlantis . . . Yes."

"And you are called Yokar?"

"Yes. That is correct."

"Is that your real name . . . spirit?" I said, attempting to provoke something of truth.

"This vibration is as it always was, given in Atlantis at the consecration of manhood. My name symbolizes the fire of three mountain peaks in Atlantis—Paathrinar, Ixuus, and Althoas. Sometimes, it's possible to retain something from the physical, which is useful even unto spirit. In your terms of time, long ago in the land of Atlantis, I served as priest and scientist. Now, as spirit from Stellar Mind, I call upon that matrix or that soul experience, for your sake."

Excitement surged along my spine like a fountain. Curiosity filled my mind.

"Wow. Some friends would give up eye teeth to ask you a thousand questions right now."

I giggled again. It felt like Christmas morning and none of my presents had been opened. I leaned back in my chair. I let out a nervous sigh and bravely continued. "I have a lot of questions. This is a real leap for me!"

Yokar smiled again. "We are aware of your resistance and stubborn quality. We perceive these traits to actually be something positive in you. If transformed, your energy could be molded into great strength. We welcome your sense of skepticism and scrutiny. We can make good use of it!"

"Sounds good to me," I said, relaxing a little. "So why me?"

"Well, this will take a bit of explanation. For now, let's say that we have a previous relationship that can now be accessed."

"What kind of relationship?"

"Your soul matrix is an extension of the same Stellar Mind as mine, but from the future."

My mind balked. My body seemed to tense up again. "Uh . . . I think I don't want to know anymore of that right now. Okay?"

My mind quickly drifted back to the subject of Atlantis. "Hmm," I murmured. "This sounds great, fantastic in fact." Maybe too good to be true! Still . . . direct contact with a spirit, accessing very old knowledge, power systems—the history, the technology of the Atlanteans! Whoa! "Yokar, if what you say is all true, this contact could advance our civilization a thousand years."

Yokar responded, "There are limits to whatever technology we can offer you, my son."

I felt like Aladdin with my very own genie. "So what can you offer me then?"

There was a moment of silence.

Then Yokar said, "We can help you with anything you desire and assist you in your spiritual development, but we cannot boost your culture's lust for power."

"Well, Atlantis was supposed to be pretty advanced, right?"

"Perhaps. In many ways, more than your culture is now. You have many wondrous things added to your achievements. But you leave a trail of residue that is polluting the Earth. There is no understanding of fundamental forces and how to balance them!"

My brain was reeling. I realized I was beginning to accept this outrageous premise, but I had no way of knowing if this "scientist guide" was who he claimed to be.

"Listen, before we go any further with this, I'm going to need some sort of proof. You know . . . something I can sink my teeth into. It can't be anything off the shelf . . . do you know what I mean?"

"So, this is your way of describing the digestion of knowledge, beyond what you already possess?"

"Yeah. You could say that."

"We'll see what we can do. What did you have in mind?"

"Okay. How about helping out with some of those waste problems you were talking about. Like uh . . . give me something to eliminate nuclear waste?"

Another silence settled over the room. Then Yokar returned. "This is a problem. For you see, once you have awakened the Elementals, it is difficult to put them back to sleep!"

I didn't really understand his reference to Elementals, so I assumed he was trying to be clever. I grunted in disapproval, "Uh huh!"

Then, another idea struck me. "Sooo . . . how about giving me a solution to the chemical waste, then?"

Once again there was a long silence. This time, I wasn't going to let him get away that easily. He took long enough to let me continue in my own thought. I went on to consider the loss of my mental balance. I began to weigh the effectiveness of several therapy alternatives before he returned.

"We will consider this problem," he said with authority. "It may be that certain Atlantean techniques for sea water desalination can be applied here." There was a pause. "We are noticing a slight rise in your body temperature. We will suspend this contact for now . . . bessings be upon you."

After the formal parting, the silence was completely upon me. I became aware of some distinct and unusual warmth leaving my body. My frame dropped automatically in relief.

A strange contraction filled me. The excitement dwindled and now turned to disappointment. War brewed in my brain: one part was calm and delighted and the other was furious over my foolish reactions to this preposterous situation. There was still a deep concern over my sanity.

To keep myself busy over the next few days, I worked out the remaining details for starting my business and then launched some new advertising. A deep sense of relief rushed over me. I had a new confidence that my business was going to be fine.

Within a week, jobs began to roll in. Even my old employer called me for consulting work. Dianne finally began to relax, for the first time since the accident. My business was no longer fantasy. We began to settle down into a new life. Quietly, a singular worry continued to nag me. My "schizophrenia" would surely reoccur.

I didn't tell Dianne about my conversations with Yokar. I wasn't ready to accept the experience for what it seemed to be. Meanwhile, I awaited secretly for some further response from Yokar.

The years of my Bioenergetic therapy and spiritual counseling seemed to be thwarted by this possibly maniacal fantasy. I had worked so hard to be practical and grounded. This was not an easy adjustment, and I was very confused.

Over the next few months, Yokar returned time after time, offering small insights to bolster my confidence. He began my understanding of the balanced use of "primary forces." For example, one day he noticed that I dragged a heavy cart along with me when I tended to all my clients. The cart weighted several hundred pounds, carrying electronic test equipment and tools of all kinds. I often openly complained about the burden of pulling it. He approached one day and calmly remarked, "You know, you could make better use of your strength with that burden you're dragging behind you."

"Oh really! How could I do that?"

Yokar seemed delighted as he went on, "Well, if you will tilt the cart backwards about an inch off vertical and then let it go, observe the results."

Dutifully, I did as he requested. The cart began to roll forward slightly before gravity pulled it downwards, grinding it to a halt on the sidewalk.

"Now," Yokar said, "what did you observe?"

"I saw the cart roll forward a short distance before it came to a stop."

"Good! If you will find the subtle point of imbalance over the wheels of the cart, between the gravity force pulling it backwards and the gravity force pulling it forwards, you will have the energy differential necessary for propelling the cart forward without any effort other than directional guidance!"

"You're kidding! Are you trying to tell me I can make gravity propel this three-hundred-pound cart, and all I have to do is direct it?"

"Essentially. But the point of imbalance will have to be developed by you, continuously within your understanding and consciousness. Do you understand?"

"Uh ... I think so. How do I find that point of imbalance, Yokar?"

"First, you will have to seek out the point of perfect vertical balance for the cart. You can do this only by feeling it. Then, by exploration, you will need to find the point of imbalance just ahead of it, that is, just slightly forward of vertical center. In this way, you will make the appropriate determination as to how much differential you will need to propel it forward, without losing control of it. This ability is largely within your own consciousness!"

"I think I get it! I'm going to learn to control the cart's falling forward continuously."

"Essentially!" Yokar said with satisfaction. "It was this concept that powered all of the Atlantean vehicles whether they be on land or over it, even in the water and under it!"

Excitement began to rise. My mind tried to embrace the simple logic of his idea. I couldn't wait to try it during the next long stretch of sidewalk.

I reached the street corner and let my cart come to a halt. I stood beside it for moment, attempting to find the right grasp of the handle for the experiment.

Next, I tilted the cart forward so that I could feel the pull forward. Then, slowly I let it fall back again, sensing the backward pull as well. I kept shifting the handle above vertical center, until the forces were just about equal. Then, I gently let the cart fall backward "off center" again, just enough to feel the gradual building up of force.

It wasn't smooth as expected. The force was very slow at first, and then suddenly it would accelerate out of control. The cart took off wildly, leaving me to chase after it. After several tries, however, I developed a better sense of what Yokar was talking about. Before long, I was able to actually walk with my cart beside me, apparently propelled by an unknown force. After several days' practice, I managed to make the cart travel beside me at any walking pace. I never had to pull it anymore.

I knew it must've looked strange. I would always draw attention from onlookers along the street I traveled. I realized now what he meant by the balance of my consciousness being so important. If I was upset or distracted in any way, I could not perform this little "miracle" of leverage, no matter how hard I tried. I would first need to settle the inner disturbance and restore the inner balance, before I could demonstrate control of any outside primary force. It was a good lesson for me on all levels. This practice also worked as an internal barometer for my inner balance.

Sometimes I would awaken in the middle of the night with Dianne asleep next to me. The air would bristle with electricity all around me and I knew Yokar would come. Hoping not to awaken Dianne, I would whisper, "Are you there?"

Yokar would not answer right away! Then I would repeat the question a little louder. "Are you there? Damn it, I can feel you. Say something! If you're there . . . answer me!"

The room would move, as if it were strangely soft and pliable. It could have been a dream, but it didn't matter to me anymore. It was real enough for me. Yokar would press his thoughts into mine, not exactly in words. At first, it was like a feeling, like words on the tip of my tongue. It took time before I could adjust to this process. It was tiring, and I couldn't really tell if the thoughts were mine or his most of the time.

I complained of this confusion. "Why must you be so evasive?" I demanded. "It's hard enough for me to grasp all this, let alone have you come on like 'The Shadow' all the time!"

Yokar responded patiently, "The pathways that link us together are young and tender. We must move slowly and with some caution. In time, this contact will grow stronger. Try to be patient. We must take great care that you adjust physically. For us, it is with great effort that we enter so close to the physical. With your existing vibrational framework, it will take some time.

"Over the next few of your days, we will give you some impressions. These patterns will help you adjust. They are also related to your scientific inquiries. We want you to explore them with your imagination. Concentrate on the connections between matter and vibration."

The first of these impressions slipped into my consciousness just a few hours later. Before me danced a complicated pattern of energy. Yokar supplied some narrative to the fantastic mental show of energy.

"All things spring forth from vibration," he said.

I began to think. If the world begins with vibration, maybe this was the hidden meaning of the Word, referred to in the Bible. Then I asked out loud, "Yokar, if vibration creates matter, then what is vibration?"

There was a brief hesitation. Then his wisdom poured out again. "Good. You've already begun your training. Vibration is consciousness moving in orderly patterns."

"I see." In a blinding flash, I could see something about the connection between spirit and matter. I became curious about the origin, the real beginning of all existence. Yokar then obliged my curiosity.

"There is a need to start at the beginning," Yokar told me. "As in all your stories that are given to children, it always begins with a long, long time ago. So, for the sake of your sense of time, we will continue in the same way.

"Once upon a time, long long ago, there was a vast sea of energy. An energy that was fully aware, but not moving. It was held in stasis, totally passive like the glassy surface of an immense pool of water. Then, the First Mystery occurred; there was movement, a shift, and expansion vertically in this pool of awareness. A ripple began from this expansion that moved across the surface of this pool. This movement was conscious thought and corresponds to what you were told is the 'Word.' As it was said in your sacred scriptures, 'In the beginning, there was the Word.'

"This wave traveled the vast expanse of the great pool until it came to a kind of boundary and returned to fold upon itself. The pool of energy began to undulate under the influence of this secondary wave. The energy mixed together and began to gather itself together, coagulating and condensing until there were more waves folding together, causing further condensation. Then a Second Mystery occurred.

"The energy continued to condense. The awareness of the pool became more substantial and solidified. Its awareness moved and became more thought. The thought developed a sense of self with the growing form. The energy became more compact and more intense until there was, in the intenseness of the self, a sense of its own boundary.

"This boundary defined the shape of what we will call a crystal. A great crystal. This crystal defined the awareness that was consuming all of formed reality. In this realization of this boundary, there was perceived a limit. And this limit was perceived by the self to obstruct the flow of awareness, the flow of consciousness and the growth of thought. Then a Third Mystery unfolded. "With this new awareness of limitation, the self-consciousness desired to break the boundary to eliminate the obstruction. It wanted to go beyond awareness, beyond thought. In one act of supreme will, the self dissolved the crystal, shattering the form with a great explosion. Perhaps this would correspond to what your scientists call The Big Bang.

"Out from this explosion exuded great energy and pieces or shards of the crystal called Stellar Mind. Even if all of the energy from this explosion and all the shards were put back together again, they would not equal the total of existence. The original awareness had already evolved into something called Witness. Now there were three components to all of reality. There was the Energy, a vast and infinite sea of it. There was Form, the Stellar Minds constituting the remaining shards of the original crystal, and there was the new awareness. The new awareness possessed higher vibrational qualities, harmonics of the original that became a witness beyond the energy and the Stellar Minds. All three were intimately interconnected.

"This trinity formed the basis of a great ring realm. A ring of experience that became a continuum. This continuous ring of infinite being folded upon itself, creating multiple rings of existence defining all vibrations past, present, and yet to become. From this moment forward, the great ring could not be reversed. The great First Self could not uncreate or unlearn itself. It was permanent, immutable, and infinite. What had been done could not be undone. So now, as the expansion of the original First Self progresses across all existing universes, the realm of what you call the Most High God is the trinity: Witness, Stellar Mind, and Energy.

"Now rest, my friend," Yokar said as he placed a comforting hand on my head.

Before I fell into sleep, I saw the room move again in a wave-like shift. The pressure I felt behind my head was gone and so was Yokar's presence. Dianne began to breathe more deeply, signaling her sense of his leaving. All was quiet. I leaned back onto my pillow and greeted sleep easily.

I was up early. There was an irresistible urge to go to the Coliseum Bookstore to browse. Bookstore browsing had become a familiar habit for me. Most of my ideas spawned on that fertile valley of books, especially the occult and science sections. The books from Moscow were my favorite parts of the science section. It always seemed to me that the Russians had their fingers into some really promising ideas. Of course, the math usually soared way over my head. I possessed only an undergraduate understanding of mathematics. Mir Publishing of Moscow had a flair for the scientifically obscure. The books they published often managed to whet my imaginative appetite.

I began as always, snooping the shelves of my favorite categories—physics and engineering science—looking for something new and unusual that stood out. Call it a hunch, but I could sense something was hiding in the recesses of the third shelf above my head. There, I found a small but thick text lodged in the back. It was unfairly smothered by other dull bindings of pulp and word not deserving front mention.

Pulling it out from the shelf wasn't an easy task. Some of the stores help saw me struggling and offered their help, but I declined. I wanted to discover this treasure for myself! With some wrenching and tugging, I finally set it free. "There you are! You little devil, now I've got you!"

It was finally in my hands. "My, oh my! What have we here?"

It was indeed a little prize of a book. Except for its extreme thickness, this three-by-five-inch wonder might have been designed to fit into a Russian hip pocket. I knew right off that this was no ordinary book. This was a real handbook . . . a physics handbook, Russian style. It was not limited to a few areas of science that you might find in the reference section of an American library. It was stuffed to the gills, bursting to offer more than it could contain within its bindings. I was thrilled. It was like a scientist's Bible, complete with Bible-thin pages. The cover, however, opened to reveal a handsome price, certainly more than I possessed at that moment.

Usually I had to put the expensive Mir books on hold, and I did this time. Letting a book out of my sight was always agonizing; there was an awful wait until I could afford to buy it. Fortunately, the next few days brought extra income, allowing me to procure my prize early.

Days later, I eagerly awaited the delivery of my prize from the basement storeroom and imagined devouring its pages over some coffee at a nearby shop. The coffee served as a prop next to the dessert-like contents of the book. For me, a new book of science was total fulfillment!

Coffee in hand, I plunged my whole mind into the little book. Immediately I was lost. I stopped only briefly, like a runner passing by, to slurp down extra black energy to carry on my adventure.

I happened upon a curious discussion about very high-frequency sound and some experimental applications. Suddenly, a feeling stirred inside. This information seemed important. The waiter poured more coffee into my cup, but I barely noticed. This theory seemed significant, but I couldn't manage to define in what way.

After I gulped down the last juice of my coffee, I bolted from the shop. It was as though I were late for an important meeting, yet I had no particular place to go!

I wandered aimlessly around midtown Manhattan. Meanwhile, curious phrases and patterns emerged in my mind from Yokar's implanted visions. They whirled inside my head like a churning fever. Yokar's words resounded over and over like a mantra. Concentrate on matter and vibration.

My preoccupation with these ideas made me unaware of the swiftness of my gait. I came to the apartment building very quickly. The newsstand nearby seemed unusually interesting, and I decided to check out the latest editions. I had to chuckle at myself for my insatiable appetite for the printed word that day. As my eyes poured over the fresh batch of magazines, the colors and patterns made me instantly dizzy and nauseous.

Yokar chimed in. "Play with shapes . . . Play with shapes . . . Play with shapes."

"Okay! Okay! I'll play with the damn shapes," I said aloud.

My outburst caught the attention of the people around me. I projected their judgment: I was one of the crazy outpatients loose on the street. The dizzy feeling persisted for several minutes. I took a deep breath to calm down. When I directed my gaze to the rack of magazines, the nauseating feeling was gone. The Scientific American became the magazine of choice. This issue had articles on Alzheimer's disease and something on photochemistry. They seemed strangely connected, but I didn't know why.

With my magazine tucked neatly under my arm, I was complete and started for home.

I arrived home with hunger gnawing at my belly.

Dianne called out from the kitchen, "Did you find what you were looking for at the bookstore?"

I jumped to pull my new book from its bag, proudly displaying it at the kitchen doorway.

"You bet! Look at this."

I presented the Mir book as though it were a captured blue ribbon.

She looked puzzled. Then she said kindly, "What is it?"

"It's a Russian physics manual."

I held the little book up, showing its thickness with some glee and rattled the Bible-thin pages in the air.

"It covers everything on the latest research the Russians have been doing. I discovered something interesting about very high-frequency sound physics. I know it's important to me somehow. I just haven't figured it out yet!"

"Oh, God, you don't have to translate it, do you?"

"No, no, nothing like that. Mir already translated it."

Dianne gazed helplessly at the maze of words and diagrams. She was not normally inclined toward technical things. Then she responded flatly, "That's nice, dear."

Her response dampened my enthusiasm slightly, but I continued to rave about my find. Then, she looked at me with a smile. "The noodles are ready. So let's eat."

Later, I sat in my chair browsing the new Scientific American while Dianne rested on the couch. An article on Alzheimer's disease appeared before me first.

The great thing about Scientific American is the attempt to be technical enough to interest the scientist or engineer, with enough lay language to carry an average person also interested in science.

I knew almost nothing about Alzheimer's, just that it was nasty if you developed the disease. I thought that Alzheimer's was like cancer—after a year or two, your brain turns to mush. It was clear that I was wrong on a good many points. The article frustrated me, however. There weren't any answers, but a lot of questions.

The questions were all posed rhetorically. It was clear that they knew very little and wanted to know more. A feeling of compassion for those afflicted entered my heart. I wished there were more help available.

A sharp pain jabbed at the back of my head. It felt like someone had clubbed me. A serious ache descended down my neck. I grabbed my neck and began to massage it, trying to ease the pain. Electrical energy crackled around me, followed by prickly heat. Yokar leaped upon my shoulders with the swiftness of a falcon pouncing on its prey. It was so startling that my composure left me.

Yokar said, "First, we will reveal to you what this disease is and how it forms. Then we will tell you how it can be alleviated. The problem starts with . . . "

"Wait! . . . Wait a minute . . . Dianne! Help me . . . quick!"

She flew out of the kitchen and gaped at me. She watched in horror as I held the back of my neck in a grimace of pain. She surmised that my injury was back with a fury.

"Should I call a doctor or an ambulance?" She asked desperately.

"No! Get a paper and pencil quickly, will you? Quickly . . . you have to write this down!"

Then she exclaimed, "Why? Are you okay?"

I gave her a quick nod to indicate yes.

She jabbered on. "What's going on?"

"I'll tell you later—just get the damn paper! Okay?"

My voice became shaky and reflected the greatest urgency. I was about to say something profoundly important, something I thought I would never be able to say again.

Yokar began, and I repeated almost word for word to Dianne.

"The problem begins with a poison . . . that is ingested through the breathing process. A metal you term aluminum is atomized and becomes airborne. The metal ions join the blood through the capillaries. The toxic metal, now attached to the blood, passes undetected through the blood brain membrane.

"The metal goes undetected because of the close ionic bond formed between the blood cells and the aluminum particulates. Once there, the blood deposits the metal ions into the neural electrolytes, a solution inside the neural synapse. The metal acts to short-circuit the energy potential of the electrolyte solution. The charge on the neural cell wall drops, triggering an immunal reaction to send proteins to wall off and isolate the 'dead' neuron from the healthy tissue of the brain.

"Since the neurons can only live by virtue of community, they eventually die off. This process continues until whole regions of neural pathways are destroyed, leaving the afflicted a mindless being."

"Did you get all that?" I shouted over my pain.

Dianne responded with dismay, "I think so."

"Well, don't stop, there's more coming!" I demanded.

Yokar continued, "If certain ranges of high frequency sound were to be irradiated to the cranium in three stages, then the protein chains would break up, freeing the contaminated neural areas from the binding action of the lymphocytes. If the afflicted person were to then ingest several whole oranges baked slowly at a low temperature or consume several ounces of fresh-squeezed orange juice heated to a temperature slightly above normal body temperature, this heating would act to convert the simple orange or its juice into a chelating agent. Later, the metal ions would be attached to the orange and would flush the toxin out with normal elimination."

"How about that? Did you get that, too?" I demanded forcefully.

Dianne nodded in confirmation. "Yes, I think so."

"My God, I hope so!"

The sharp pain left as quickly as it came. Dianne began to read back to me what she had written. She looked puzzled as I listened carefully.

"Wow! That's amazing stuff," I declared.

"Don't you know what you just said?"

I looked back at her slowly and shook my head. "No! Not really."

Dianne's eyes widened with surprise and began to fill with tears. "What's going on, honey?"

"It would seem Yokar has decided to give me my first proof."

"Oh my God! You mean you can hear him . . . he's been talking to you now?" She asked in a shaky voice.

"Well, he was, a few minutes ago. You know, as I listened to what you wrote, it didn't make a bit of sense to me!" I said, with a sheepish grin.

She listened quietly while I went on.

"This is so strange. We're going to have to get another opinion on this information. I think I know the person who can do it. We'll have to copy all this down into a letter. I want to send it to Dr. Kurtz, a neurophysiologist, in California. She'll be able to make sense out of it, I'll bet! First, I've got to find her address. Mark's aunt in Greenwich will know." I looked at her. "You okay?" I asked softly.

Dianne peered into my eyes. "When were you going to tell me?"

"Uh . . . I'm really sorry about that. I didn't say anything because I wasn't sure if I might be going crazy! To tell you the truth, I'm still not sure!"   A call was placed to Greenwich, which revealed that Dr. Kurtz was in California, working an extended professorship at Stanford. I sent Yokar's information.

Three weeks later, Dr. Kurtz's response arrived. She wrote that our letter flattered her, but she regretted to say that this aspect of physiology was not her field. She refrained from commenting on the contents of our letter, but forwarded it with an introduction to the Alzheimer's Institute in New York.

Two more weeks passed and I had given up validating Yokar's information. Yokar was conspicuously silent. I began to turn bitter about the whole affair.

Then one night, while Dianne was attending a business meeting, I received a call from the institute. "Mr. Morgan, this is Dr. Reynolds calling from the Alzheimer's Institute. We recently received a letter from Dr. Kurtz regarding some information you had passed along."

"Yes," I answered cautiously, waiting for the ax to fall. My breathing was short and shallow.

"Would you mind repeating to us now, as close to verbatim as you can, the information you relayed to her?"

I took a deep silent breath. "Of course. But you must understand that this information was given to me through paranormal means."

"Yes. We understand that, Mr. Morgan."

I took another deep breath and settled into my story. She listened throughout, without comment. When I had completed the last of the information, she broke in. "Okay. Now let me tell you what we've been doing. First of all, we had to abandon the approach of the blood brain membrane, very early on, for practical reasons. It was not because we considered it an unviable approach. When we receive a patient, the patient is already dead. The membrane ceases to function once the life processes have been terminated. You understand?"

"Yes. I believe so."

"Secondly, we have been using sonicators, ultrasound devices, to divide the protein chains so we can observe their formation in the laboratory, under controlled conditions. We were immediately struck by the corollaries in your story. We also investigated some possibilities that metal toxins may be at the root of the problem. We suspected that copper or lead were prime suspects. We hadn't tested aluminum yet."

I could feel electrical charges building around my neck again. Yokar was not far away. Suddenly, I felt nauseous.

Then Yokar chimed in. "Tell the woman if she will provide the technical specifications of this sound device, we will provide the necessary modifications that will make it a healing instrument."

"Uh . . . Dr. Reynolds, I realize what I'm about to say is unprecedented, but if you can provide me with the specifications of those sonicators, my 'source' is ready to modify the designs for experimental healing purposes."

There was only silence on the other end. After several moments, I was sure we had been disconnected. Her voice finally broke through the awful quiet. "We would have a problem with that. Our position is noncommittal and we have a responsibility to the National Institute of Health, our parent organization. If we were to engage in such unauthorized activity, we would lose our funding. Do you understand? It's simply out of the question! We are, however, compelled to investigate all avenues of information. Actually, the only item in dispute is the use of orange juice as a relieving agent."

"But it's not just orange juice," I defended. "It's heated to increase its ability to detoxify. Don't you think that has any merit?"

"Well, quite frankly, we doubt that orange juice, in any form, can have any significant effect!"

I was shocked to find her so rigid on this point.

"Yes. Well, it's clear enough where you stand. Try to understand where I'm standing at the moment. I'm trying to validate some of this information. Can you tell me, what you think, overall?"

"I'm sorry, Mr. Morgan. We're not at liberty to comment on the value of the information, only that there were significant similarities to our work at present."

Pressing her further would have resolved nothing. I thanked her for her feedback, what little there was. Later, I sifted and analyzed her remarks. It was a marginal validation, even though somewhat backhanded. The whole thing was fascinating. My appetite was definitely stimulated, but I was going to need a lot more than this experience to spark my enthusiasm.

Dianne arrived home later in the evening. I told her of my conversation with the institute. She was tired and only mildly excited. I found that disappointing. I wanted someone to share in my partial success. I plopped onto the couch, although it provided little comfort. My eyes turned inward. My body began to vibrate and the nausea began again. I was annoyed at this recurring physical discomfort, and I added this complaint to my plea to Yokar for a response.

"So, what's the deal here, Yokar?"

Yokar approached, filling the room with his usual blast of rapidly vibrating energy. "Relax. It won't be much longer."

"What are you trying to do . . . torture me?"

"No. It's not designed to torture, but we are trying to prepare you."

"Prepare me for what?"

"You need to learn how to behave when you are receiving. As you can perhaps see, you have a lot to learn. The male force in you is seriously out of balance. You have almost no patience! Now begin to breathe. Breathe in a regular and deep pattern. Let your mind follow the breath inward. Concentrate near the area of the crown. Make your attention gather there. There will be the intake of the Life Force. Uncross your feet, let your hands fold together, and keep your spine straight. You cannot hope to improve your ability to receive if every aspect of your energy is hopping around!

"While you are practicing, this would be a good time to talk of consuming this bubble water. It is essentially a disaster to your digestive process."

"You mean the Coca-Cola?"

"Yes, Michael. We believe you may have real possibilities for awakening, but this bubble water affects everything. It would be better that you eliminate or reduce your consumption as soon as possible."

"You can't be serious! Are you trying to tell me that Coca-Cola is standing between me and enlightenment?"

"In a manner of speaking. You might say that. Although the average concept of enlightenment is a myth!"

I was stunned by this remark more than the idea of Coke standing as a deterrent to my spiritual awakening. I remained silent for a moment, trying to digest what he said. I wasn't ready to give up one of the main staples of my sugar-energy diet. So I shifted the focus of discussion.

"What do you mean, enlightenment is a myth?"

"This expression, as it is generally understood, indicates a final state of complete and blissful satisfaction—that is, the utter fulfillment of all knowledge and wisdom about self and its relationship to the rest of reality in a single stroke. A goal which many are seeking! But I tell you this, it is an illusion. Truly there is no such final state. True enlightenment is an ongoing living experience of an ever-increasing, evolving discovery of the unlimited Self, moment by moment.

"In other words, if you knew everything and possessed all wisdom at once, what else is there for you? Nothing! The duality of possessing all wisdom and possessing nothing leads one only to another point on the circle of endless frustration.

"The 'true' state of being is continuous. If there is a condition of enlightenment, it is only in the momentary discovery when the self is revealed in some aspect, and only in that moment. Those moments are always occurring now and forever, continuously. The true self is infinite and ever changing, therefore unknowable in totality.

"There can arise a true or kinesthetic sense of the infinite capacity of the unlimited Self and that realization is perhaps the closest feeling to an ultimate and complete joy."

My mind buckled under the weight of Yokar's words. I felt like a lump was caught in my throat and I couldn't swallow. I felt uncomfortable and noticeably squirmed. I quickly shifted the discussion back to Coca-Cola. "You're treading on my comfort zone. I'm not so sure I'm ready to give up Coca-Cola just yet."

"Perhaps if you come to understand its effects, then you will relinquish?"

I frowned. "I doubt it very much, really."

"Michael, your digestion is a wondrous process of cooperation. The body has the ability to ingest raw materials, which are quite foreign to its integrity. It can transform those raw materials into needed energy through a process of alchemical transmutation. The molecular structures are altered through vibratory adjustment. These processes rotate the molecular structures through a mass-energy cycle, releasing enormous amounts of cosmic solar forces. The result of that release maintains the body's structure and provides cosmic motive power for your existence.

"Your digestion accomplishes this feat by combining a series of subtle and sequential vibrations. A process I believe you already understand called 'heterodyning.' Yes?"

"Yeah, I think so. Go on!"

I knew that "heterodyning" is an engineering term used in radio theory. It describes what happens when two frequencies, which are at different rates of vibration, are mixed together. The result produces a shift in frequency above and below the base frequency, simultaneously.

Yokar went on. "If you introduce sudden explosive forces to this delicate process, the process is all but destroyed. In other words, the entire fabric of digestion will be disrupted. This is what happens when you consume the gaseous bubble water. The bubbles explode randomly, discharging intense and chaotic forces that disturb the vibratory patterns needed for conversion of raw materials. From this action, you are robbed of vital energy critically needed for higher development!"

"Okay. It seems to make sense, but that doesn't change the way I feel when I drink it. It's enjoyable, Yokar!"

"Very well, as you wish. We cannot violate your free will. Perhaps in time you will come to embrace the wisdom in this.

"There is also the matter as to the elimination of toxic chemical substances. In Atlantis, a process was developed to desalinate seawater. This involved generating sound forces at vibration frequencies that exceed your current understanding. In order to accomplish this, we produced sound at frequencies normally attributed to the energy spectrum of light, in your science."

"You mean sound operating at light frequencies? I was under the impression that sound is sound and light is electromagnetic!"

"Yes. We realize your views are somewhat limited in this respect. Eventually, you will come to understand that these hyper-sound vibrations speak to the binding forces of matter and can re-order the structure in any way desired without unwanted byproducts. In addition, you will find the energy required to accomplish this is quite small compared to anything you have yet developed. Sound vibrations in the visible portion of the energy spectrum can, when properly combined, act as a key to unlock all the mysteries of fundamental forces. We will impress upon you patterns of understanding so that you can grasp the operating principles of these concepts."

My head began to pound furiously as strange visual patterns of light darted back and forth across my mind. It made no sense to me whatsoever.

"Yokar, I don't understand these patterns you're giving to me."

"Just try to relax now and allow their entry into your mind. They will work in a subtle way, to bring about greater understanding. Soon, we will have to terminate contact for a while. Your body continues to exhibit a lack of tolerance for great heat."

The patterns stopped and I could feel Yokar's presence leave. The pressure lifted from the back of my head and the uncomfortable warmth subsided. The unusual "thought pattern shapes" from Yokar puzzled me. I tried to make sense of them but the effort was making me tired and drowsy. Again, it was clear to me that this new idea of hyper-sound changing structural bonds was similar to the Alzheimer's information. I couldn't evaluate the viability with my limited knowledge of physics. This evaluation would need someone in the pure scientific research field, perhaps someone really brilliant.

Two days later, I contacted my old mentor, Conrad, through another friend, a machinist. Conrad was a German scientist who had a doctorate in electrical engineering as well as physics. I knew his schedule wouldn't allow for such an investigation, but he would know of someone who could help me.

We met for coffee at a small restaurant in New York. I outlined what I had in mind and pushed Conrad for some of his contacts in this country. Since the project was going to be just a feasibility study, Conrad felt that a scientist in the academic community would do nicely.

Then he smiled. "Ya . . . Well, I think that a friend of mine who is teaching physics at the university in New Jersey might serve well in this case. Ya . . . his name is Heinrick Geothe. I'll give a call to him and make the necessary introductions."

A week went by before I could meet Dr. Geothe. He had been on holiday in Germany, visiting friends. Conrad called me and reported that Hein, as he referred to him, would be more than glad to speak with me for a cup of good coffee. I had a feeling, as Conrad went on, that I knew Hein would become a good friend too.

One evening, a little after six, I met Heinrick in lower New York at a small coffee house that was well known for the best specialty coffees. Heinrick was dressed casually. He sported a cardigan button-down sweater with soft leather patches at the elbows and casual slacks. His slightly dusty tan fedora revealed a thinning, silver-white mane growing unkempt at the back of his neck. Thin-rimmed glasses perched lightly above his nose.

He appeared young and energetic, with his umbrella in hand. He extended a warm handshake and said, "I'm Heinrick Geothe. You are Michael?"

"Yes. Welcome to my favorite coffee house, Dr. Geothe."

He nodded with a warm and gentle smile. "Call me Hein. All my friends do."

The glow appearing from behind his soft blue eyes gave me a sense of his unpretentious genius. A thrill went down my spine. My body was already pleased with this meeting and I knew he was the right man for the job. After a second cup of coffee, we shared many mutual feelings over knowing Conrad. Then Hein offered help in answering my inquiries.

I began to brief him about the "new idea" I happened upon. Knowing his traditional background, I thought it wise not to reveal the nature of my source. He listened without comment during my introduction.

"This is no small task you're asking for, Michael. I'll have to give considerable time to this study. My teaching schedule is very busy just now with term papers, projects, and the like. You understand."

My heart lurched, as I waited for his refusal. Grasping for a solution, I countered, "Hein, I realize this is not something you can whip up over the weekend. I'd be willing to pay for your time, to do this feasibility study. How much time do you think you'll need?"

I held my breath as he paused to consider my offer.

"Well, a month might do . . . actually, there will be some time just after the finals are finished at the university. Yes . . . about a month or so, I could do it then. Are you are willing to wait until then?"

"How much would you want for a month of your time?"

"Well," he paused again, "I make about seventy thousand a year as a professor of tenure. But this is not quite the same, I think. I would accept five thousand as a fee for this time. That would be fair I think."

He looked at me, expecting a heartfelt rejection. To his surprise, I agreed. Moments after, we both realized the hour was getting late. We shook hands on the deal and then Hein left. I was so excited that I ordered another cup of coffee.

Later, I returned home with the news. Dianne was less than pleased.

"And just how do you expect to pay for this?" she scolded.

My eyes dropped to the floor. "I have no idea." Then I returned, "Don't worry, I'll think of something. Besides, I've got until August to come up with the money. The way I figure it, if spirit wants me to prove this stuff, they've got to give me the cash to do it!"

Dianne grumbled, "I don't know about this. I don't like it. It's five thousand dollars! That's a lot of money."

"I know how much it represents. I've decided. If I'm going to work with this, then I have to have something real I can count on. Further, I don't intend to starve to do this, either! That's my deal with Yokar! If spirit wants me to play ball, it has to be, in some respects, on my terms."

She softened to my confident manner.

"Well, I feel better about that."

I went on, "I didn't spend ten years in therapy making all those changes just to throw it all away! I tell you, this is going to be a two-way street as far as I am concerned."

My words sounded real enough, even to me. Although I spoke with courage and defiance, in truth, I was like a warrior singing a song of victory to drum up the courage to fight.

It was July. A large contract came in, providing me with the funds I needed to hire Hein. I was delighted. I contacted his office to remind him of our arrangement. He was in Europe. A week went by before Hein called to say that he had been delayed unexpectedly in Europe, but was ready to begin the study for me.

We met again at the university to go over the project.

Hein began by introducing another element. "With your permission, I'd like to bring in a colleague. He's affiliated with the university as well. His name is Dr. Gunnar Hecht. He's a specialist in liquid state physics, whereas my specialty is solid-state physics. I believe collaboration on this is helpful. You don't have to worry. I'll pay him out of my end of the funds."

My body began to relax. Excitement filled me. I had not one, but two German physicists working for me. I felt a rush of ego gratification. I was imagining myself as a great entrepreneur. At that point, I handed Hein an envelope. "Half now and the other half upon completion. Okay?"

He looked at me and smiled. "Of course."

"So how long before you have something I can look at?"

"Michael," he said slowly while he placed his hand warmly on my shoulder, "these things can't be hurried. Scientific investigation must plod along step by step, leaving no stone unturned."

My vision as an entrepreneur dwindled. He sounded more like a grandfather, though he was rapidly becoming my hero. I waited anxiously for the next two weeks without any word. In fact, I did not hear from him for nearly a month.

Late one evening, in the latter part of August, I received a telephone call. It was Hein. His voice was urgent and excited. He wanted to meet me in New York as soon as possible. His excitement was contagious.

We met at the coffee shop of our first meeting. He came in, fedora and umbrella in hand, dressed as casually as ever. I stared at him for a moment and mused to myself, When you have that much gray matter sitting on your shoulders, you can afford to be casual.

Hein jumped right into the news. "Michael, Dr. Hecht and I have discovered some really exciting prospects about your concept. It seems that it represents a major breakthrough. Highly focused hyper-sound energy along the wavelengths of certain molecular bonds can bring the respective molecules to disassociate without having to go through the classic photo coupling laws. We don't have to worry about all the other excited states! Do you realize what this means?"

"I'm afraid not." I said, looking bewildered.

Undaunted, he went on. "We can break molecular bonds and direct them into any other combinations, with very little energy required! There will be no byproducts to worry about. We've already conceived of at least five hundred applications for this new technology beyond the original concept!"

Yokar's words re-entered my mind. Hein's words were almost word-for-word identical. I was in shock. I murmured under my breath, "I'll be damned! I guess the 'ol' giant' is for real after all!"

Then I broke out of my own personal considerations to greet Hein's expectant face. "Gee, Hein, that's great," I said, enthusiastically.

While I was still trying to process this astounding news, he went on to really blow me away.

"The other point I wanted to tell you is that Dr. Hecht and I are prepared to quit our tenure at the university and work on this project full-time! Will you raise the funds for that?"

I was dumbfounded. I stood up spontaneously and left the table. I wandered outside the coffee shop, needing to breathe some air. My head was dizzy with this new development. Hein soon followed. The whole thing was a dream—Hein, Yokar, the accident, everything. My mind reeled. Then Hein broke into my internal mayhem.

"Obviously, you need some time to think about it, Michael. I'll go now. I'll call you in a couple of days and we'll set another meeting between all of us. Okay?"

"No. Wait. Hein, you have to realize, I have no prior knowledge of the actual technology. It was only a conceptual study. At best, from what I know about present photo-chemical engineering and acoustical research, the know-how is at least two orders of magnitude away from such technology!"

Hein was crushed by this news. Obviously, he thought that I already possessed some prior knowledge of the apparatus to achieve these results.

"I'm sorry, Hein. I thought you realized."

"Don't blame yourself, Michael. I'm the one who got carried away." He seemed to recover his composure quickly. He sighed deeply. "Well, at any rate, this study is worthy of a National Science Foundation grant! Let me know what you want to do, okay?" Moments later, a cab whisked him away into the night.

I was left to ponder the importance of these unfolding events. A few weeks later, I called Hein to tell him regretfully that I was not capable of raising the kind of funds that could finance a scientific project of that magnitude. I went on to say that, as interesting as the concept was, I would not have the personal time to pursue a grant for continuing the study. He expressed some disappointment with this news, but he understood. We parted then with a fond farewell. That would be the last time I ever spoke to or saw Hein. There were times later when I wondered if Hein ever pursued the project.

Armed with this new confirmation of Yokar's knowledge, I realized I would have to seriously consider the impact of Yokar on rest of my life!

Master of Fire

It was 1986. A year had passed since my accident. My connection to Yokar continued to develop. My Pathwork was becoming less important to me as I worked through my issues with Yokar's help in advance of my personal sessions. The time for the advice of a helper was rapidly coming to a close. Burt, my conceptual helper, had already recognized the coming closure of our work together.

Yokar came to me one evening to offer further insight into my negative emotions—my fears and guilt—which complicated my relationship with my children. First, he scanned me quickly. Then he began to quote fondly one of the immutable esoteric laws of existence: "As it is above, so it is below. As it is inside, so it is outside."

"What do you mean by that, Yokar?"

"It is a hidden statement to the uninitiated. It means the nature of all things behaves consistently throughout reality, regardless of the level of vibration. In other words, all things are subject to the same laws relative to their vibratory level."

"How does this apply to my life, my problems?"

"It applies to all life experience. You have heard me say to you many times that you are responsible for everything that comes into your life, that nothing can come to you that you do not invite. Yes?"

"Yeah. You mean I'm totally responsible for creating my life, right?"

"Yes. So now let's take another look at your personal work from that perspective. Do you remember your indignant proclamation many years ago, just before your marriage to the woman called Mary: you didn't want any help from spirit, you were going to live life on your own for a change, you were going to marry regardless of the consequences. Although spirit tried to advise you to the contrary at the time, you wouldn't listen. Do you remember this?"

"Yeah, I remember. But I was pissed off and tired of being

sensitive to suggestion. I wanted to feel the power of my own decisions, my own mistakes!"

"By your leave, spirit had no choice but to comply. Now, after more than ten years of behaving unconsciously, you have seen the light, as you would say. Yes?"

"Yes, Yokar. I have learned the hard way!"

"Now you long for freedom and you can't wait until you get past these awful feelings. You are still feeling guilty about ending a marriage, about hurting the children. We remind you that it was out of your willful decisions that you created a life of unconsciousness with this woman. And you involved children in the process. Though we hasten to add, the children have their own responsibility in this, as well as the woman called Mary!

"Now you have awakened to a problem. You fantasize about being something more or even something else. Certainly, you always fantasize about more than what you are! You're tired of the unworthiness and self-doubt. You want to be rid of your fears. The fact is, you have spent many years building up this terrible burden. You are impatient and want it all to go away! Right?"

Yokar's words were painful, not easy to hear. My body cringed. I wanted to run away from him. Then I became angry. But I resolved not to run . . . not again, not ever, no matter what. I knew he wasn't trying to hurt me. He was smashing me down to make something new. So I tried to embrace his confrontation.

"Yeah," I said humbly. "I see what you're getting at. But I don't really expect it to go away, not like that! But I do wish it didn't have to take so long to fix."

"You weren't considering this when you were busy building up the unconsciousness, the numbness?" Yokar snapped.

Again, Yokar's words entered like a knife. Again I buckled with humility. "Yeah, I know . . . hindsight is always 20/20 and I'm even feeling sorry for myself right now!"

"Exactly! Listen, Michael, in reality, the All and Everything doesn't care what you do. The Most High God does not judge you here . . . not like that. You know that now. Even if the action is negative! You are free to do anything you like. You have free will!"

"Is that really so?" I asked.

"But remember," Yokar, warned. "Negativity is self-limiting by nature. If you do decide on something negative, then you had better be conscious of what you are doing and when you are doing it. You better be prepared to accept the consequences of your actions. This is responsible living!"

"You say I'm allowed to do anything, positive or negative? Why is it that I'm allowed to do that? I always thought there was some kind of law preventing me from doing negative stuff!"

"The law you speak of is the Law of Cause and Effect. But you misunderstand this law. With your understanding, you would have no free will. You would only obey, or disobey. That is all. This viewpoint eliminates personal responsibility and reflects the workings of outer law, not unlike the Law of Moses."

"But didn't Moses say that there was an eye for an eye and a tooth for a tooth? Speaking of cause and effect."

"Yes, he did say that. And for good reason, too. At the time, there was no law or model for right behavior. So, Moses sat on Sinai for many years and pondered how this might be changed. The result was the code of Moses. Others, in other times, also realized there was a need for boundaries and moral and social modeling, such as Hammurabi. He also developed a code of conduct, a social guide for living.

"These outer laws serve their purpose. They provide a strong day-to-day guideline for everyone during a time of inner and outer lawlessness. In this way, there is a greater peace with less violence and less confusion. The individual can rest, knowing that practical and spiritual issues are settled nearly at once and meet with swift justice whenever necessary."

"I always felt that those old laws were harsh and uncompassionate, showing no mercy. They didn't suggest any room for the possibility of remorse to arise!"

"That's true, my son; you are correct," Yokar continued. "It was often that this kind of justice was indeed harsh and meted out swift punishment. The old laws indicated little mercy. But such is the case with the outer law. It is only an approximate simulation to the inner law."

"You mean like, as it is above . . . so almost below?"

"Hmm, yes. Something like that."

"So, if and when I screw up real badly, how does the karma fit in?"

"You believe you live your whole life like a good man and you will expect to go to heaven, as you would understand it. Meanwhile, you might be surprised to learn that there is, down the road, a murderer, liar, and thief carrying on without any consideration for his actions or their effects, and that this negative man may end up standing next to you in your Heaven! Karma, the active principle and recorder of Cause and Effect, would not be implemented. Because he may not exhibit remorse or consciousness of his negative actions."

"What!" I said, feeling suddenly outraged. "Wait a minute! You mean to tell me that he just gets away with whatever he does and there is no retribution for his actions?"

"Not until there is remorse," Yokar confirmed.

"So, let me see if I got this straight. You're saying that if a bad man does lots of bad things in his life and doesn't feel sorry about it, he just gets away with it?"

"Essentially. At least, in the context of your sense of time, he gets away with it. Until he feels remorse."

"But why is the bad man allowed to be in Heaven, next to the good man?"

"He is in Heaven long enough to reconstitute his being for another round of incarnation, as set down by his Stellar Mind's intention. Try and consider this: what purpose does retribution serve, if there is no consciousness to warrant learning from the punishment? Also, realize that a man does not grow while he is unconscious, either. He will remain stuck in the vicious circle of his unconsciousness, until he experiences remorse. Then, and only then, will the karmic debt begin to unfold for his further development. It is through the karmic action that greater sensitivity is developed."

I was silent. Inwardly, I could feel wheels turning, but I felt strangely quiet. As though something else was weighing Yokar's every word.

Suddenly, I felt my feelings explode. "That sucks! I feel cheated. I can think of lots of times when I felt abused by somebody. I wanted the other person to pay for it, somehow. Now you say that may not happen? Maybe, even for a long time!"

"Yes. That is possible. In accordance to your marking of the passage of time, anyway. But you see, that is why man often distorts the inner laws. Because man has a lust for revenge. He does not trust the wisdom of the All and Everything, the Most High God. He sets out to mete out his own form of justice. Then, he will most likely create further karmic debt for himself."

"I see."

"The more you grasp the timelessness of the moment, the more this won't matter to you. Then you can let go of your lust for revenge. We are not saying that there is no karma for this negative man. We are only saying that the karmic action does not begin until he calls it up out of his remorse. In other words, it's like saying: when you feel remorse, you're ready to learn. So life responds, by unleashing the karmic response appropriate to the level of your remorse. This brings about a change in being.

"It is also possible that, should your remorse be great enough, the fire of your consciousness can change your being instantly, in the moment. You can even burn karma before it even unfolds. There is no point in torture! Where is the learning with the torturing? Ponder this." Yokar commanded as he left me.

I began to experience a new feeling: the need to share Yokar's wisdom with others. My doubt was shifting into the background, and I felt that it was foolish for me to hold all this wonderful insight to myself! I needed to consider the problem of how to communicate Yokar's wisdom directly with the public.

Often I did not feel Yokar's presence. This meant only one thing that he was not in the vicinity of the Earth at all. Often, when I didn't need his help or advice, he would visit other star systems to offer his services, in a similar way. He told me that when he was absent, I should just think of his presence and that thought would be sufficient to call him.

So, wanting to ask Yokar about sharing his wisdom, I sat down on the couch, took a deep breath, and closed my eyes. I began to inhale, turning my head from side to side to balance the air in the left and right nostrils. Yokar had taught me that turning the head with each breath would build up neutralizing force along my channel of perception and aid in contacting him. As I began to breathe, my body began to calm down, and I could easily visualize him. The memory of the essence of his being filled me and I became warm all over. My scalp began to bristle with prickly heat, indicating that I had made contact.

I knew that it would only be a matter of minutes before he arrived. Moments passed into minutes until I felt the familiar warm current run down my spine. A complete and utter sense of safety surrounded me. He was here!

"Greetings to you, my friend. How are you doing?"

"Hi, Yokar. I have a special problem I want to work out with you."

"How can we help you today?" He asked.

"Out of curiosity, where did you go this time?"

"A small planet in what you are calling the Rigel system, a planet called Riaseda."

"Is there someone like me on Riaseda contacting you in the same way, Yokar?"

At this point in our conversation, he became slightly visible. He seemed to be leaning on something. It was tall and cylindrical like a tree, but it was blue in color and changing, almost like marble. The other features around him were difficult to define.

"Well, not exactly." He went on: "Let us just say that we were assisting with bringing clarity in a dispute. But never mind about that. We sense that you have something else on your mind . . . out with it!"

"I've been feeling that I want to bring this wonderful information you possess to others."

I waited for a response but there was only silence. My vision of him seemed to waver for a moment. Then he spoke again.

"What you ask will require a great deal of change, and mostly for you. We are not so sure you are ready for this. We have not come to teach others on the Earth! We have come to help you.

"In order for this direct communication with others to occur, we would need to enter your body. We would speak with others in a bold, honest, and sometimes harsh way. You would not allow this on a conscious level. You often desire to placate others in order to avoid conflict. Yes?"

This time, I was quiet. I knew that it was true. Being a Libra, I would try to avoid conflict at any cost. I continued to press him for a solution. After a brief pause, he suggested a demonstration.

"If you are willing, we will attempt entry now, to see how you feel about it. Are you willing to do that?" Yokar challenged. I hesitated for a moment, but then agreed.

Yokar told me to begin my breathing as though I were attempting to make initial contact with him. I started to rotate my head from side to side as usual, while I gathered neutralizing energy. Yokar's image faded, and I began to feel a most peculiar sensation. I felt full, as though I had eaten a large meal. A peculiar pressure was building deep inside my abdomen. There was a sensation of a bubble forming. Then the bubble started to move slowly upwards, toward my throat. As it rose I began to feel nauseous. The higher it climbed, the sicker to my stomach I felt. At a certain point I couldn't take it any more and demanded that he stop.

The sensation ceased, but I felt lightheaded and dizzy. A wave of heat rushed through my body like a fever.

"I can tell you this," I declared. "We won't be doing that again real soon! That was awful! Disgusting! Oh man . . . what a horrible feeling."

"Well, we warned you that you were not ready for this. There are far too many toxins in your body to continue an entry at this time. Let us just say that it is not our purpose to teach others, Michael. We are here to help you in your development, in whatever way we can."

Still holding my stomach, I walked around a bit trying to stabilize the queasy feeling. Despite my pain, I believed strongly that this amazing knowledge needed to be shared. I continued to press for some other way. "Isn't there some other way that you could offer this to others? Don't you see . . . you would be helping me, if you can help me to help others see the truth!"

Yokar paused. After a several seconds that seemed like hours, he spoke again. "We have decided that it might be good for you to do this. Very well, by your wish, we will comply. But you will have to follow our instructions to the letter. Do you understand? The consequences will be most distressful for you if you don't!"

I wondered for the moment what he meant by "good for me," but I decided not to ask just then. I believed the answer required too much concentration, which would increase my nausea.

Yokar began to give me a list of instructions: "First, you will need to go on several fasts of raw vegetables and vegetable juices. The fasts must follow a natural pattern of change, which your body is structured to handle—always in cycles of 7. The first cycle will be 7 hours, then 7 times 7 or 49 hours, then for 7 days, and so on. You will need to eliminate your consumption of fermented liquids for at least three full days before you attempt such contact with us again.

"The main problem will be the uncontrolled rise of heat in the body. We must control it! Otherwise, your nervous system will fry and sizzle like a pig's belly on a hot iron."

For the next few months I followed his instructions carefully. Time after time, I reluctantly attempted intimate contact, again suffering the awful nausea I felt, with almost the same results. Each time was a little better, but the progress was painful and slow.

Meanwhile, I continued to consciously relate Yokar's words to others. He felt this attempt would be good practice. He was right. Very often, I would try to censor his comments. They were too shocking or provoking. I felt I didn't have the right to say shocking things to other people. I was afraid of the confrontation or I was embarrassed.

Eating was the biggest problem. If I ate, the digestion process really caused tremendous heat. I had to skip meals just to let him speak for a minute or two. When he did, I was still conscious but somewhat removed or distant from the action. It felt as if I was talking to someone while I was half asleep. I could remember speaking, but I couldn't remember exactly what I said three minutes after.

One afternoon, I went to visit my children. After we had returned from seeing a movie together, we sat in my car, speaking casually. In a moment of courage, I told them about Yokar. I received from them a range of mixed reactions—from total disbelief to faint and idle curiosity.

I suggested that I could bring him out enough for them to feel him, if they were willing. My youngest, Melinda, wanted no part of it. She got out of the car and bid us goodnight. My older daughters, Michelle and Stephanie, stayed to accept the challenge.

I asked them to close their eyes and I would try to transmit his image. They both saw a figure with little or no hair, looking a little like Mr. Clean from the detergent commercials on TV. Then a strange thing happened. I passed out! A half-hour later, I awoke and apologized for napping.

To my utter amazement, I learned that my children had carried on a complete conversation with Yokar while I was out cold. They couldn't believe that I didn't remember what "I" had said. Moreover, Stephanie was very agitated.

I inquired gently about the matter. "What's up, kiddo . . . why are you upset?"

She began, almost in tears. She was wondering if I wanted to insult her, or was it this strange visitor I called Yokar!

"Yokar called me a bigot! He even said that all my friends are bigots!"

I was horrified. Then I thought suddenly, Yokar how could you do that to my own daughter?

Before I could defend Yokar, or myself Michelle began to admit that she also knew some of Stephanie's friends. She agreed with Yokar that they were indeed bigots! This comment instigated an argument between them, which I had to referee.

The incident ended with my offering consolation. I assured her that Yokar meant no malice in his comments to her. I went on to say that he wanted her to be conscious of her judgments.

Later, I drove back to my home in New York in shock. It had happened! I had gone totally unconscious and Yokar had spoken freely to another person. The feeling was so strange. I felt out of control of my own faculties. Alarms were going off in my head. The worst part was that my fear had been realized—something was said that upset another person and I had nothing to do with it!

Then Yokar chimed in. "We wouldn't be too concerned about the incident. You are concerned that she will not love you because of it?"

"Yes," I said.

"Her love has not been influenced in this way. She will recover and we believe she will see the truth of what was revealed."

"I sincerely hope you are right about this."

I learned from Stephanie later that she had accepted the comments in stride and had calmed down. She was able to see some of what Yokar had revealed to her and was considering it. I was relieved.

My full-trance training with Yokar continued. I was able to extend the length of time he could stay inside my body. Abstaining from meals allowed me to maintain contact with Yokar for as long as an hour sometimes. When the time came for the first full session, where Yokar would lecture and offer answers to questions for a group, I needed to fast for a full day before the group began. Even then, participants would acknowledge that upon my re-entering the body, I would flush red with heat.

As I would leave my body, I found myself entering a blue field. It was blue everywhere. There was no definition or detail to compare with anywhere, just the color blue. It was like being in a fog bank lit with blue lights!

During one of the first lectures Yokar offered, I decided to explore this "infinite" blue field to see if I could find anything at all. Curiously enough, the lecture subject was on death! Toward the end of the lecture, Yokar bid everyone farewell. He telepathically called me so that I could return to my body. It was a spiritual law that spirit could not leave a physical body unattended. So Yokar waited for me to return before he could leave. But I didn't return!

Yokar suddenly returned to the body and declared that I couldn't be found! Dianne was shocked and the audience began to laugh nervously. Meanwhile, Yokar assured everyone it would be a minor delay.

Yokar began to call upon the Life Force in Astral Kingdom for a kind of "all points bulletin" for my whereabouts and return. I suddenly felt a force clutching me and pulling me back to the point of debarkation. I could see my disgruntled teacher staring at me with a scolding expression.

"Sorry, Yokar. I just couldn't resist exploring the blue field. But rest assured, my curiosity has been satisfied."

He grunted an acceptance as he ushered me back into my body.

From that time forward, my acceptance and adjustment progressed. In the beginning, there were some difficulties for me in doing group sessions—the sense that I was losing precious time out of my physical life while I was in trance, and I couldn't shake the fear that I was going to sleep in front of a group and nothing was going to happen, that Yokar would abandon me, leaving me to simply snore in front of everyone.

My paranoia about the lost time made me compulsive about listening to the recordings from those first sessions. I would get very upset if the recording were lost for any reason. As time passed, I finally relaxed and consoled myself that the information given was worth the sacrifice. Later, I would often joke about the possibility of lapsing into snoring to ease my nervousness in front of the groups.

Serving Two Masters

In the spring of 1987 . . .

It was a bright and sunny day in New York. I joined Dianne for an afternoon stroll and some bookstore browsing in Shakespeare's, one of our favorite bookstores in the neighborhood. I was drawn to look through the philosophy and self-help department. While I scanned for interesting new titles, a large white book slipped off the shelf above and fell squarely on my head. It had no unusual markings, so I placed it back on the shelf without further consideration. Later, the incident wouldn't leave my mind. Regardless of where I looked, I kept returning to the white book. As we stood on line for check out, we shared our discoveries.

"Did you find something?" Dianne asked, staring at the white book under my arm.

"I don't know, really. This damn book hit me on the head. Afterwards, I couldn't shake the compulsion to read it. So I decided to buy it!"

Several months later . . .

I was lying on the living room floor of our apartment. It was a lazy Sunday afternoon, and my mind drifted. As my eyes rolled past the bookshelf, I saw it. It was that darn white book glaring at me! I declared silently, I guess it's time I take a look at you.

I began to leaf through the pages casually, with little interest. It was a treatise on Taoist Chinese Yoga. I began to shiver inside. I realized my body knew something I hadn't discovered yet. These new sensations made me look at the book's content more deliberately. It was like nothing I had ever seen before.

The text inside revealed strange practices that stimulate an internal energy. The energy is called Chi. The descriptions of energy flow began to sound very similar to my experience at the Center. As I read further, the text revealed more. I learned that I could stimulate and control it.

Oh, this is too good to be true! I thought, as I sank into my chair with mixed feelings of excitement and anticipated disappointment. This guy probably lives in a cave somewhere on top of Mount Everest! Right?

I turned the book over to look at the author's picture and brief biography. "Hey! Look at this!" I blurted out. "Master Mantak Chia, Huntington, New York." I suddenly jumped with excitement. "Jesus, he's right here in New York. He lives on Long Island, for Christ's sake!"

I leaped to the telephone to call Master Chia, still doubting this discovery. I expected another screwball to answer, giving me the runaround. Again, I was surprised. Master Chia himself answered. This was bizarre!

He was from Thailand. His English was pretty rough. I really had to tune my ears for "pigeon speak." I didn't really care. My solution was close at hand and I was happy. Within minutes, he gave me his schedule for classes at the high school near Chinatown. I was prepared to throw myself into the Taoist study with the same zeal I had given to the Pathwork.

Soon I was taking courses four nights a week and loving every minute of it. The first thing Master Chia confirmed in my training was that my energetic incident in the Pathwork was actually quite common among students in China and Thailand.

"What you experienced is called Chi," He said with absolute confidence. "We can show you how to make it flow, to control it!"

This was music to my ears. He began to teach me the beginning meditations of the Taoist Yoga system. It is called the first formula in the practice, the Micro Cosmic Orbit. The purpose of the meditation is to lead the energy called Chi up the spine to the top of the head by focusing the mind on several energy points along the way. This pathway is called the governor channel.

Here the Chinese Yoga practice takes a right turn from my theoretical study of Eastern Indian Kundalini Yoga practices. In both cases, the goal is the same: to get the Chi energy to travel up the spine to the head. The alleged benefit is a profound stimulation of certain endocrine glands, offering the practitioner a boost in conscious awareness.

In the Chinese system, I was taught that the Chi energy needs to return down through another hidden energy channel so it can safely return to its point of origin at the base of the spine. This other channel is called the functional channel. Curiously, the Eastern Indians never talk about this channel or its importance. I concluded it is a secret or they just don't know about it!

The functional channel is a path from the throat down through the heart, solar plexus, and navel to the male or female genitalia and finally meeting at the bottom point of the governor channel called the perineum (a point between the anus and sexual organs).

For it to reach this channel, a physical bridge for the energy is needed. This bridge is formed by touching the tip of the tongue to the roof of the mouth behind the gums of the upper teeth.

In the meditation practice, the Chi energy is directed by mind focus to drop through the tongue into the throat, following the front path back to the bottom of the spine. Thus it forms a loop, or "orbit." Master Chia called this the psychic safety valve. Without this meditation as a foundation, the other energy practices can become precarious or even dangerous for the practitioner.

Later, through other formulas, I learned an effective way to balance negative emotional energy in the body. The theory is based upon the five elements: Fire, Water, Wood, Metal, and Earth. Each vital organ is related to these elements in a complex flow of energy, i.e., the heart, kidneys, liver, lungs, and stomach respectively. I won't go into the details of the theory of these paths as it extends well beyond the scope of this book. Please refer to the number of books available by Master Mantak Chia on Taoist yoga.

The Chinese believe that when the vital organs become unbalanced, the vital Chi becomes spoiled or toxic. The result is negative emotional energy. For example, when the liver is unbalanced the negative emotional energy produces anger. The liver's positive energy complement, when it is balanced, is kindness.

When the heart is unbalanced, there is excessive cruelty or bitterness present. When the heart is balanced, the positive energy condition is love and sweetness.

The five elements can be fused through mental visualizations, creating opposing centers of stored negative energy from the various unbalanced organs. This mediation in Taoist Yoga is called the fusion of five elements. A neutral or natural form of Chi energy is derived from these opposing negative qualities by combining them at the lower navel, through the use of another special visual pattern called a pakua (pronounced pah-kwa). Once neutralized by this method, the Chi is restored to its positive healthy state and stored at the base of the spine and is available for deeper practice later.

The heart of Taoist Yoga is based upon the recovery and preservation of all forms of human and elemental energy. This technique of blending the various negative emotional energies of the vital organs is a form of this preservation practice. When the blending is accomplished, a most amazing energetic calm is reached inside the body. This calm is essential to the success of more sophisticated (higher level) meditations practiced later on in the Chinese Yoga system.

I learned that the Taoist philosophy of energy cultivation is based upon the principles of farming; in order to plant seeds and grow a fine crop; one must monitor and manage all of the natural elements. By metaphor, harmonizing the elements (emotional energy) within the body is like managing all the natural elements for good farming. The student can make the body ready for something fantastic: the beginning of a new spiritual growth, the essence of a spiritual "light body." A "spiritual seed" could conceivably be planted through the practice and caused to grow within the individual.

The various higher formulas or alchemical practices center on mastering the gathering and flow of the subtle energies necessary for the planting, growth, and further development of the spiritual light body.

In the ancient times of this tradition, the student's physical body, even before learning the meditations, would be strengthened and his sense of timing would be improved. Specific methods of exercise and breathing, which were based upon animal movements, were used.

This knowledge was held in secret tradition and allegedly began more than 8000 years ago. It has been said by scholars of Chinese history that the basic spiritual techniques were brought into China by the Buddha and introduced to the various monasteries. Although the true origin is unknown, the Shao-Lin monastery is considered one of the first to reveal this ancient tradition. The Shao-Lin monks were responsible for developing the five animal forms—the tiger, monkey, crane, dragon and eagle claw—out of the original techniques. This exercise style became known as Wushu or Gung Fu.

Eventually these practice forms became the rudiments of martial arts used by the monks to defend the monastery against marauding bandits, a distortion of their intended purpose. This history explained why Master Chia used the Chinese martial tradition for much of his students' physical training. He often declared, however, that he would not accept students who were interested only in the fighting techniques.

Master Chia often described the average human nervous system by metaphor, as a house with regular electrical wiring, allowing only 110 volts of electricity to flow. He declared that, with preparation, the body could conceivably handle 220 volts of electricity, or more, without burning down the house (student).

As I reflected on my experience in the Pathwork intensive, it all made perfect sense to me now. That's why I doubled up on the floor shaking violently. I was running 220 volts. Hell, I thought, maybe it was even lightning!

The practice of mental visualization in Chinese Yoga was exhausting for me, often taxing my patience. It was also my first introduction to the concept of energy meridians. The practice encourages Chi to flow through an ever-increasing complexity of meridian pathways in the body.

The Chinese system of medicine uses these meridians to treat illness through the application of small needles. The needles are inserted at various points along the meridians, called acupuncture points. In this way, a Chinese doctor siphons off the energy of the toxic

Chi and thus helps the body back into balance and restored health.

At first, I found this concept very difficult to believe. Even the Chinese admit that the meridians don't actually exist in a physical sense, but rather as a series of energetic responses between the connective tissues of the body. I had to accept this "fact" in my imagination first! It would be several years of practice before I would actually feel the energy running along these paths. Then it was gratifying to know that my efforts were not for naught!

Mantak Chia was not an easy man to know. He was cordial but seemed stiff and held back. He resisted talking about his personal life, keeping at a certain distance. I suspected this reticence was due to the nature of the Asian culture in itself. In my experience, Asians tend to keep to their own and do not trust other people easily.

I have found that this lack of trust can easily be reduced by an unusual amount of personal effort. Americans tend to expect all other people to accept them warmly and automatically, without such effort. I have learned a difficult lesson: to the Asian, this lack of personal effort can represent a lack of respect and will undermine a relationship without the American ever-knowing why. My friendship with Master Chia developed beyond the teacher/student relationship very soon, but the real deepening took several years.

I believe that my progress in the Taoist Yoga system progressed very quickly because of Chia's warm personal caring and friendship toward me. I began to feel that I was more like an extended member of his family. This part of my training helped to further heal aspects of my emotional split with my father and other general difficulties with men.

My preparation and training continued for three years, nonstop. Then I finally reached the intermediate level. I was ready for advanced Iron Shirt Chi Kung and Five Finger Gung Fu practice.

One day, in the middle of my Iron Shirt practice, another Chinese master approached me from the side. He had been observing me for some time without my knowing it. His name was Master T. K.

"I have been watching your practice very carefully. If you will keep up this intensity, your energy will be great enough that I will be able to teach you Iron Palm."

"Iron Palm?" I blurted out. "I thought that was a myth!"

I knew about Iron Palm from Kung Fu films: the bad guy punches the good guy once, and three months later he dies a mysterious and awful death.

Master T.K.'s eyes narrowed. After several seconds he turned quietly. "Oh, it is quite real!" he said. "But not many have such ability. To conjure and master the energy to this level of perfection is a great feat. And I see that you can be one of these with the proper training."

I sat down on one of the nearby benches. My belief envelope was being stretched again. I looked at him with some tolerance.

"Listen, Master K., your offer is very kind. I've heard of you and your abilities. I really hold you in the highest regard, but I don't think I want to turn this energy into a super weapon. You know? I didn't start this to fire up my martial skills again. You know what I mean?" Then I added, "No offense."

"None taken," he said softly. Then he smiled at me and continued, "I'll be around from time to time, should you decide to change your mind."

"Thanks, Master K., I appreciate it, but I don't think so, just the same."

In the following year, through the Iron Shirt practice, I doubled my body strength. My fingers had become so strong that Dianne couldn't stand a deep massage from me anymore. I had to be careful and mindful of the pressure. I felt an incredible sense of health.

The practice also increased my "rooting power." Rooting comes from learning how to strengthen the relationship between one's body and the Earth. I learned to sink my Chi energy into the Earth and the Earth, in turn, sends energy back into my body. This strong Earthly connection gave me the ability to walk on ice and not slip. My enthusiasm for the Taoist practice was soaring.

One night, Yokar appeared to me in a dream.

The time has come to begin the preparations for your deeper training. Soon you will undergo an initiation with fire. This will be the beginning of your inner transformation. Ultimately, you will embrace all of the elements in a similar way. I awoke in a sweat!

Two days later, Master Chia called me at home to tell me about something urgent. "Hello Michael."

"Hi, Master Chia. What's up?"

"I want you to walk the fire with me."

"What do you mean walk the fire?"

"Come with me next week and we shall walk the fire together."

"Are you talking about a real fire walk?"

"Yes, that's right."

I began to laugh nervously. My dream was looming into view. All I could do was hem and haw. No words. Finally, I blurted out my denial. "Listen, Master Chia, I don't know about this. I can't see myself as a firewalker. You know what I mean? I'm a dedicated student, you know that! But walking on fire is not my cup of tea."

Master Chia did not accept my denial. He continued to press for an agreement. He kept saying it was very important for my training. I felt he was taking unfair advantage of my loyalty. I wanted to continue my training very much, but this was something else. I was entering into shock. I said I would think about it. Then he gave me instructions to meet him one evening the following week at a small elementary school auditorium in lower Manhattan.

Later that evening, I called my Pathwork helper Bob, and asked him what he thought about Master Chia's request. Bob didn't know what to say at first. But later he suggested in a laughing tone, confirming what I already knew, "Mike, it sounds like an initiation to me, a rite of passage of some kind!"

Dianne already knew that I would go, so she decided to join me for support. For me, it was strictly a reconnaissance mission.

When we arrived, it was a little past six in the evening. Many of Master Chia's other students were already taking seats in the auditorium. We took some seats with a pretty good view of the stage. A few minutes later, Master Chia showed up with another man. His name was Lar Short, an American monk of the Tibetan tradition. Lar was a short man and appeared rather ordinary looking, not unlike Chia. Lar also brought along an assistant.

Master Chia first made a few announcements. Then he turned the floor over to Lar. Lar wasted no time. He called for six volunteers. I did not raise my hand. I had learned from my military service experience; the one who volunteers is usually about to get the short end of the stick. It was later that I realized how ironically true this would be.

I watched as an assortment of people, male and female, climbed upon the small stage. He handed each an arrow, the kind used for target shooting. The arrows were made of hardwood, having feathers on one end and a blunt metal point mounted on the other end.

It was like the beginning of a magician's act. Lar presented one of the arrows to a member of the audience to test its "true grit." The person checked both ends and even flexed the arrow's shaft for strength. All was apparently in order. Now Lar began his pitch. He described the feats of endurance of the Haitian firewalkers. He went on to describe the altered trance state they would enter before beginning their walk. Then he described the rudiments of this kind of trance state.

Lar explained how the trance could be achieved by anyone. But first there needed to be a preliminary introductory breakthrough. In short, he called for a demonstration.

Lar placed one of the arrows in front of his body, with the feathered end lodged against the wall. The other end, with the metal tip, pointed at the hollow of his throat. While in this position, he went on about the importance of looking up and finding the point of mind where there was no fear. Then, without further delay, he lunged into the arrow with his full force of weight. The arrow shaft snapped into splintered pieces. Then he presented his throat for everyone to see. No blood and no hole. Amazing!

At this point, you could hear a pin drop in the auditorium. Lar went on to place the same kind of arrows in front of each one of the volunteers. One by one, he encouraged them to follow in his footsteps. If they could do it, the point would be driven home, so to speak, no pun intended.

Well, to my utter amazement, each one performed the same task without a hitch. I could tell that my mind was beginning to twitch a little. Then something remarkable happened. One of the first volunteers, wearing a black t-shirt and jeans, which sat only two seats from me, raised his hand to get Lar's attention.

"Uh, Lar," he stammered, his voice choking. Then he cleared his throat to speak louder. "Uh, Lar!"

Lar raised his hand to acknowledge the young man's request. "Yes, can I help you?"

"Lar," he continued, "I'm having a problem here. I think . . . I think my mind won't accept what I've done here tonight." I watched incredulously as tears began to roll down his cheeks. He was obviously very upset. Then it happened. Blood appeared at his throat, where there was no mark before!

I started to quake inside. A sharp blast of sound exploded from me and a kind of mad uncontrollable laughter followed. Dianne started to cry. Then I knew it. My God, we were on the edge of something here! I kept repeating under my breath, over and over, "Holy shit! Holy shit!"

Hours later, the fire had been built and reached its peak. It was estimated to be about 1200 degrees. A minimum safe distance of six feet from the coals could be maintained without peeling the first layer from my face.

We were instructed to write down all of our fears regarding the fire, on paper. Then we had to throw the paper into the fire, making a sort of homage to the "fire elementals." Afterwards, we were all lined up behind the gymnasium, shoes off and pants rolled up. We were all ready to walk on red-hot coals! Lar and Master Chia led each participant to the edge of the coals, one by one, re-instructing them on the fine art of trance induction: look up, find that point of fearlessness bordering on ecstasy, then march onto the coals,

When my turn came, I gulped. As I approached the fire, Master Chia looked at me kindly and said, "I'm really glad you came tonight. This is it! Go for it."

I looked up and with all my heart, mind, and soul reached for that point of fearless quality. Then a strange thing happened. I felt a rush of icy warmth rush along my spine. An extreme sense of happiness suddenly filled me. I knew I was ready. I turned to Lar with bright shining eyes and said, "Yeah, all right. Let's do this thing!" Before I knew it, I was across. No blisters. No burned clothing. It was a miracle!

Three hours later, we sat having refreshments and talked of our experience with the fire. Then I began to feel odd. It was like my left-brain and my right brain were at war. I could actually feel a tugging inside my head. Chills were beginning to run up and down my spine. Now I knew what the young man in the black shirt had felt.

I tried to ward it off, but it was too strong. My right foot started to get hot, but my left foot felt fine. I ripped off my shoes to get more comfortable. The itch became intense on my right foot and that's when I found them growing. There on my right foot, several huge blisters, three hours later! I glanced at my left foot; it was lily white with no adverse signs. How odd., I thought. I leaned back in the chair, stunned at my curious condition. "Weird," I said quietly to myself. Looking around, I commented to the others, "Well, guys. I guess I still have some work to do around this!"

After five years, my intense day-to-day work with Master Chia was over. Now I looked forward to the summer retreats where the advanced alchemical meditation training of Kan and Li began. Once in a while, Master Chia would offer some minor preparation work in the city, but the courses dwindled and became less important.

Six more years passed, and it was 1989 before I reached the summit of Master Chia's training program, the Greatest Kan and Li. This was the highest alchemical meditation practice he was prepared to teach anyone at the time.

Everyone at the retreat was excited to receive this training. We were at the old estate of Guru Rudyana in the Catskill Mountains. We had all waited patiently for this offering. On the second day of the retreat, I couldn't help but notice that the meditations were very similar to my own full trance contact with Yokar. After the morning exercises, Yokar came to me in my room.

"Hi, Yokar. Have you come to watch my work this morning?"

"Actually, we have something else to tell you."

"You know," I went on, "it's good that you're here. I have some questions about this Kan and Li practice. I seem to already know this meditation. It's identical to the techniques you've taught me to prepare for making contact with you!"

"That's what we're here to talk to you about. There comes a time in each student's practice that defines a substantial shift. You have reached this stage."

I felt myself unconsciously gulp to catch my breath. "Okay. Can you explain a little more?"

"The progression of spiritual development takes a certain path. First, the student has to recognize that there are many 'I's that make up the ego-self. Each I believes itself to be the only self. With each physical awakening, a new I comes forward and claims its supreme position of conscious control.

"As long as this separation continues, there is very little chance for any growth in the student. When the time comes that the student realizes the separation of his consciousness into many 'I's, his opportunity then is to remember, when the next I comes on board, the previous I's agenda, which may be very different. It is said that the student has reached a shift when he can command at least 51 percent of all the individual 'I's to follow him under one banner of purpose."

"Go on, please," I said eagerly.

"The next level describes the proper use of the 51 percent of the student's consciousness. When used properly, it becomes a kind of magnetic center. This magnetic center can attract events to the student that will benefit his progress, such as attracting certain knowledge and or a teacher or teachers relating to his continued training. Are you with me so far?"

"Yes. I understand."

"The next shift comes when the skill level of the student attracts the inner teacher and the student begins to establish a firm contact with the inner teacher."

"Okay. I'm starting to get the picture, Yokar."

"Michael, you have discovered that your training on the inner level has gone beyond the outer teaching. You're at the next point in your development where your training will only come from the inner teacher!"

"I see. Is there another shift that occurs after that?"

"At the appointed time, your inner teacher will dissolve."

I suddenly felt insecure. "Does that mean that you will dissolve someday, Yokar?"

There was a long pause. Yokar finally answered, "Eventually, we will withdraw. Then you will be the Master!"

I was silent. Yokar let me ponder that thought while he kept silent. I pondered my position with Master Chia. I knew what I must do. My student relationship with Chia was now at an end and I felt sad. The sadness intensified when I began to consider the time Yokar would withdraw from me.

Then Yokar added, "You don't need to worry, my friend. Only at the appointed time, when your skill is sufficient, will we withdraw from your training but we will not abandon you . . . ever!

"Now we will continue with matters more important, your training! Since you now have the fire element burning within you, it's time to learn the language of the elementals that you may speak to them from your heart. Even from ancient times the adepts learned the sacred tongue of spirit. This way of communicating is called Vril (pronounced Veh-rill).

"This form of language isn't spoken in the same way as the words of gibberish spewing from your mouth. Humans are the only creatures on Earth that do not communicate! The Vril is a spiritual vibration uttered from the origin of communication, the entire being. It's directed from a point just below the hollow of your throat. Actually, this is where you begin to really communicate now, before you utter your words. This place of directed vibration is called the unnamed organ!"

"Why is this organ unnamed, Yokar?"

"Because the term in Atlantean is unpronounceable by you, so this unnamed term will suffice for now!"

As I pondered this, I wondered what the real name might be. I felt challenged that Yokar didn't think I might be able to speak the real name. Yokar went on with the teaching.

"The real name can only be uttered in Vril," he said. "You do not have the skill, my boy."

"Okay. I see what you mean."

"The language of Vril has 72 sounds. Fifty-two are verbal and the other 20 are silent. In ancient times, each temple initiate would receive a particular sound that would best represent his bloodline from Stellar Mind to begin his path of training. But all initiates would learn how to use Vril eventually. So out of that same tradition, you will also learn how to use it.

"As you enter through each elemental rite, relating to each of the elements, you will learn special formulas combined from the uttered Vril, that will give you dominion over those elements."

"What are the other rites?"

"During your training, you will merge with the others one by one, as you did with the fire. The others are water, air, and Earth."

"I understand, Yokar," I said solemnly.

I began to tremble inside, thinking of what I must do to merge with these elements. Yokar's vision for me was grander than I had imagined. My sense of him was changing from my long-lost grandfather to an ancient grand master/teacher. This relationship was proving to be a lot more than I bargained for!

Pilgrimage To The Sun

Yokar appeared before me unexpectedly while I sat at the kitchen counter, writing an overdue letter to a good friend in Japan. I was startled to see him. He appears to me so rarely in visual form that I had grown accustomed to telepathic communication. He interrupted as I was sharing my thoughts with him about my relationship with trees. I had always liked trees very much.

"If you look very closely, a deeper relationship exists between the Earth and Man," Yokar said.

"What do you mean by that, Yokar?"

"The Earth has a nervous system too, in many ways very similar to your own body. Many wise men of ancient times discovered this and mapped it."

"Mapped it!" I blurted out in surprise. "For what purpose?"

"In many of your belief systems, you furiously seek the attributes of heaven, yes? By this we mean you chase after it and long for its favors. Yet when you succeed, it consumes you!"

"But isn't that the goal, to be consumed by heaven?"

"Well, that's one way of looking at it," Yokar went on. "The problem is, as it consumes you, you lose the ability to assimilate it into your consciousness. In other words, you can't digest it very well. So we mean that it consumes you or burns you up. Do you understand?"

"I'm not sure what you mean," I said. "Can you explain further?"

"You see, this is an old problem. It was well known to wise men of the ancient past that the consumption of spiritual energy was limited by the capacity of the individual to take it in or otherwise digest it. They knew that integrating the incredible surge of insight and the higher vibration of this energy could easily overwhelm the normal nervous system. Too much heavenly energy in the body without preparation would result in a kind of toxicity which causes mental illness or madness."

"Is the madness permanent?"

"In terms that you can understand, it is sometimes permanent for the individual life, yes! But in the overall scheme of things, it is only a temporary setback."

"Yokar," I continued, "does this explain why some people who pursue a spiritual life, devoid of all other earthly experience, get a little wacky or crazy? You know, like celibate ascetics or monks who believe they should renounce their regular existence for the sake of spiritual purification?"

"Yes. This can be the case. A certain perception developed that heaven was the opposite polarity from that of the Earth. The two regions of existence were separated by the vast difference in their respective potential energies." He encouraged, "Are you following so far?"

"Yes, please go on."

"Thinking this, seekers of long ago set out to develop a way to accommodate this potential energy long enough to gain the benefit from it without these obvious hazards. The seekers determined that a way to accomplish this was to increase the amount of Earth potential in the body. They felt that this approach would provide a kind of safe path or extended neutrality for what they called the raging Fire dragon. This was an image quickly adopted to describe the terrible effects of the heavenly energy's blazing passage.

"Therefore, these wise seekers set out to find a corresponding dragon in the Earth realm. The Earth dragon, they reasoned, had to be very different than its fiery counterpart and must demonstrate the opposite qualities. They began to look for this Earth dragon that moved through the Earth as easily as the Fire dragon moved through the heavens.

"The Earth dragon was finally seen after they traveled for many years looking diligently in many places far and wide. This Earth dragon was like a great sea serpent. It rose out of the Earth quite suddenly, catching them by surprise, and then plunged back again almost as quickly as it had come. Once they recovered from this amazing sight, they discovered that it didn't rise very often. It was more rare than they had anticipated.

"The Earth dragon seemed to rise only in a few special places and only at certain times. After realizing this, the wise seekers resolved to decipher and understand this fleeting appearance. Knowing this problem, their hopes of harnessing the heavenly energy seemed more remote than ever. But, undaunted, they were vigilant and marked the passage of the great serpent, noting where and when it came, writing it down in their sacred scrolls.

"Cyclical patterns emerged, related to the timing with the seasons, the arrangement of the stars, and certain unique dwelling places. After much discussion amongst themselves, they concluded that dreams of controlling the Fire dragon would have to be restricted to locations where the Earth dragon appeared most regularly. They reasoned that a system to synchronize their spiritual work with the exposure times of the Earth energy would have to be developed.

"Before long, the seekers realized that their efforts to chase after heaven were apparently unnecessary. They observed that the Fire dragon naturally chased the Earth dragon each time it appeared. From then on, they concentrated their efforts to capture and harness the Earth energy and finally storing it into their bodies. Then, they reasoned, heaven would chase them!"

"Was this during your time in Atlantis, Yokar?"

"Yes. That's correct."

"How did they know where to look for the Earth dragon?"

"It was known by psychically gifted men, since the earliest times, that certain places were marked by unusual energy. They also discovered that energy traveled in lines."

"Could they see this energy?"

"No, not really, but they could feel it."

I felt the warmth of Yokar's eyes as they twinkled at me.

He continued on. "The dragon's presence was discovered by the rumbling sensations and nausea in the bellies of the special men. They had the gift of the inner sense. Because of these gifts, they were chosen to become the overseers of the various tribes. These overseers decided that they would set out and follow the lines of energy to learn where they would lead. The seers believed these lines of energy were in fact tracks made by the great dragon as it moved through the Earth."

"How long did it take for them to find the dragon?"

"Oh my! Well, in terms that you will understand, it was many thousands of years. It was many generations that wandered through the wilderness meticulously tracing and recording its passage. Then, much to their surprise, they discovered that the lines intersected in some places. Sometimes they found as many as three lines that would conjunct together. At first, they thought the dragon was trying to fool them. Later they agreed, after drawing a map that it was more like some kind of giant web stretching over the Earth. This is what you now call the Ley Lines of the Earth.

"The paths of the Earth dragon were completely mapped. They found from their analysis that the patterns would change over long periods of time, roughly every 2000 years. In these rare places of three conjunctions, they also discovered that the Earth dragon hesitated above the surface for an unusually long time."

"How did they finally capture the Earth dragon, Yokar?"

As I awaited his answer, I sensed a smile forming at the corner of his mouth while he readjusted his robes and stroked his beard.

"Well," he went on slowly, "it turned out to be more difficult than expected. At first they tried to block the dragon's return by creating patterns of stone built into the Earth. This only succeeded in creating earthquakes as the dragon stampeded through the barriers. The overseers then tried incantations of all sorts, attempting to bind the dragon, but it only resulted in their becoming very ill. After all their attempts to subdue it, they realized the only way to capture the great dragon was to cooperate with it. They needed to study and make use of its movements, enticing it to stay.

"The clue to their solution rested in the places of the great triple conjunctions, where the dragon seemed to hesitate. Many meditations and deliberations were held in these rare and sacred places. It was finally determined that the place of the triple conjunction was defined by a special arrangement of the mountains, valley contour, and the flowing water in the region. In addition, the rocks in these areas contained a special mineral. This mineral seemed to store unusual amounts of a special energy believed by the overseers to contribute to the sustenance of life itself. This energy was called the Triune Stream, or the Life Force. The overseers concluded that the Life Force also originated in the places of the triple conjunction.

"The overseers began to imagine temples constructed out of this mineral to honor the dragon, built with the same wisdom and understanding of the elements that shaped the regions of the triple conjunction. Their idea was that the temples would reflect the same harmony and vibration of this Life Force, thus making the temples a temporary home for the dragon. They reasoned that the dragon would be tricked into hesitating inside their temples, long enough for them to absorb some of its properties."

"Wow! That's an amazing story. So, did it work?"

"Actually it took many more years to perfect the temple designs. The improvements included a rounded dome that had sloped walls, which were truncated. This made the dragon spin inside, forcing it to stay longer."

"What was this mineral they found?"

"Later the mineral became known as auriculum. It was used for many other marvelous applications at a later time."

"Does it exist now?"

"It still exists, but only at the base of certain volcanoes deep within the bowels of the Earth. It is well out of your present reach."

"So this web of energy they discovered, was it the nervous system of the Earth?"

"Yes. They continued to study the web throughout all of the Atlantean experience. And, during that period, they observed no less than one hundred cycles of change in the web through eight sojourns of the sun!"

"You mean the web was changing all the time?"

"Yes! That's correct."

"Changing in what way, Yokar?"

"Every cycle lasted some 2000 of your years, carrying its own pattern and quality. With each twelve cycles completed, a single sojourn of the sun was complete!"

"Yokar, you're talking about astrology! The cycles represent houses of the Zodiac and the sun's sojourn is the sun's path, the solar phalanx or path of the dragon, right?"

"Very good, you're learning quickly!"

I just sat there dumfounded and silent. Bits and pieces of esoteric hodgepodge came together in my mind like some fantastic jigsaw puzzle. Chills ran down my spine, confirming my recognition. My body jumped up spontaneously with excitement. I began to giggle. Slowly, I murmured, "Wow! Yokar, that really ties a lot together for me. Okay. Now tell me more about these temples."

"Our presence has begun to increase the temperature in your body beyond your capacity. We will break off for now."

As Yokar's energy subsided, my excitement calmed and the intense heat slowly drained off. My body slumped.

It was just past noon. My mouth was so dry from the session that I felt like a desert had blown through it. I smacked my lips, trying to muster some saliva, but none was available. My mind rolled around the thoughts of traveling for thousands of years.

God, I thought. What incredible persistence! It's hard to believe someone could track something for that long.

My mind reeled at the thought of it. The dryness in my mouth was suddenly unbearable. I slugged down some cold water, still imagining an endless journey. While I sipped my remaining water, I fantasized about stopping at an oasis and pondering the long quest.

Then there was the sound of an engine. The mail had just been delivered. There were several important items expected and my anticipation broke the lingering thoughts of Yokar's story.

My mind quickly turned to the practicalities of the moment. Poring through the junk mail, I tossed most of it into the wastebasket. The disappointment sucked the wind from my sails. Nothing had arrived. I continued dispersing all the superfluous mailings into the waste with all the excitement of a plodding government employee. I tried to quell the pain.

"Damn, I didn't get what I wanted."

Then one surprise package emerged. Having been wedged between two pieces of junk, a letter fell to the floor.

That was close, I thought. It was almost lost with the rest.

It was a letter from Japan. My disappointment left in an instant. The envelope was like a predator's first bite of a long-awaited meal. I ripped it open. My eyes raced along each line and consumed every word like a firestorm. It was from a man called Masumi. He had been scouting for new material at the Los Angeles New Age Exposition some four or five months earlier. While there, he met a friend of mine who happened to be in possession of some of Yokar's audiotaped lectures. There was a friendly exchange between them, and my friend offered his copies to Masumi out of a gesture of good will.

Masumi had listened to the Yokar lecture material and wanted to invite me to Japan on tour. His business involved organizing New Age guest speakers from other countries to come to Japan giving lectures and private sessions to the participants of his events. He was especially looking for trance channels with interesting stories and/or information. The Japanese people were hungry for this kind of experience.

Shaking my hands wildly in the air, I yelled out spontaneously, "Yes! Yes! Of course I'll do it."

I couldn't wait to answer him with a fax. I had so enjoyed Japan during my military duty in Southeast Asia. My squadron of fighters was called on duty early in the game when the Gulf of Tonkin incident happened. Japan was our landing strip of choice in a remote part of the North called Misawa Air Base.

Later, when things got really hot, my squadron's duty was right in the middle, in such places as Quang Tri, Ben Hua, and Dhnang. As during the Korean conflict, during the Vietnam War, Japan was chosen often as a close site for welcomed relief to the stress of war. My experience of Japan had happened more than thirty years ago. I was sure it was now very different there.

Masumi Hori answered my fax immediately. After a few days a flurry of faxes began to shuffle between us. Masumi's English was a little rough. If I forgot myself, I could easily overwhelm him in sophisticated English nuance and detail, but he was not too embarrassed to tell me right away. My Japanese, what little I remembered of it, was of no consequence. In the North, I had learned to speak a very different dialect than what was spoken in Tokyo. It had been slightly more than a week when Masumi called me one evening very late.

He first proclaimed a warm greeting in his usual polite manner.

"Ah, Michael-san, how are you?"

"Oh, I am fine," I responded jovially. "It's good to hear from you. What's going on?"

I wondered if he had changed his mind about the tour or some other serious problem had arisen. He chuckled a bit shyly and then went on. "I wanted to ask you if you would be willing to lead a tour for me with the Japanese people to Egypt and Greece?"

Well, I could've been knocked over by a feather. No words came out of my mouth for several moments. I could hear Masumi's voice speaking ever so faintly. "Michael-san! Are you there?"

"Huh. Uh . . . oh yeah, I'm sorry, Masumi. You surprised me a little."

"Hmm!" He said with another chuckle.

Surprise was hardly the word to describe how I felt at that moment. My mind was trying to rationalize his request. He had never met me, and we had been in contact for only a week. This was truly bizarre!

He was most insistent. He continued about how he wanted me to design tour themes for these places, so that he could inform his clients right away through mailing advertisement. It seemed this practice was quite common for the trance channels with whom Masumi had previously worked. He would use the spiritual import of the trance channels as a basis to conduct spiritual journeys to other lands of interest to the Japanese people. Quite frankly, the concept boggled my mind!

He continued to express urgency with his tone and said he wanted to do it in February. That was six months after he wanted me in Japan. Japan was then only four months away. My mind was still swooning in shock. He was talking, but the words weren't making any sense.

Finally, I said, "Okay! Sure. But I'll need a little time to put it together."

I was still desperately trying to think of a polite way to stop him from talking. Masumi responded quickly. "Please call me, will you . . . as soon as possible?"

After I hung up, nausea crept in with certain fear. Now my excitement about Japan was greatly overshadowed by the exotic and intoxicating thought of Egypt and Greece—two places I had dreamed about but never had seriously considered visiting.

That night I couldn't sleep well. I didn't want to get up the next morning. A knot had appeared in the middle of my stomach. I couldn't shake it. It was noon and Dianne had prepared lunch, but I wasn't very hungry. As I was telling her of the new wrinkle in the Japan exchange, she could hardly believe it. I had called Manos Angelakis, a client of mine, about the practical side of these tours for Japan. I felt that since he was Greek, he might be able to shed some practical light.

I was right. Immediately, Manos concluded that a joint trip to Egypt and Greece in the month of February was not a good idea. The weather in Egypt was fine but Greece would be most unpleasant. The freezing rain and snow, as well as the cold, would prove to be unwieldy for traveling he said. I contacted Masumi by fax right away to let him know of these impracticalities. He was not pleased. In his response, he seemed very reluctant to believe me. I assured him that my resource was very experienced; he was Greek, after all. Still, Masumi was not entirely convinced by my claim. I concluded that he should seriously consider splitting the tours and running them at different times.

Later, I felt concerned. Here I was, already giving Masumi problems. The fact that he and I had not actually met weighed heavily on me. My mind kept harping on this fact. The more we interacted with business about the tours in Japan and now with Egypt and Greece, the stranger it seemed. It was as though we had been doing business for many years!

In the midst of these new entanglements, Yokar stepped in one day, to add to the milieu. Again he appeared visibly and startled me.

"Michael, sit down," he said abruptly. "Now we have to inform you of what is really going on."

Yokar's tone seemed somewhat ominous and carried a serious quality. My body felt nervous and began to tremble. He had never before spoken so directly. Waiting for his next words, I quickly pondered if I had done something wrong. Feelings shifted to self-blame and accusation. Memories of my early school years rolled in front of me. I expected a strong reprimand. Then, without notice, he interrupted my thoughts again. "Michael, you need to get a map of Egypt . . . please get one now."

I could feel the rush of shame that had scorched my face rapidly fading away. Without question, I jumped to get the atlas, grabbing my book on pyramidology, too. Secretly, I hoped that my brisk obedience would hide my stupid thoughts.

"What we are about to show you is not well-known in your time. It is good that you pay close attention. We purposely stimulated your attention with sharpness."

"Oh, thanks!" I returned sarcastically. "You really put me through some old feelings I had forgotten."

"Yes, we know. Sorry for that."

Then I moved on quickly to the matter at hand.

"So, what's with the maps? Okay. I'm looking at Africa. Now what exactly am I looking for?"

"We want you to examine the river called Nile."

My eyes squinted to find the Nile River coursing through the middle of the country. The map wasn't all that good. It wasn't very detailed, but I continued to follow the river's path as it moved from the gulf all the way to the Aswan. "Yokar, I still don't get it! What is it you want me to see?"

"Please to find another lighter, more transparent, paper to lay upon the map. We want you to extract from the map certain details if you can."

This was becoming an adventure. My imagination began to picture various movies where the hero discovers an ancient secret design, which points the way to the hidden treasure.

Then I commented with a smile, "Are we looking for buried treasure?"

Yokar's lips twisted as his brow went up.

"That was a joke," I said quickly.

The atlas was pretty big, so I had to tape the book open to the right page and tape the tracing paper to the page, in order to keep it straight. I felt like I was five years old.

"Okay. Yokar, what's next?"

There was a long pause as if he were taking a breath. The atmosphere became heated around me and very close. Yokar seemed to peer down around me to get a closer look.

"Hmm," he said. "Now trace the flow of the river from the delta to the dam. Be as accurate about it as you can. It's important."

"Don't worry, I'll be real careful," I said reassuringly.

My hand began the trace along the river, and I could feel my nervousness trembling through the lead point as it wiggled from time to time. I began to make excuses for the uneven line.

"I'm usually better at this!"

Yokar guided. "Just try and relax, steady your focus, and concentrate." He encouraged me, "You're doing fine."

A warm affectionate current trickled along my spine. My love and appreciation went out to him.

After I was finished, he went on. "Now, encircle the delta near the point of Cairo."

As I completed his last request, he quickly stepped back

"What do you see?"

My eyes fell onto the page again. Only this time, much of the terrain was clouded by the tracing paper. All I could see was the outline of the river. The circle around the delta was important and again I glanced back, trying to catch something significant.

After several minutes, I was about to give up. Then it hit me! "Oh my God!"

My words almost choked me on the spot. The river formed an almost perfect replica of a human brain and spinal nervous system.

"You can't mean this is true?" I cried. "This is ridiculous. It's a river, for Christ's sake! You don't mean that the Nile traveled like that on purpose, do you?"

"Yes," he said quietly.

Then he motioned for me to look again at the map as he continued to speak.

"The water elementals are conscious and offered this pattern as a gift to Man. This special river is so marked so that Man might learn and develop. But there's more. If you now observe, there are various places where the river takes a small diversion from the regular flow. Then it continues on . . . yes? It is this necessary detail that we wanted you to pay close attention to. Don't you see?"

"Sorry!" I lamented. "Yokar, I don't get it. What's your point?"

"Ugh!" Yokar grunted in disappointment.

"The ancient seekers realized that the Nile presented places where the dragon comes up out of the Earth several times on its way to the triple conjunction, just before the Delta. Further, they realized that these points were not accidental. These places describe windows of energy called Pukkas (pronounced pookahs in Atlantean). Flowing in and out of the Earth, the great serpent exited and re-entered the Earth through these windows. In the same way, the Life Force enters and exits through the 'pukkas' of the physical body. These pukkas in the body are what some have come to call energy centers or chakras (pronounced chak-rahs). They are not centers but rather places where the energy flows from other spiritual realms into this physical realm.

"From the starry patterns in heaven they made their calculations. The celestial influences and their seasons indicated the timing of the dragon's movements. With this exact natural replica built for them, it demonstrated the arrangements for human spiritual growth. At these places, the jogs of the river that you can see, they built their temples. Using the knowledge of harmonic shape and special intoned energy patterns, they enticed the Earth dragon to join them in their spiritual development. This became known as the Solar Path of Initiation or the Grand Canal of Light in the land you call Egypt."

I was speechless. The pattern on the paper seemed to jump out at me even more than before. The more Yokar told me of this incredible story, the more the tracing made sense! My mind was rebelling, but my body seems to completely agree. The nervousness was replaced by a tremendous sense of joy and excitement. I couldn't explain it. At that moment, my body knew more than I. Then, after several minutes, I managed to squeak out a question. "So where do these temples and this path lead?"

"Only one place," Yokar said. "The plateau of Gizeh, the great octahedron known by you as the Cheops Pyramid."

"Yokar, you mean that the pyramid is a temple? I thought it was a burial chamber."

"This is the confusion of many of your scientists. They would like to think that it was the last and final culmination of hundreds of years of practice by a Stone Age culture. It was actually the first pyramid built. And not built by the Egyptians at all. This temple was manifested much earlier by the remnant of the population of Atlantis using technology far beyond your comprehension."

"How did they do it, Yokar?"

"It was the sacred sound Vril, my boy. A form of sound vibration you are not yet familiar with. By the use of this sound vibration, they made the stone molten. Each stone was made to float in the air, as light as a feather. When the stones were formed, each one was fitted to the next while their surfaces were still hot and soft. Once cool, you could not pass even the smallest edge between them."

"I couldn't help notice that you refer to the great pyramid as an octahedron. That would mean its apex has a mirror duplicate that enters into the Earth, as a reflection of that above the ground, with four sides buried?"

"Good for you! You are correct again. This temple was built to reflect both Earth and Heaven. So now, if you examine your records of the great temple, you will see a path that leads to the 'chamber of the greatest ordeal' below the Earth."

On the table next to me was a plan of the Gizeh pyramid, which contained drawings of the known internal structure. I had already opened it. The marker indicated an illustration depicting the ascent and descent along the great hall to the upper and lower rooms, respectively.

Yokar went on. "This lower chamber rests precisely in the same harmonic area as the so-called King's chamber, its heavenly counterpart."

"What was the chamber of the greatest ordeal used for?"

"Many thousands of years later, it was used to test Egyptian neophytes for their worthiness to become priests in their secret brotherhood."

"So, if they were tested for worthiness below, what did they use the upper chamber for, Yokar?"

"This was the place of the greatest infusion. Knowledge was imparted to the one lying inside the resonator by the transmuter positioned above."

"By transmuter, are you talking about the capstone, the missing piece that was on top? And the resonator is what's called the sarcophagus in the King's Chamber?"

"Yes, that's correct. The capstone was a smaller version of the Taoi stone, one of the great power crystals of Atlantis, which rested on top of the pyramid and was encased in auriculum. But it remained closed and unavailable to the uninitiated. The resonator was constructed of a solid piece of crystal with harmonic proportions.

"We will have to separate soon," he interrupted, "as the body is suffering. There is just one more thing. You are going to go to this place Egypt. You will proceed to each temple along the Grand Canal of Light. You will perform the original rite of Solar Initiation in each of the temples, including the high temple at Gizeh, while we will assist you by moving the stones of initiation in the temples using the sacred Atlantean intonations of Vril. This has not been done since the time of the priesthood of Karnak and Dendera, more than twenty-five of your centuries before the common era."

Yokar left me alone to stew with that information for several days.

Later that week, I was at an advertising agency in New York, taking care of some last minute repairs before their video editing session was to begin. Steve, another engineer, overheard me talking about the trips to Egypt and Greece. He interrupted to express his interest. He had no background in mystical subjects and was unfamiliar with most of the terminology. But he was really fascinated by the idea of Egyptian initiation. The other engineer had left to tend to some pressing work. I continued my discussion with Steve, recapping the highlights. As I finished, Steve offered a friendly gesture of good wishes and success. Then he expressed an interest in hearing about the trips later, upon my return.

He walked away but then stopped and turned back. He looked at me. This time his gaze was piercing and unfriendly.

He said, "Are you not concerned with the Jackal?"

I just stared at him, cocking my head for a moment, trying to figure out what was going on. After composing myself, I firmly returned, "The time of secrets is over!"

Then I smiled at him and watched him carefully. The engineer's face turned blank and sallow. He turned away, saying nothing. He paused and then started to leave. I stopped him again by asking, "What did you say?"

He merely glanced over his shoulder and spoke flatly.

"I didn't say anything."

Later in private, I called upon Yokar to explain about this incident.

"So who the hell was that, Yokar? He confronted me with the Jackal."

"This was a temple guard," he confirmed telepathically.

"Temple guard from where?" I asked, somewhat startled.

"He represents the priesthood of the great temple of Karnak."

I found myself unconsciously sitting down.

"How can this be?"

"Oh, there are many such spirit guardians in the Egyptian temples," he said casually. "But we have a small problem. You are being challenged." "A small problem, huh! And challenged by whom?"

"The temple guards are concerned that an infidel is going to serve as high priest in the temples. They are calling for a ritual initiation ceremony, a trial for you, to find you worthy."

My body shook spontaneously with chills down my spine.

"What does this mean for me?"

"You will have to be tried and initiated in the great pyramid, alone, before the grand council, before we can begin the Grand Canal of Light. We will need to plan for this, yes?"

I found myself whispering, "Holy shit!"

Yokar interrupted. "Why do you prefer to proclaim your fear or excitement with an expression of excrement as being something sacred?"

"It's just an old expression of mine. You'll have to forgive me. I need some time to give it up, Yokar. It's an old habit." I apologized and began again. "Tell me about the capstone from the great temple."

"The secret of its key lay in the sacred intonations uttered by the worthy. Thoth engineered it (pronounced Teh-ho-teh) as a legacy from Atlantis. A great library of knowledge and insight, if you will, was stored there. Thoth wanted to make it available to man when he was found ready to evolve to a higher plane of consciousness.

"The stone was programmed to operate from the sun, controlling the weather by providing a rich and fertile valley. It functioned in other ways as well. Thoth believed this pyramid would set the stage for an easier life. He thought this would allow the Egyptians ample time to prepare themselves for development beyond simple survival."

"So this explains why the Egyptian civilization suddenly started at a high point and declined?"

"That's true," Yokar confirmed softly.

"Yokar, when did the Atlanteans come to Egypt?"

"Marking time is difficult for us but perhaps it was 15,000 years before your common era, prior to the sinking of the last Atlantean island, Alta."

"If Thoth was Atlantean, who were the others?"

"There were four others. Isis, Anubis, Osiris, and Nepthsis. All were Atlantean priest/scientists save for Nepthsis. She was not yet ordained. The only remaining female priestess from Atlantis, in Egypt, was Isis."

"But Yokar, these are attributed to be the Egyptian gods, by the hieroglyphic records."

"That's correct. They were 'Lords of the Shining.' From the Egyptian point of view, they were gods. They built the pyramid as their home away from home, so to speak. You might even say, in your terms, that the pyramid was a kind of spaceship sitting on the Earth. A place where they could reside peacefully beyond the profane Stone Age world where they had landed. It represented a nether world of interdimensional beauty suitable for pure energy beings like themselves."

"You mean they were invisible?"

"To the outside, yes. But one, Thoth, decided to venture outside. A great argument ensued among the five. Thoth wanted to share the knowledge. The rest thought that he was crazy to think that the primitives could ever reach their level of accomplishment. Thoth argued that their knowledge would come to nothing and stagnate if it remained locked up amongst themselves. He tried to persuade them to develop a new Atlantis in the heart of the Nile valley.

"Despite his friends' advice, Thoth left the pyramid. He shifted his energy and reshaped himself as a baboon, speaking to the primitive Egyptians through telepathy.

"He started to plant ideas of mathematics, science, and the harmonics of shape. Even a new language was given, complete with writing symbols. He wanted to instruct them about the laws of vibration. Soon it came to pass that the stone culture grew to a great civilization unheard of anywhere.

"He told them of the Earth energy and the promise of heaven if they pursued efforts to develop further. He instructed them on the art of temple making and directed their attention to the important places of the Nile River. He promised them, if they obeyed, that he would provide them with long life and fertile land. Their life would be easy and abundant. And if they were found worthy, the chosen would be allowed to enter the great pyramid, the abode of the gods."

"Yokar, the capstone is missing! Don't we need to have the capstone for the initiation?"

"We will use the pituitary and pineal glands as the human counterpart of the capstone. After all, it was made in the image of a human brain."

The months went by like the flapping of a bird's wing. January was only days away. The number of Japanese participants for Egypt was staggering. There were seventy-five on the go list and another fifty waiting to go. Masumi was beside himself. He had never seen such response to a tour before. There was only one hitch. Conditions in Iraq weren't looking favorable. We looked on as the relationship between the U.S. and Iraq continued to deteriorate. I had called Masumi and stated that I wouldn't cancel the tour unless shots were actually fired. But then we watched in disbelief as CNN broadcast live the battles in Iraq.

I was saddened that the tour was canceled. It would be another year before Egypt and the Middle East were quiet enough to attempt another tour.

Sadly for Masumi, the loss of the tour was financially damaging. Even worse, many of the participants lost their money to the airlines and ground operations, and many lost their jobs! The Japanese could not arrange for time off for the trip, as the trip was fourteen days long. In Japan, vacation allotments are never more than a week in length. To accomplish a ten-day journey, the participants would add several single holidays, advanced from the following year, to make up the difference. In the case of a fourteen-day trip, it wasn't possible. So they simply quit their jobs to go on the tour. When I learned they had done this, I was shocked. I felt a deep sense of commitment, and I matched that feeling with my own sense of responsibility. Wow, I thought. What a price to pay for spiritual development. But I also knew that this was no Disneyland experience. Yokar meant business.

The reality of the impending trip, which had been rescheduled for February of 1992, was hard to believe for all of us. It was hard not to believe it was only a dream.

Several times, Masumi called me and asked, "Uh . . . Michael-san, what does it mean that Yokar will open the stones of initiation? Is he going to really move the stones in the pyramid?"

I couldn't answer because Yokar refused to describe the experience inside the pyramid. He would only repeat the same words over and over. For me, it became a real test of faith. I was really sweating this one out.

I kept telling Yokar, "I'm really out on a limb . . . I'm really trusting you on this one, big guy!" I had hoped to coax him into revealing more, as I told him how much was riding on what he was claiming. But Yokar would just smile at me and say nothing.

Meanwhile, a year passed.

It was January and the guns were rattling again in the Middle East. So everybody held his or her breath. Yokar assured me that it would never come to anything more than rattling this time. The participation for the tour was down from the previous year in both Japan and the U.S. The economy in the U.S. was in the dumpster, and the Japanese economy was getting ready to follow suit. In addition, many never recovered from their losses and disappointments from Desert Storm, the U.S. military code name for the Iraqi engagement.

In Egypt, there was a new wrinkle to deal with. Political unrest gave rise to threats of terrorism. The target was foreign tourism. The terrorists felt the only way to bring down the government was to seriously impair their financial resources, of which the tourist trade represented a substantial part. It was difficult to ascertain the truth about the situation. Though there were isolated incidents, the activity seemed to be near Alexandria in the Muslim communities there.

The problem for us was that the international newspapers were carrying inflated and often false reports of terrorism without actually checking the sources. This sensationalism sold newspapers. It was strongly believed that the so-called reliable sources in the Cairo news bureaus were pro-militant Muslim supporters. Regardless of the probable inaccuracy, the effect was making people nervous. War was one thing, but terrorist activity really stepped up fear of traveling in the Middle East. Whatever the case, it was working. Even though the government advisory was not redlining the area, they exercised caution by issuing a warning.

Japanese participation was reduced to two groups. One was forty in number and the second was twenty-eight. These were still reasonably sized groups but definitely much smaller than the groups planned the previous year. The American contingent amounted to only twenty-two, reduced from forty in the previous year. Clearly, the economic slump had taken its toll. I defined these three groups as "true believers" considering all of the atmospheric flak coming at them!

The Japanese were to be the first to arrive in Cairo. I met them promptly at 4:30 in the morning, at the airport. They were grateful. They had not seen such dedication in a tour leader before. I assured them that I would make sure they would get everything they were hoping for, to the best of my ability. The orientation meeting was set for mid-afternoon.

Before the meeting began, I had asked Yokar another question. "How could it be determined that an individual was ready? I couldn't imagine having to select each participant's worthiness by myself."

Yokar responded, "Nor shall we in spirit decide. The determination may come from many lifetimes, not just this one. So the determination comes out of their choice to come. This is when the initiation begins. If they arrive at the time and place of initiation, they belong there."

Learning this, I decided that once the preliminaries were taken care of, I wanted to have each participant get up and introduce himself or herself to the others and describe the struggle of the journey to initiation. The result of this was nothing short of amazing.

For example, several participants had taken the bullet train in order to arrive at Narita airport on time. There was a terrible snowstorm. The train had stopped on the tracks still several hours away from the airport. Some of the participants intuitively sensed a problem and decided to move forward by several cars. The others stayed where they were. Shortly thereafter, the train was separated. Only the forward cars continued on to the airport, leaving behind the others, who therefore missed the tour.

There were many other trials and tribulations, including all-night cab rides and the like. At the end, everyone felt somehow joined and bonded in his or her mutual struggle. I concluded the meeting with tales of my own struggle and then described the special trial that was about to unfold for me.

I explained that at 5:30 that evening, I was to leave the hotel by special cab and be taken to the pyramid area. Once there, I would enter the pyramid alone after all the tourists had gone and the pyramid was closed for the night. Inside, I was to begin a ritual trial of my worthiness by descending to the chamber of the greatest ordeal, thus providing a ritual sacrifice for all the others.

No sooner had I finished my story, than two Arabs poked their heads through the conference room doors and motioned for me that it was time. I stood up somewhat sheepishly and smiled at everyone. I asked that they pray for me so that the unknown forces waiting inside that immense and mysterious structure would not consume me. I left with the Arabs as I listened to applause trailing off behind me. It seemed as though I were being taken to the lion's den to test my faith.

The Trial

The setting sun lit up the dense haze of gas fumes and sand dust in the Cairo streets, offering a mystical appearance to the hustle and bustle of evening traffic. I was told that the ride to the plateau would be more than an hour because it was quitting time and everyone was going home. I sat cramped in the back seat. The tiny cab bore no recognizable markings as to its make or model. It bore multicolored paint, indicating that there had probably been damage while negotiating busy Cairo streets. There was a continuous flow of Arabic in the car, as the two who met me, as well as the driver, were deeply engaged in conversation. Once in a while they would laugh. This was the only sign that it was friendly.

Hussein was my main contact. He was a man of short stature, dark complexion, coal-black curly hair, and hazel eyes. When he stared at you, it was hard to look away. He sat in front with his arm draped easily over the front seat. He would turn from time to time, to give me an official Omar Sharif smile. He spoke English, but it had a distinct British flavor. He was smartly dressed and wore strong cologne, indicating a preference for the Western culture over his own. I began to comment on the brazen behavior of all the pedestrians in the street, especially what I perceived to be foolish attempts to negotiate traffic by women and children, crossing in the middle of the road.

"How many people die a day doing this?" I asked.

Hussein responded with a chuckle, "Oh, they do it all the time, really. They think nothing of it. To them it is just another part of their life. Whether it's mule-drawn carts or motor cars, it's all the same to them!"

I felt Yokar over my left shoulder and he whispered quietly into my left ear. "You must prepare yourself now. We are nearing the temple. Close your eyes and focus your attention equally between your heart and brow."

As my attention drew deep within, the conversation became a low drone in the background.

"Good," Yokar confirmed softly.

A tingling sensation began to move along my spine; it felt like ants crawling along in a line. It was very uncomfortable and made it more difficult to maintain my concentration.

There was a sudden jerk as the cab swerved to just miss colliding with a small truck. I opened my eyes to check on our status. To my left and jutting upward like a mountain was the great temple, the pyramid of Gizeh. Its blunted peak pierced the haze gracefully and offered a majestic stance. Quite naturally, I bowed my head and experienced a trembling that shifted across my abdomen.

Hussein called the great pyramid to my attention and mentioned that I should not say anything regardless of what I see. I felt puzzled by this admonition. I had made the financial arrangements on the official level and paid the bakshish (bribes) on the unofficial level. His smiling nature seemed to shift to cold determination.

This new sense disturbed me, so I inquired, "Are we okay with this? Is there any problem?"

"No! No," Hussein said, gesturing his hand in a quieting manner.

The little cab strained to carry all of us up the steep grade leading onto the plateau. Finally, a clearing appeared, only to be closed by ominous looking troops dressed in dark blue heavy uniforms and toting weapons. They surrounded the little cab, preventing its further movement. As the driver began to show his identification, Hussein pulled a set of papers from his small valise. One of the soldiers stuck his head into the window and looked back toward me. Then he turned and began a loud exchange of violent words. I couldn't understand, but I think I was the subject of discussion. I believe it went something like, what is the foreigner doing here?

Through his body language, I gathered that Hussein had stated my official desire to go into the pyramid after-hours and that I had all of the needed approvals, including one from the director of the plateau. Another burst of argumentative discussion ensued. I felt a distinct air of complaint by the officer in charge of this little platoon.

At this point Hussein got out of the car and walked a bit with the officer and slipped him a wad of bakshish, enough for him and his men. The officer's argumentative tone again shifted and now seemed to say, okay, but I warn you, there had not better be any violations. Hussein waved his hands in a reassuring manner with humble overtones sprinkled excessively in the officer's direction.

Then there was a simple nod. A chain that had blocked our path dropped, and we slowly nudged our way to the entrance of the great pyramid. It didn't take long for me to get the idea that what I had seen was a way of life here. Everything was based upon an exchange of bakshish. Later I learned that almost anything could be accomplished in Egypt if enough palms were greased.

I took a deep breath, thinking that the worst was over. Soon, I would be inside. I hated the yelling and screaming of negotiations. My parents were screamers and I just never got used to it. Out of my window the view was astounding. I noticed that the moon sat squarely over the peak of that almost vertical structure. The moon was full. Night was growing darker and the moon's pale yellow light cast the pyramid into a dark rising silhouette. Oh my, I thought to myself, this is going to be a whopper of an evening! My body began to tremble again. For a moment, the shaking seemed like it was never going to end.

I sat in the cab as instructed by Hussein. He said, "Now I have to negotiate with the pyramid guard and the keeper."

"What! You must be kidding! Jesus, how many people are involved in this deal anyway?"

"Michael," he said resolutely, "you must try to be patient with these things. It is our way!" I just nodded. We had arrived more than half an hour ago and I was still trying to get inside. I looked on as more bakshish transferred hands and then Hussein looked bewildered as he returned to the cab.

"What's wrong now?" I said with my anger leaking between my teeth. Hussein looked apologetically toward me and shrugged his shoulders. Then he exclaimed, "The steel door to the entrance has been locked already. The key must be obtained from the director's house!" For the first time he looked sincerely worried.

"Is that a problem?" I inquired.

Hussein again shrugged his shoulders and expressed some reluctance. "I don't like to disturb the director now; this is his dinner hour."

I nodded in acknowledgment. Quietly I called Yokar. "Listen old boy, I think we need a little of your magic right about now."

Yokar moved his energy upon me in a slow undulating wave of heat and then a thought shape appeared in my mind of the director smiling as he gave the key to the keeper.

I turned to Hussein and remarked confidently, "Don't worry. It'll be okay."

About twenty minutes later, the keeper appeared out of the night with the keys jangling from his hand. Hussein and the guard began to climb the huge stones. Hussein motioned for me to get out and come up.

I had to climb almost vertically, more than fifty feet on several large stones, to arrive at the entry point. After I arrived, I looked back at the panoramic view of Cairo. It was strangely beautiful and enticing. Middle Eastern music lingered faintly in the air, mingled with the melody of a Muslim call to prayer. I had to force my attention back to the pyramid. A heavy iron gate creaked opened before me, marking the beginning of a very dark and craggy passage. Just before entering, I arched my back and looked up one more time. I strained to define the outline of this enormous mountain of stones. The perspective was staggering.

Hussein and the others had already disappeared into the darkness of the passage. The pictures I'd seen had failed to transmit the feelings of this place. My hands crawled along the stonewalls, trying to provide reconnaissance of the unseen terrain.

"Where is everybody?" I asked tentatively.

Voices echoed unintelligibly out of the darkness. Suddenly, the passage was illuminated by several small incandescent lamps placed strategically behind certain large stones for maximum dramatic effect. The light was shockingly eerie.

As I was trying to adjust, Hussein explained that I would have to pay bakshish to the keeper when I finished. I simply nodded.

The keeper was a large rotund man obscured only slightly by his draping tan garabia, a kind of single-piece caftan robe worn by most Egyptians. The sandy floor of the tunnel seemed to reach up to him, giving the impression that he and the floor were one. He was very dark-skinned, but his turban was hiding most of his face. His eyes were also dark but very friendly and seemed to glow like jewels by the dim light.

He spoke to Hussein briefly in Arabic, with a deep melodious voice.

Hussein translated. "Do you want all the lights on?" he asked.

"No! No lights at all. Please tell him that there must not be any lights while I'm here. By the way, does he speak any English?" I asked.

Hussein went on to translate, ignoring my question. Even with Hussein, the cultural differences were so strong that some requests in English were never quite understood.

"Look, just tell him, I'll let him know when to turn them on...okay?"

Hussein nodded and left quickly with the guard. The keeper stood quietly staring at me for a moment and then motioned for me to follow him. We followed the winding passageway deeper into the entrance vault. The walls were not smoothly hewn but naturally very rough. The ceiling dropped occasionally. The impression given was that you needed to duck. We ended within a small anteroom, with one set of steps leading in a spiral upwards to a narrow ascending ramp, another set of the spiral steps descending downwards. Both ramps entered foreboding darkness.

To my surprise, the keeper turned and spoke to me, in English. "You want to go up?"

He pointed toward the ascending passage of darkness.

"No," I said. "I need to go down, please."

I pointed toward the downward passage as if he needed sign language. He smiled. His turban had become partially undraped from his face, exposing his mouth and a healthy set of teeth, unusual for this country.

He turned to reach for the switch box that would turn on the lights, planning to illuminate the descending passageway. I rushed to stop him. Now I realized that he really didn't understand my request through Hussein at all! I waved my hand in front of him with a gesture, suggesting in Western terms, "Never mind."

Then I said, "No lights!"

He still looked puzzled. Then with one last desperate attempt to communicate, I motioned toward the lights and crossed my hands one in front of the other, suggesting a crossed "X" pattern. It must have been universal. He leaned back in surprise and nodded in acknowledgment.

He said, "What time you come up?"

I pulled back my sleeve, exposing my watch. I pointed to the clock face and shrugged toward him, throwing my hands aside. I was hoping that he would get the idea this task was not time dependent. He turned and headed for the doorway out. I hesitated to begin, wondering if I had transmitted my ideas effectively.

I turned to face the descending passageway. With grim determination, I entered upon the ramp. The passageway had been cut very low, forcing me to assume a crouching position. The position was so low that I was practically "duck walking."

The ramp was an endless smooth slope descending into absolute darkness. The descending stone path was rigged with continuous wood planking, having struts mounted crosswise, simulating a crude kind of ladder arrangement. On each side, mounted to the stonewall, was a wooden railing.

How on Earth did the early Egyptians manage to negotiate these steep passageways without this ladder-like planking? I thought.

I recoiled at the thought of descending this smooth ramp without planking. I was horrified by the prospect of sliding down without the possibility of coming back up. It was later that I would deeply appreciate the added handrail feature, too. The descent continued endlessly, and I wondered about the duck-walking posture. I figured that the Egyptians were pretty smart. No one would tolerate this kind of torture for very long.

The deeper I traveled, the greater the silence. It was deafening. Each step downward seemed to also increase the pressure.

I blurted out loud, trying to comfort my sense of growing claustrophobia and loneliness, "Oh God, I'm descending to hell for Christ's sake!"

The pressure was coming from everywhere. Not just upon my ears but all over my body. I kept trying to adjust. It became almost intolerable. Then Yokar interrupted my concentration. I welcomed the companionship at this point even though it was only telepathic.

"The purpose of this posture is to force the candidate into a position of humble respect for what he is about to do. It is not designed, as you've imagined, to be a kind of torture!"

I added comically, "You wouldn't happen to know if there is a stretcher down there? I think I'm going to need one, when and if I ever get there!"

"Hardly likely!" Yokar said as he warned, "Although, you do have a bit of a crawl once you arrive."

"What kind of crawl?"

"About twenty yards on your belly I should think!"

"Great!" I cried. "That'll be good for my claustrophobia."

Yokar was right. The ramp ended finally at the foot of a huge stonewall. Solid in every respect except for a shallow crawl space at the bottom. I felt around like a blind man looking for his cane. The hole was about thirty inches high and roughly three feet in width.

There was something terrible about getting down on my knees that really sent terror into my heart. Only then did I fully consider how much was on top of me. It was excruciating. I couldn't wait to get through that damn tunnel. Then I noticed a slight odor as I assumed a prone position, my face close to the tunnel floor. A foul stench of something dead filled my nostrils. I prayed that I wouldn't come into contact with it while still in the tunnel.

To my surprise, the tunnel did not end at the floor of the anteroom or chamber of ordeal. I sat at the tunnel's edge, leaning out into the room, letting my legs dangle. I was not in a rush to jump down into the darkness! Actually, I soon learned that the distance to the floor was only five feet.

Yokar chimed in. "You may light your way for a moment so that you will avoid the pit."

I took out a small penlight from my pocket and pressed the switch. It was hardly as I had expected. The dimly lit scene reminded me of war pictures revealing an old bombed out cellar, very rough with huge stone rubble lying about. The walls, ceiling, and floor were hewn with only slight consideration for mobility. The floor and ceiling seemed to ascend gradually and meet together in the back.

Before me, the floor dropped suddenly. A small round hole descended to a depth of forty feet, ending abruptly as a pit. The diameter I estimated to be five feet or so. It resembled a well that had gone dry. A crude iron railing had been built to prevent anyone from falling in unexpectedly.

Yokar indicated telepathically that I should move toward a crevice dividing two large stone seats. After I wedged myself between the seats, he began to explain.

"The priests would sit in these stone chairs and chant. This would occur after they had lowered the neophyte into the well pit. From time to time they would lower some water but no food. There, the neophyte would sit and ponder his decision to be a priest. Meanwhile, the priest would chant special intonations of Vril, designed to conjure elements of emotional and psychological portent. Hence, the ordeal would begin."

I could only comment with brief grunts of dread.

"Ugh! Do I have to go down there?"

"No. Sit here in the crevice. It will be sufficient! Oh, and please extinguish your lamp."

"Sure," I said.

The loss of light left me totally blind again. My mind considered the density and closeness once more. Then I felt the heat begin to build up around me. As I was wondering when my ordeal would begin, air ceased to be available. There was no question now as to my ordeal. With a deep inner groan, I realized that I was to suffocate to death. Fleeting thoughts of making a run for it vanished as my reasoning concluded, I would never make it to the first set of ramp planking. I decided, If I'm gonna die here, then I want it to be in this room and not in that damn tunnel.

A strange feeling came over me. I began to giggle nervously. I thought, Man found dead in the bottom of the pyramid, film at eleven!

It all seemed too unreal somehow. Me, here in the bottom of the pyramid in Egypt, and my stupid ordeal. My irritation gave way to thoughts of my wife. I wondered about my life with Dianne and whether or not I would ever see her again. Breathing was really getting difficult now. The sharp crags of rock that had gouged me in the back grew softer. I kept making my inhalation shallower and began to feel dizzy. I tried to conserve whatever air there was left. I didn't want to make a bad show of it with choking and gagging all over the place.

The warmth that was around me now entered me. It felt soothing and strangely comforting. I was beginning to lose consciousness. I felt totally at ease. With my last conscious effort I thought, If this is it . . . well, so be it. I could think of worst places to die. Just then a breeze blew past my face as if someone blew on me! I sat up in a jolt. The great weight lifted, and breathing was easier. I smiled. This ordeal was apparently over.

Pride and satisfaction coursed through me like a river. But while I was patting myself on the back for a job well done, something furry brushed passed my face. I sat motionless and startled.

"What the hell?"

My thoughts broke off in fear as my body stiffened. Many possibilities raced in front of me. One by one I dismissed each as an implausible explanation.

Great, I thought. Something is in here with me, hasn't eaten in three thousand years, and I'm lunch!

I determined quickly that my trial was not yet over. This was a new wrinkle. Suddenly, I knew that I had to get a handle on this before this thing began to nibble. My eyes closed and I entered deep within to calm myself. I began to systematically sort out my feelings of intolerance and separation.

Yokar had taught me early that fear is a mind killer, a disrupter of the flow of Life Force if it is not properly digested. So, as I swallowed this new fear and let it fill up my belly, I knew the key was to embrace this unknown thing. I needed to allow it to be in my presence without reservation or doubt. In order to do that, I would have to allow it to be whatever it was and not try to make it into something else. Even if it was hungry and wanted to eat me!

A sense of calm swept over me and feelings of love and compassion began to leak into my heart. I willingly reached out to make contact. I offered myself to the void. Not acting out of fear, I let my fear join me, while utilizing its energy to give me strength and courage.

There was a rustling noise at the place of the pit. It sounded like something was struggling to claw its way out of the deep shaft. My mind offered several awful suggestions as to its appearance. Calmly, I thanked my mind for sharing those images and asked it to support me in a different way. Judging from the differences in the noise, I determined that it was free of the shaft and was scurrying across the floor toward me.

I held firm, continuing to digest my fear, channeling it for strength and support. I tried not to anticipate the outcome. It was excruciatingly difficult. The noise grew louder and obviously closer. Then, as if to test my last ounce of courage, the bloody thing, whatever it was, sniffed at me! But as I waited to be ravaged, a remarkable thing occurred.

Suddenly, a sensation of something warm and wet began to pour over me. My mind reeled, and then collapsed. For once, my mind was silent. And I appreciated that. No sooner had I caught up with my impending demise, than it stopped! There was nothing but silence. There was nothing at all! . . . It was over.

I could hear a new sound far above me, apparently coming from the top of the pyramid. It was the ringing of a great gong. It sounded three times before I could realize and believe what I was hearing. In that moment, I completely forgot about my ordeal.

Yokar interrupted. "This is the ancient signal of release. Now you are to make the ascent to the upper chamber. Do not forget that you must stop and pay your respects to the feminine principal. You must enter into the so-called Queen's Chamber. We will instruct you from there!"

"Can I use my light for a moment to find the crawl way?" I asked.

"Yes, but only briefly. The temple guards do not take this form of illumination lightly."

On my way out, I could not resist the temptation to scan the chamber one more time with my little light. My mind demanded that I seek evidence of my last encounter. This request seemed fair because my mind had been obedient and had not failed me. Not surprisingly, there was nothing but an empty room.

Are you satisfied? I said silently to my mind. My mind said nothing.

The climb upward was long. With each step, I developed a greater respect for the priests who must've climbed this ramp every day without the benefit of the wooden ladder and railings. I tried to pace myself accordingly. But despite my measured effort, my legs felt rubbery. Soon they grew to be unstable, responding to each request irregularly. My breathing was labored, also.

When I finally arrived at the top, I found the physical guardian of the pyramid waiting for me with a warm smile. He gestured to the entrance.

"You want go out?"

I paused for a moment, raising my index finger indicating time out for one minute while I caught my breath. Still gasping for more air, I thought I'd better speak.

"No. I have to go up."

I punctuated this with my hand pointing to the upper ramp way. This time he seemed to understand and just nodded. As I turned to face the upper ramp with dread, I watched the guardian shuffle his way into the darkness, gently stirring the dust along the floor behind him.

"Oh boy," I commented sarcastically to myself, still heaving with each breath.

The upward climb seemed formidable. The ramp ascended into the same unending darkness I had experienced on my descent. I conjured greater determination to poise my flimsy legs onto the first plank.

After an eternity of agonizing steps, I found myself standing upright. I had entered onto the Grand Gallery. In the plan of the pyramid's inner structure, I had seen a drawing of a taller space leading to the King's Chamber. The drawing didn't begin to prepare me for the impact of the sudden and expanded view. My puny lamp illuminated a mammoth hall jutting straight up into a series of progressively narrow and truncated walls layered one onto the other. I was awe-struck by the vision, and tears filled my eyes.

The ramp was interrupted only by a horizontal platform that huddled over the entrance to the Queen's Chamber.

I was so winded by this time that my lungs were wheezing. I coughed to clear my chest. The gallery absorbed my coughing sound and amplified it by an order of magnitude. The reverberating shock wave returned with all the fury of a rabbit punch right to the back of my head. The pain quickly extended into my neck. I reached up to massage the area, trying to ease the trauma. My thoughts cried out to Yokar, and he answered my unspoken question.

"You must take care what you say or do from now on. The temple is extremely sensitive to all of your movements."

"What the hell was that, Yokar?"

"The Grand Gallery corresponds to the medulla oblongata and brain stem. Certain intonations here will create very powerful effects as you have just discovered."

"But all I did was cough, Yokar!"

"Ah yes . . . but the violent expulsion of your breath articulated a certain shape from the 'unnamed organ' at the base of your throat. You have uttered your first Vril my boy! In so doing, you have activated the great hall, which now aligns to your intonations. Now you must move softly and swiftly to the Queen's Chamber without further delay."

I was spinning within a vortex of my own confusion. But I obeyed without any further hesitation. The entry to the Chamber for the Queen, as the archeologists call it, lay straight ahead. Again, the doorway was blocked by an iron gate. At first I thought it was locked, but with some minor pressure I finally opened it. I had to duck into the crouching position again to avoid banging my head on the overhead lintel. This time, I presumed on my own that it was customary for the initiate to bow one more time before the Queen.

I leaned my body against one end of the room where there had been carved some kind of alcove. There I sat for some minutes, quietly waiting to see what would happen. There was nothing. I was about to ask Yokar, when the left side of my body began to violently shake without warning. It was most peculiar. Some kind of palsy had suddenly consumed my left side. There was nothing I could do to stop it.

The firm but wise voice of Yokar said only one thing to me. "Just try to relax into it and allow it to happen."

Just as I thought I was getting into the rhythm of the shaking, it stopped. It had gone as mysteriously as it had come, really testing the patience of my mind. I wanted to know what was happening. The not knowing seemed to be the greatest torture. Still, I kept my demand at bay.

"You can proceed to the upper chamber now," Yokar said matter-of-factly. "There we will teach you the nature of the workings of the crown."

Without fanfare, I left the Queen's Chamber. I wondered why my body responded with such trembling. I wasn't afraid. I reasoned that it wasn't fear that caused it. It seemed to be something much deeper, perhaps at the cell level. It was definitely outside of my conscious attempts to understand.

The ascending passageway narrowed into a single-person path. The final ascent to the upper chamber was nearly complete. The long ramp ended abruptly with a short vertical "cat climb" to another level of stone. I turned back and flashed my little lamp once again to catch a glimpse of where I had been. The view down was as astounding as it was looking up!

I was standing at the edge of a stone precipice several hundred feet above the Gallery, yet I had no fear. I turned and took a deep breath. The stooping had become entrained in me. Automatically, I ducked down to accommodate the low-hanging lintels of the king's entrance. As I grasped the lintel to balance myself, I noticed that the surface was different. It was smoother and actually seemed polished. I was tempted to shine a light on it, but Yokar quickly advised me not to.

Five or six steps in the crouching position brought me into the King's Chamber. It seemed larger than I imagined. I was dying to see the inside detail.

"Yokar, I must see the inside—please."

"If you must light the lantern, aim its beam at the floor. Under no circumstances should you lift the beam into the open space."

"I understand."

Much to my surprise, the detail was almost nonexistent. The floor was as plain as the walls and ceiling. It turned out to be a very simple rectangular box. There was one thing, though. The King's Chamber stone was the same stuff as the entrance lintel. It was hard to tell exactly what kind of stone it was. My light was very dim and aimed at the floor as requested. But the chamber had a distinct reddish tone to it.

To the right of the entrance and at the end was a large stone case. "Hmm . . . that must be the sarcophagus," I murmured under my breath.

Yokar quickly corrected me.

"It does not serve this purpose! We remind you that this is not a tomb. If you will notice, there is no lid and it does not bear the inscriptions characteristic of burial preparation.

"The stone berth resided precisely beneath the axis of the capstone that was atop the pyramid. Its line of transmission was aimed at the initiate's head. Its construction is unique. I will show you. Please approach the cubicle and, remember, do not shine your lantern into the cubicle."

"Okay."

It was hard to define, but I felt some trepidation during my approach. With each step, many graphic scenes from horror movies ran through my mind. Only by constantly reassuring myself that these scenes were from Hollywood, did I manage to boost my courage. My mind kept reminding me emphatically—this is not Hollywood!

The stone cubicle was larger and more ominous up close. I was feeling nervous and resisted looking into its depths. It seemed to be constructed out of one piece of rock, again the same stuff as everything else! It was rough on the outside but smoothly polished on the inside. The length and breadth of the cubicle suggested that it could easily hold a large man, perhaps six feet tall or larger.

Yokar then said firmly, "You must climb into the berth . . . after you have entered into it, you must ready your mind."

My teeth clenched with a shudder. This was no easy task. First, I had to douse my flashlight and try to negotiate the cubicle's wall in the total blackness. It was well above my hip level, so I had to hop up to swing my legs into the interior. Once inside, I adjusted my body with my head pointing to the West, positioning it for an indefinite stay. Calming my mind turned out to be a formidable task. Despite Yokar's insistence that this place was not for burial purposes, I felt a distinct sense of finality in my present position.

Yokar said, "We promised that you would come to understand the workings of the crown chamber. The berth you are lying in is made from red granite. So is the interior of the chamber as well as the tuning mechanism. There is a symbiotic relationship that exists between these two aspects, as you will soon realize."

Then he commanded, "Form your hand into a fist and strike the wall of the berth."

I followed Yokar's instructions carefully and struck the cubicle wall softly. Since it was stone, I was concerned with bruising my hand.

"Harder!" Yokar demanded.

Once again I formed my hand into a fist, striking the wall but with much harder force than before. To my amazement, the cubicle began to vibrate all over. Heat rushed over my body as the sound vibration continued.

I realized that another sound was joining the first. This new sound was not coming from the cubicle! It was coming down from above. The cubicle rang like a bell and was rich with many overtones. The overtones reached out above me and danced with the tones ringing down from above. It was wonderful. Suddenly, the King's

Chamber seemed to be warmer, and I began to sweat.

"Yokar, what is that other sound coming from above?"

"This, my son, is the effect of the great tuning mechanism. Above you are constructed several chambers . . . five altogether. Each one has been designed with a particular and unique set of vibrations relating specifically through proportions representing four-fifths and eight-ninths. These will reverberate if the proper intonations are set in motion.

"If you'll recall, we told you that the pyramid was not built by Egyptians, but by Atlantean adepts. The great octahedron is designed to provide a path of reconstitution or a reordering of consciousness. Through Thoth's arrangements, these chambers have been designed to align the subtle bodies of every individual who lies within the berth through these combined harmonic vibrations. By chanting the proper intonations, the priesthood would engage the great tuning mechanism to prepare the initiate for the infusion of knowledge from the crystal capstone. Now you can see why the berth you are lying in has a sonic relationship to the chambers above."

"So that is what you meant by moving the stones of initiation?"

"Yes. That is correct."

"What are the intonations that move the stones in this way?"

"It must be done in the ancient Vril, the sacred tongue of the Atlantean priesthood."

"Yes, I can see now. It makes sense to me," I said, suddenly flooded with understanding. "Thoth would have to code the crystal capstone with keys from the language he knew best. It would insure that only the ones who possessed the knowledge of the coded patterns could access the library of knowledge. Right?"

"Yes." Yokar continued, "Those keys were given by Thoth, inscribed on the emerald facets of the great Ruune stone, the library crystal atop the temple. Later they were secretly copied and written down on papyrus scrolls and kept hidden by the high priests of Karnak and Dendera in the underground chambers of the Great Sphinx. It was the knowledge of these keys that provided the greater influence of the priesthood. Later, in your antiquity, they became known as the emerald tablets."

"What happened to the Ruune of Thoth?"

"The Ruune capstone was vaporized when the encoded signal for its self-destruction was implemented."

"Who gave the signal for its destruction, Yokar?"

"Thoth prescribed the nature and time of its destruction as part of the crystal's programming."

"And the scrolls?"

"The scrolls eventually found their way into the great library of Alexandria. Since they were written in ancient Turbin Egyptian, the scrolls became an enigma to later generations. Those who could translate the scrolls eventually died out. Their final fate was decided by the fire that destroyed the Alexandria library, started by the Romans when they conquered Ptolemy's Egypt."

"Oh . . . That's terrible! What a loss."

"The loss was significant but appropriate." Yokar added, "Trace fragments were eventually found and translated into the heiratic form. The faithful then transcribed the scripts into Arabic. These scripts were transported out of Egypt in great urns to Greece under the code name of Hermes, Thrice the Great.

"The Earth would enter into a darker time when man would suffer greater indignities. The capstone and keys were wisely removed from man's reach until he could rediscover his wisdom to use the knowledge properly.   "Let us now begin to prepare you for your alignment to the temple's crown. Strike the berth wall again and record in your mind the vibratory tone you hear. Once you have secured the frequency of that vibration, we want you to resound that tone with your own voice. When you begin the intonation, do not veer off of that frequency . . . it's important."

Once again I struck the side of the cubicle with my fist and studied the sound coming from it. Then I hummed a little to get the right pitch. As I began a long and slow tone with my voice, Yokar encouraged me to go deeper into my throat with the sound. He wanted me to use the bottom-most part of my vocal cords; close to the place he called the unnamed organ.

While I intoned the chord, the cubicle began to vibrate a little. Then I got nervous and my voice broke into sudden discord. The cubicle stopped its reverberation instantly. A shock wave immediately reached down out of the ceiling and struck me in the chest.

Yokar interrupted my moment of pain by warning me again. "I told you—you must keep the intonation steady! Now begin again."

Still trying to catch my breath from the shock wave, I humbly began again with my practice. This time I started slow and easy. Trying to steady my voice deep within my chest, I realized that it was the fear that caused my loss of concentration. At the same time, it was strange to recognize that the pyramid had its own way of teaching a neophyte how to communicate with it. It was effective and swift with its punishment if the neophyte failed.

This time I focused my mind on the sound and directed my mind to go into the sound to keep it busy. Deeper into my throat I went. The image emerged that my throat was an extension of the cubicle. For a moment, I realized that the cubicle was now vibrating much louder. I dared not let that discovery break my concentration. Curious as to where this vibration might lead, I applied my inner will with greater effort and shifted deeper into my throat. The upper chambers began to resonate in response, offering their own harmonic melodies. A definite sensation of pleasure filled my body.

The whole process was hypnotic. The multiple harmonics began to carry me up and out of the cubicle, and I experienced a distinct sense that I was floating in midair. My eyes were closed. I did not want to open them to look; for fear that it would break this wonderful flow.

Then out of the ceiling I felt a force that gently twisted at my forehead. A cool wet substance poured down from the ceiling and funneled through the vortex that was screwing into my head. My brain at once felt cool and full of mint. It was delightful. I wanted to know what this substance was but the effect was so amazing that I couldn't form any words to ask any questions.

A gong rang out loudly from the ceiling. Three times it sounded. This sudden intrusion into my personal orchestration startled me. My intonation stopped. I squinted my eyes, waiting for a terrible backlash. But there was nothing! The harmonic melodies simply faded into obscurity. It was over.

Yokar stepped in to comment once again.

"You are complete. The temple guards are satisfied with your qualifications to lead the Canal of Light ceremonies . . . you are no longer an infidel! You can leave now."

I felt grateful. "Thanks," I said.

My body was buzzing all over. I sat up, feeling somewhat stiff. I think it was harder to get out than to get into this stone box. Before I exited the chamber, I turned and gestured into the darkness a farewell and gratefulness for the temple guards' help in my preparations. I descended the ramp of the Grand Gallery as the electric lights began to switch on, one section after another. For the first time, I got a view of the ascending passage in its full glory. The pyramid guard had anticipated my completion.

When I arrived at the bottom point of the pyramid's entrance tunnel, the pyramid guard stood in front of me like a statue with a wide grin. His eyes burned like fiery jewels. Then he spoke. "Are you happy?"

Startled by this question, I paused for a moment before I responded.

"Yes . . . very. Now I know the secret of this temple," I declared. "It has all been built with sound."

I didn't expect him to respond. He looked at me and his eyebrows turned up in glee. He reached out and grabbed me, pulling me into a bear hug. I was totally engulfed by his enormous body and garabia. I fell limp in his forceful clasp. He laughed from the bottom of his belly and then spoke to me.

"I am Mabrouk, the keeper. You are a good man."

Again he hugged me and then kissed me on both cheeks as he continued, "Will you be returning here?"

"Yes, Mabrouk. And I will bring many who are worthy to receive the blessings of this place."

With that, I said that I was very grateful for his patience in waiting and passed him some bakshish. He simply nodded and gladly took the money.

"I have many children. Thank you." He said.

"Blessings to you and your children," I said. "May they all be well and prosper by Allah."

He just continued to smile at me. Then I gave him the traditional Egyptian expression between friends.

I touched my lips and heart and said, "Masalam, Mabrouk."

"Masalam, my friend," he returned.

As I began my descent through the great stones to the plateau, I looked back and wondered about Mabrouk. I suddenly had the feeling that he was not working alone. Egypt was full of mystery, and this meeting was no exception. I am now convinced that he belongs to some secret network or brotherhood. These unsung guardians watch over the ancient temples and protect them from the true infidels, whether they are Egyptian or Occidental.

I was never to see him again. Although I inquired about him many times along the Nile, no one seemed to know of him or that he served at the Gizeh complex. Strange! Another mystery.

Grand Canal of Light

On the morning of the third day, our first day out of Cairo, we had to fly south to Aswan. There we met the bus that would begin our trip down the Nile to all of the temples. Our first stop in the late morning was the Aswan Dam and the ancient quarries where the great stones had supposedly been carved and sent down river on rafts for the building of the temples.

We stood upon a colossal pylon of granite now prostrate along the quarry floor. It had been chosen for a great obelisk. According to the guide's story, however, during the construction a major flaw was discovered. The guide went on to say that the Egyptian engineers knew it would never withstand the stress of erection, so it was abandoned during the early stages.

Everyone milled around the site while the guide continued through the standard explanations about the carving and polishing process. Someone asked how the engineers had determined the existence of the fault in the obelisk. The guide pointed to a small hole cut into the side of the giant stone, five or six feet deep.

As I looked into the observation hole, I noticed that the inside surface was as smooth as glass and that the shape was a perfect circle for the entire length of the hole. I thought, Even more amazing is the hole's entrance, a well-defined sharp edge. The entrance suggested the tools that were used had to be sophisticated. I couldn't imagine hundreds of quarrymen chipping and grinding by hand. I finally asked Yokar, "Yokar, how this was done?"

Yokar was quick to respond. "It was made by sidereal vibration, a vibration that is not heard but is melodious to the elements, appearing as a beam of light. Only the priesthood of Karnak could have made this orifice."

"So," I continued quietly, "the priesthood was involved in all phases of temple construction?"

"Yes," he said.

I called out to the guide. "How do you explain that this deep hole is too narrow to polish so smoothly and so accurately by hand? Also, why would they polish the inside if it is only an observation port?"

The guide mumbled something about being able to determine the flaw more accurately. But he didn't explain away the mystery of its accuracy.   I spoke to the group, confirming Yokar's words. "This hole was created by some kind of laser fire conjured by the priests."

There were some soft "oohs" and "ahs" from the Japanese participants.

Later at the Aswan docks, we boarded our cruise ship, The Nile Princess. Almost two days later, we docked at Kom Ombo. It was early evening. The dock was overwhelmed by a horde of cruise ships, so our captain docked further down the shore near a high grassy knoll. The first temple was fifteen minutes away on foot.

The deep red sun had already dipped below the sand-filled horizon. A dramatic reddish-orange glow was painted onto the temple stone. When I saw what shape the temple was in, I was shocked. It was hardly standing. Most of the pillars in the hypostyle, part of the front entrance of the temple, were still standing. The rest of the complex looked like it was falling apart. The complex appeared wide open, exposing the stone floor. I wondered how I was supposed to do ceremonies in the open, in front of everyone! Somehow, I had imagined it to be more intact. I smiled at myself, trying to lift my disappointment.

Morgan, I thought to myself, you have such a movie mind. I guess I was expecting something more like a Hollywood set!

As the gangplank rolled out to the shoreline, I was the first to leave the ship. The plank swayed dangerously and wiggled as I stepped quickly. A small chill ran down my spine. There were ropes on either side of the plank, but they didn't help much to keep my balance. There had been numerous rumors of nasty microorganisms called schistosomaisis or bilharzia polluting the shores of the Nile. They were allegedly strong enough to penetrate the skin on contact and capable of heading straight for the liver! I had no desire to test the rumors of these vermin.

Trying not to look awkward, I leaped off the final step, landing on a small outcropping in the tall grass. I looked back. A crowd of Japanese huddled hesitantly by the gangway. They looked with reluctant smiles, watching me lead the way to their first initiation. The guide handed out the boat passes and hollered to everyone to follow.

The grassy knoll led to a higher ridge on the riverbank. The climb along the riverbank was difficult. A young Egyptian boy waited for me at the upper ridge. With his hand outstretched toward me, he gestured a warm smile. Then, with one easy movement, he hoisted each of us onto the trail, a narrow dirt passage that dissolved into river reeds and tall ferns. The final way to the Kom Ombo Temple lay just ahead.

I stood quietly at the entrance for uncounted moments. Everyone in the group bunched up behind me. With their tickets clenched into tight fists, I thought I heard them smacking their lips in anticipation. Just to gape at this magnificent place was enough. The serious nature of what I was about to do heckled me like some invisible parrot from hell. Then I realized, with diminished zeal, that I didn't know where I was going.

I whispered desperately, "Yokar, where am I going? I've never seen this place before . . . you've gotta help me out here. Come on . . . I feel like I'm making this up as I go along!"

"Relax," he said telepathically. "You're doing fine. Just keep walking ahead."

I proceeded cautiously onward as Yokar guided me on like a traffic cop. "Left . . . now right," Yokar went on. "Go straight ahead for a bit. Okay, now turn to the right and go to the second from the last chamber. Here it is! This is the place."

Before me was a long stone building with a series of small "storage rooms" reminiscent of a galley of garages. Not very impressive! I thought. There was nothing to mark their significance, no writing or artifacts, nothing. The workers had even stacked bags of sand near the entrance, as if to add to the unimportance of it!

"Yokar, what is this place, anyway?"

"This is the birth-origin where the seed stones lay hidden."

"Seed stones? What the hell are seed stones?"

"Temple construction is not an easy matter. These are not like your ordinary dwellings for living. These structures are alive when completed. Not unlike the birth of a human, their existence is determined by a birth cycle and death cycle. The priesthood determines by sacred geometry and astrology a perfect time and place for the temple's erection and destruction.

"Most of these current temple remains are relatively new, built in your Greco-Roman period. The originals were simpler and built some thousands of years before.

"In order to create a new temple on top of the old one, the laws of rebirth and regeneration have to be considered. As the farmer takes seeds from an ear of corn to sow the Earth for another cycle of life, so the priesthood took the seed stones out of the original temple and began the new life of another temple. The location of the seed stones was a closely held secret . . . even to this time."

"I was expecting something a little more dramatic, Yokar."

"Listen, my boy, someday you will learn that everything is not what it seems. Bring each neophyte into this chamber, one by one. Here, we will utter the sacred intonations that evoke the Earth currents out of these stones, preparing the neophyte for induction into the mysteries."

The temples corresponded directly to the pukkas (an Atlantean name given to energy windows in the body). Yokar pointed out that the pukkas correspond to the spiritual subtle bodies and their energies. As we moved along the Nile to each temple, Yokar would conjur the energies out of each temple and stimulate each subtle body in turn through a series of endocrinal secretions, raising the individual's natural vibration. This process would prepare the neophyte for the final ceremony performed in the great pyramid temple at Gizeh, back in Cairo.

After a few minutes, I began to explain to Kasa, my Japanese interpreter, that I was going into trance while standing and to be at my side, ready to catch me when Yokar left my body. He suddenly seemed concerned.

I placed my arm around Kasa. "Anything wrong?"

"Yokar is going to stand up erect in your physical body now?" He asked.

"Yes," I confirmed, "it's great isn't it? It's the first time for me."

Now Kasa became excited. "I've only seen you channel him while sitting! Wooow!" Kasa shouted. "This is amazing. I feel so honored."

"Don't worry, my friend," I said. "You're going to do just fine."

Everyone waited outside patiently while I entered the chamber and took my position at the north end of the room. Kasa then stood on my left side as I requested. I winked at him, saying, "Well . . . here we go!"

Kasa rolled his eyes back indicating his nervousness. After a few moments, I achieved full trance while leaning against the wall, another first for me. Yokar then entered my body and leaned forward immediately into a freestanding position. He placed my left foot forward slightly to set his balance. Then he proceeded with each candidate, uttering the sacred Vril language.

Each blessing began with the phrase that sounded like Balaam shiitock (pronounced bah-lamb-shee-tock), followed by a series of unintelligible consonants and a set of strange sounds that varied with each individual. The impact varied widely and in some cases was quite dramatic. Some complained of dizziness and nausea, while others experienced a temporary paralysis.

Yokar explained that each candidate needed an individual adjustment. It was necessary that the conjured Earth energy of Kom Ombo enter each individual's body correctly in order to stimulate the endocrine gland secretions in the right sequence. This adjustment also prepared each for the next transmission at Edfu.

I had asked Yokar about a discrepancy regarding the number of subtle bodies existing in the body. I was aware of only five subtle bodies in my study of Atlantean theology with Yokar: from the physical upwards there was the astral, emotional, mental, etheric, and finally the causal body. I couldn't help noticing that there were six temples in the Canal of Light tradition along the Nile.

Yokar quickly agreed that there was the possibility of a sixth subtle body. The sixth body had not been formed as yet. He explained that the original human matrix was composed of five subtle bodies extending from the fifth root race, or the Atlantean race. But the Orions imposed genetic alterations to the female of the fifth root race, during the time of Atlantis, creating the formation of the sixth root race and the possibility of another subtle body. Yokar said that the new human matrix was hexagonal, suggesting the phantom body, or the inter-etheric body. He called it phantom because it really isn't formed yet, but its influence is already felt. The inter-etheric influence is between the etheric and causal bodies. It is called the light body.

Our Japanese tour guide entered with an attitude that she was not a believer. Although she agreed to share the group's experiences, she freely admitted before the initiation started that she was interested only in Yokar's archeological knowledge. Afterwards, she had to be assisted out of the chamber. In the end, all had been affected in some way.

When all was done, Yokar exited my body in a flash. It was so sudden that Kasa, caught off guard, nearly dropped me in the process. When I came to, I was very hot and had to be assisted out of the chamber.

I walked around for a few minutes, held up by Kasa, just to cool off. This new experience of Yokar animating all of my body was very taxing.

A few minutes later, I signaled that it was time to leave.

I began the journey out of the temple, following the path from the inner sanctuary. The Egyptian caretakers all behaved strangely and bowed their heads toward me. Embarrassed, I nodded and smiled back, not knowing what to say. One Egyptian guard approached as I made my way to the main gate. I heard him say to me, "Blessings to you, Doctor Morgan." Then he bowed with his hands clasped in the usual position for devotional prayer.

I wondered at this adulation. Perhaps because I knew more about their temple than the average tourist? They certainly didn't treat the other tourists in the same way. It puzzled me. They seemed to know what I was doing there.

By the time we arrived at Edfu it was early morning. The temple was more than a mile from the docks. Carriages had been hired by the boat operators to take the people sightseeing.

The simple life at Edfu had awakened. The clopping hooves and the clatter of metal wheels tapped out their uneven ring on the stone streets, attracting the beggars and artisans out of their little huts. We were suddenly caught up in a wild current of carriages filled with tourists.

When we arrived, I found the temple erect and intact. Now this is more like it! I thought. My expectations had finally been met. As we entered, I couldn't help but notice the Egyptians. They were already staring at me and making obvious adulations. A chill went down my spine. I'm becoming paranoid! I turned to Kasa for comfort and confirmation.

"Kasa, do you see what I'm seeing?"

"Do they know you?" he asked innocently.

"No!" I yelled. Then I continued on in a loud whisper, "How could they know me, for Christ's sake? I've never been here before!"

"This way," Yokar quietly interrupted.

He wasted no time in telling me the right way to go. This time the chamber was well marked and just to the right of the inner sanctuary. There must have been fifty tourists milling around. I felt a squirming sensation in my stomach. This time, I knew the ceremony would be in full view.

"Jesus, Yokar," I snapped mentally. "Do we have to do this right here in front of God and everybody?"

"Michael, your embarrassment is unbecoming!" Yokar declared sternly. "It is precisely because of this anticipated reaction that we wanted to draw you out of the closet, so to speak. You must bite off the head of your fear and swallow it!"

"Great!" I snorted as I stomped off toward the Japanese guide.

I quickly worked out a schedule, letting the guide offer the usual rendition of archeological history and myth. Her monologue gave me a chance to muster more courage for myself. I wasn't quite sure how

I was going to overcome my fear as Yokar suggested.

When the guide was done, she signaled me to take over. My heart skipped some beats, and my breath became shallow. My fear sat in my throat like a giant egg. I glanced around, trying to locate onlookers, and felt sweat trickle down my neck. I tried to will away the pressure in my throat. It just wouldn't budge. Then I imagined the egg being swallowed. But it remained stubbornly lodged.

I beckoned Kasa to gather everyone into the chamber and closed my eyes, trying to hide. Somehow, I knew I wouldn't achieve trance until I smoothed this new wrinkle in my training.

"You must allow the fear to coexist with you," Yokar hinted softly.

I forced my lungs to take a deeper breath and centered my thoughts on yielding to the egg's presence. A strange sensation began to tickle my throat. It was small at first but grew to be intolerable. I wanted to cough to clear my throat, but Yokar demanded my continued concentration.

"You must resist coughing. Don't cough. Do not cough," he demanded repeatedly.

"But Yokar I have to . . . urgh . . . ugh."

"Use your inner will, boy. Use your inner will to resist the outer belief," he went on.

Now it was thousands of ants crawling down my throat and my mind was screaming to cough. I could feel Yokar's energy bearing down on me like a drill sergeant. I knew I had to obey my inner will . . . it was important.

Just as I was about to cave in, the ant sensation left me. The terrible itch was replaced by a sudden coolness. The new feeling was so soothing that I thought I had taken a drink of cold water. At the same time, a flash of heat soared up through my nasal passages and across my eyes. It was over!

Now, I was suddenly energized. "Amazing!" I murmured quietly with a smile. I opened my eyes briefly to find the main body of tourists gone. Now I didn't care about the people watching. I was fearless! Kasa had formed the initiates into a semicircle facing me. Then he leaned over to me.

"Did you say something?"

"Oh, it's nothing," I said. "I'm just reveling with my teacher."

Once again, I leaned against the wall and set myself for trance. Yokar entered and raised my body up to the standing position. Taking advantage of the acoustical geometry designed into the room, Yokar again spoke the sacred sounds of Vril to the group. The room vibrated in cadence, resonating in choral undertones, making the whole group swoon.

After Yokar was finished, I exited into Kasa's arms, finding myself resting on his outstretched knee. Everyone was clapping and beaming at me with smiling faces and shining eyes. Draped over Kasa's shoulder again, I exited the temple with him. The others followed close behind. Above the Egyptian caretakers' cheerful "Masalaams," I thought I could hear another sound. The temple was humming!

Later that afternoon, the boat set sail for Esna. There we would begin jockeying for position to enter the Nile's locks, designed to bypass the cataracts. The Nile was at two different levels this time of year. We needed to go through a series of locks in order to meet the lower river level at Luxor. It was not until we sat down to dinner that the bad news emerged.

Two of the Japanese participants approached Kasa and informed him that they had missed the Edfu initiation. Kasa came to me very upset and explained the situation. "Michael, two women were taking pictures in another part of the temple while the initiation was taking place. What are we going to do? Is it possible that we could eliminate this initiation for them this time?"

"Absolutely not, Kasa," I said with surprise. "Listen, you know that no one can miss even one ceremony. Each step is built on the previous experience."

"Oh my God, what are we going to do? Does this mean they can't go on?" Kasa lamented.

"I really don't know. We'll have to ask Yokar about this one! First, we have to talk to the captain to see what are our options."

The Japanese tour coordinator in the captain's office joined Kasa and me later. I was the first to speak.

"Excuse me, Captain, I hate to bother you right now. And I'm sure you have your hands full. We have a bit of a problem. It seems we have to get back to Edfu to handle some unfinished business."

The captain turned, his eyebrows raised.

"We've already begun our positioning for the lock. We cannot dock. We have to remain in the middle of the river. I'm afraid there is no way for you to leave now."

All eyes seemed to meet together. The options were narrowing quickly. The coordinator then asked about other transportation.

"Can we obtain a taxi in Luxor to take us back?"

"Perhaps. But you'll have to spend the night as well," the captain said.

There were five of us. We would probably need two taxis and then rooms for the night. Additionally, we had to consider the problem of coordinating a rendezvous with the boat the next day. The Japanese coordinator rapidly concluded that the expense was too high and the risk too great. We might miss our connecting flight back to Cairo.

There was some desperate Japanese spoken between Kasa and the coordinator. Then they both turned to me. Their expressions said that the burden of the decision was in my hands. If the Japanese women didn't get their initiations in the lower triangle, they would not be ready for the upper triangle.

Yokar had defined the arrangement of the spiritual energy centers working in two groups, each set of three in the shape of a triangle. He divided them by their order of vibration, declaring that they must be opened in sequence as with the temples along the Nile.

I shuffled over to one of the tables in the main lounge and closed my eyes to begin a telepathic dialogue with Yokar again. "Yokar, what can we do about this? Frankly, I know it's their responsibility to be where they need to be, but it will be a great loss if they can't go on."

Moments later, Yokar broke in. "This is clearly resistance to completing the final initiation. They are unconsciously frightened of the decisions they've made. Are not both women scheduled for private sessions shortly?"

I quickly thumbed through my papers and confirmed his inquiry. "Yes, Yokar. They are scheduled. One at 5:30 this evening and the other at 9 P.M. tonight, after dinner."

"Good. We shall observe and examine the nature of their resistance. Depending on their willingness to embrace this resistance, we will determine the course of action to take."

I got up from the table feeling a little better, knowing that the news from Yokar wasn't crushing yet. But the outcome was still unknown. This conference left me feeling that there had been only a small stay of possible excommunication from their final rites of initiation in the great pyramid.

The sessions came and went and the result was inconclusive.

I stood outside of my body waiting for Yokar to comment. "What do you think, Yokar?"

"There was adequate and genuine remorse in the review of their negative intent, but we feel that this needs to be tested once more." He seemed to pause, taking the time to stroke his beard carefully. Then he continued, "You will take them to Karnak when we arrive in Luxor tomorrow. You will lead them to a neutral point we will have chosen. If they resist the forces applied to them, then all will be well."

Later, while sipping on some cold coffee, I pondered silently Yokar's decisions. Karnak! I thought. My God. This must be serious if the old boy wants me to take them into Karnak.

I had remembered Yokar's warning. Everyone had to stay out of Karnak. He had implied the old spirits were restless and some energy had even become demonic in that temple. I wasn't exactly overjoyed about the prospects of going in there. Especially, to a so-called neutral place.

Yokar chimed in to interrupt my concerns. "Stop worrying and get some rest. You're going to need it."

The next morning we set out for Luxor, the twin sister temple to Karnak. The temples were like polar opposites, Luxor being the temple of the good heart and Karnak the dark heart, the center for all black magic in Egypt. All Pharonic curses emanated from there. The

Karnak priesthood was the most powerful of all. It was in this part of Egypt that Moses struggled to defeat the Pharoah and free the enslaved Hebrews.

Although the initiation went smoothly for the group in Luxor, I could feel the tension mounting. There seemed to be an invisible force tugging at me to hurry up and finish my business at Luxor. It was decided that everyone would go to Karnak, although minimal sightseeing would be conducted. The orders for the Japanese guide from Yokar were quite clear: stay out of the old areas!

The temple at Karnak was quite complex. There were three temples in one. The two older areas contained altars where blood sacrifices had been performed. Yokar seemed to be directing me to a point equidistant from the two. The two women in question stayed close behind me. The rest of the group dispersed in the direction of the guide, already preparing for her regular spiel on the temples and its artifacts. Before she started, I noticed her glancing in my direction. Her expression seems to indicate a quiet affection, as if to say, take care.

I found myself walking cautiously through the grounds. I felt more like a detective on the prowl than a spiritual leader about to perform a sacred ritual. My fear suggested that the boogieman was about to take a huge chunk out of my backside any minute. Despite this feeling, I managed to maintain a rather calm exterior.

Just when I was about to relax, thinking that all the fear was for naught, one of the women suddenly left me. I quickly turned to speak to her, but she had already broken away and was running. "Where are you going? The neutral position is not that way."

She ignored me. She began to mumble something unintelligible. Her face looked blanched and her eyes had become narrow. She stopped and was pointing down the main corridor of the oldest part of the temple. "We must go there," she demanded.

Ah Shit! I muttered to myself quietly. I turned to the other woman. She hadn't budged from my side. I brought her several more steps to the designated neutral position and spoke scoldingly, "Stay right here and don't move from this spot." She looked frightened but

I could tell she wasn't going anywhere. I thought to myself, One loose cannon on deck is more than enough!

I ran after the other woman, yelling at her to come back. She was transfixed. Again I called out, "The neutral place is over here, come on back." She still refused my calls.

Then, Yokar interrupted my attempt to go further. "You must not try to stop her. She is already held captive by the presence here. There is not much you can do. This was the potential that we perceived in her heart on the boat."

"Yokar," I pleaded, "I can't just let her run off to be possessed by that thing out there. I feel responsible for her!"

"We understand how you feel. It's unfortunate."

At that point, my friend Kasa approached to see what was the matter.

"What's going on, Michael-san?" He asked.

"I don't know, really. Yokar said, we need to let her go in there, to let her take this to its ultimate conclusion. I feel very concerned for her. I want to pursue her anyway and make sure she doesn't hurt herself."

"Okay. We'll go in together," Kasa said bravely.

The woman was kneeling at one of the older stones. She was leaning with her head on the stone as if she were trying to remember something. Her face was all contorted now and grimacing. As we approached, she jumped up and ran to one of the smaller chambers off to the right of the stone walkway.

We followed her in.

Kasa remarked, "It figures. A foul thing would pick the one chamber where all of the workman had been urinating and defecating."

We entered, trying to ignore the obvious stench permeating the atmosphere. The woman was speaking in a strange tongue. I asked Kasa if it was a dialect of Japanese.

Kasa shrugged his shoulders. "I can't understand her, either!"

We watched as she continued her antics. She ran first to one corner of the room and then to another, trying to explain something to us in this strange language, which apparently seemed to her obvious. The entity seemed to grow restless and irritated with our ignorance.

I decided to go into trance, thinking Yokar could help. Minutes later, Yokar was in and looking on. Kasa thought that the woman was psychologically disturbed by the awe and mystery of the trip, and that the excitement had set her off.

Then Yokar began to utter blessings into the air as the negative spirit became angry. Something akin to obscenities were hailed at us. When that didn't work, the entity tried to seduce Yokar.

The entity went on, "Oh Yokar, Yokar, I love you, I adore you, please make love to me."

But Yokar, unaffected by this ruse, continued to spread blessings throughout the chamber. It was at this point that Kasa realized that the woman was not just disturbed, but possessed by something. Kasa became concerned. Then Yokar comforted him. "Kasa, just relax. This spirit cannot harm you. If it should decide to strike you, just allow it. Do not resist or defend yourself. Let your body go limp and relaxed."

Kasa reluctantly agreed. But he inquired on behalf of the woman. "Is there something we could do to help her?"

"Unfortunately, no," Yokar proclaimed. " She has invited the spirit into her body, and this is her free will. She has chosen it. There is not much we can do about that until she rejects it."

In a final attempt to control the situation, the negative spirit approached Kasa and screamed more obscenities, which Kasa couldn't understand. He believed she was speaking some form of ancient Egyptian dialect. When Kasa ignored the outrageous behavior of the possessed woman, the entity raised the woman's arms and struck Kasa over the shoulders. Kasa went limp but did not collapse, just as Yokar had instructed.

Then, with more fury, the entity formed the woman's hand into a blade and uttered some kind of incantation. Then she plunged her blade-shaped hand into my stomach. Kasa looked on in horror, wondering if I was all right.

The entity stomped out of the chamber, mumbling and giggling more unintelligible gibberish. I returned to my body, propped on Kasa's knee like some giant marionette. I immediately scanned the room for the woman, but it was empty. "What happened?" I asked.

"Come on, let's go. I'll fill you in as we walk," Kasa said.

I felt weak and was glad Kasa was there to help me. I began to complain of an extreme coldness in my side, pointing to where the woman had jabbed me with her hand. When Kasa informed me of what the spirit had done, I became alarmed. Sensing my fear, Yokar chimed in telepathically.

"Michael, do not worry. We have neutralized the effects of this spell cast upon you. You will be cold for a while, but that is all."

By the time we had reached the rest of the group, the possessed woman was already weaving another scheme to undermine the group unity. She had picked out our Japanese guide, sensing her meek demeanor, pulled her to certain stones in the temple, and commanded her to kneel before them. The poor guide didn't know what was going on and decided to placate her until I could help. When I arrived, the guide informed me that the woman was trying to divide the group, claiming that Kasa, Yokar, and I and the Egyptian guide were all evil.

The possessed woman and the Japanese guide would have to take over the group under the possessed woman's tutelage.

After a brief explanation of the past events in the old temple, the guide proceeded to explain to the others that the woman was possessed temporarily with an ancient spirit from the temple, that they were to kindly allow her to carry on but not to pay her any mind. Everyone was sympathetic and seemed to understand the situation.

Having failed to rally the group, the spirit tried to grab other passersby, commanding them to kneel before the stones she had picked out. The Egyptian police were called in and prepared to take her away. We interceded, telling them that she wasn't herself. We managed to convince them that we could handle this situation and there would be no more trouble from her. I told Kasa to gather some of the women to usher the poor woman back to the boat, where we could watch her. I was hoping that the spirit would not be inclined to leave the temple and would release her.

Unfortunately, I was wrong. The spirit had decided to cling to her!

Later that afternoon I inquired about her condition to Yokar. "Yokar, what are we going to do about this woman? The spirit refuses to leave and is content to stay with her."

There was a long pause before Yokar answered. "We will see if the connection can be broken later. The mind is strong with this woman. This makes the bond between her and the spirit strong. Perhaps it will be broken on the plain of the will, the anvil of the mind, at Saqqara."

Saqqara was located near the Gizeh complex in Cairo. This would be the place of the final trial for the initiates before the approach to the great pyramid temple. We eagerly boarded a plane to Cairo, and the trip proved to be uneventful. The woman remained docile and quiet and slept on the way back. I think everyone was relieved that no more adventures were planned for this day.

It was early evening in Cairo. I had just finished a hot shower before dinner. I answered a knock at my door to find two Arab strangers. I let them in, thinking they were from the travel agency or ground operator. I was expecting a fax from America and I asked if they had the reply. They declined, explaining that they had come only to ask me a few questions.

Puzzled, I offered them a seat and a drink from the bar. Again they declined, proclaiming their allegiance to Ramadan, a Muslim high holiday dedicated to prayer and fasting. I apologized for my ignorance and encouraged them to get on with it.

They began in a solemn but ominous tone, "We know that you are not who you say you are. We also know that you possess the ancient knowledge. We have been told of your attempt to revitalize the ancient temples. We have seen many foreigners come and play their silly games at the temples. This is not our concern. But what you are doing is different. We cannot allow the ancient Egyptian religion to be resurrected in the heart of Muslim holy ground. We will stop you by any means necessary!"

I was stunned speechless. I began to laugh nervously, probably not a particularly good idea under the circumstances. Laughter could have been interpreted as an arrogant challenge. Calling up my inner will training from Yokar, I took a deep breath and recomposed myself into a serious demeanor.

"Sadly, you have been misinformed," I said. "I am not an Egyptian Priest. I am a tour guide from America." This is no time for secrets or theatrics, I thought. These people have come to stop me, even kill me if necessary! Muslim fanatical behavior was well known and not to be taken lightly. I was just glad they had decided to ask first and shoot later.

I continued on, holding back nothing. "I have brought a group of people to Egypt who wish to experience an initiation similar to the ancient rites. That is all. I have great respect for your religion and have no desire to replace it. I am deeply sorry, and regret that you have been offended in any way."

They seemed unmoved by my proclamation. Then I spoke what little Arabic I could. "Al ham du lil'Allah." The phrase—translated "May it be Allah's will, that we meet"— indicates a Muslim declaration of the ultimate authority of Allah to another Muslim.

My words brought on an obvious reaction. It was strange and incongruous to them that an Egyptian priest would offer public adoration to Allah in Arabic. They stood up, still looking disturbed. As they let themselves out, they warned, "We will be watching you carefully. Do not forget. Our warning still stands."

I simply nodded.

Before the door closed behind them, I spoke again. "Listen, you have nothing to fear from me. As soon as I'm finished, I'll be gone, leaving you with your country and your religion intact."

Then I closed with another Arabic phrase, indicating I was not an infidel. "Masalam." They just shook their heads in disbelief and walked away.

After they were gone, I shuddered. Man, oh man. This country is just full of surprises. I can't wait till I'm out of here! I followed that thought with a stiff belt of scotch from the room bar.

We arrived on the buses at Saqqara, at 8:30 in the morning, just as it opened. I stared at the sun now beginning to turn white with heat. "Perfect," I said with some satisfaction. When I left the bus I was shocked. There was hardly any sand! The guidebook explained that Saqqara was very difficult for tourists to see because all of the sites were separated by vast stretches of deep sand. Now, it had been all cleaned up.

I had planned this part of the adventure carefully as a test of the neophyte. The "trial of Argna" was to challenge them to walk quickly through the sand dunes that stretched from one place to another. They were to do so after they descended straight down a certain well tomb 180 feet below the surface and returned with their legs unsteady. The distance, according to the guidebooks, was a minimum of 300 yards of deep sand between artifacts. But the government had swept up all the extra sand to make the site easy for the tourists. What was I going do now?

I turned to Abraham, our Egyptian guide, and bubbled over with frustration. He thought to himself for a moment and looked over to the step pyramid of Zozer, a major site in this place. He said, "You know, the perimeter of the Zozer pyramid is about 1500 meters. You could have them walk around it, maybe several times." Then he smiled sardonically.

"Good idea, Abraham. Okay. Let's get this show on the road." Historically, this was the place where a Pharoah was tested for his right to continue rulership over all Egypt. It seemed appropriate that the initiates should be tested here too. Everyone gathered at the foot of the pyramid to listen to my instructions.

Yokar had offered a little more to this ordeal to make it interesting. First we had to descend into the Earth to gather the Earth current. Nearby were the underground well tombs of some ancient Egyptian dignitaries. This was the planned 180-foot ordeal straight down an iron spiral staircase. Going down for them wasn't so bad, but climbing up was the real trick!

When we arrived at the bottom, one of the women who had missed Edfu became nauseous and complained. I began to work with her energetically, helping her to ground the flow of energy from the Earth through her feet. She trembled violently and became faint. Her body fell limp in my arms and suddenly broke into a cold sweat.

Then, she opened her eyes and smiled and began to cry. The ordeal of Karnak was over for her. As we ascended the spiral staircase, she couldn't stop thanking me. Now I just had the hard case to deal with.

Once this woman was cleansed, the group was ready for the pyramid ordeal. They had to make seven rounds about the base of the step pyramid within thirty minutes. But each had to carry a stone, about the size and weight of a person's head, the whole way.

I had planned to take the walk myself because I was very concerned about the other woman who had missed the ceremony at Edfu. When the walk began, I purposely walked close behind her, looking for signs of the dark spirit. I watched carefully for any signs of difficulty or rebellion. She continued walking without incident for the first three rounds. Then on the fourth round I could hear her mumbling and giggling to herself. She began to twitch from time to time, bursting into laughter. I expected the worst.

By when we came to the final round, she stumbled and almost crashed flat upon her face. I rushed to help her, but she managed to recover by herself. As I assisted her to her feet, I looked into her face, scanning for any telltale signs. Her face had become soft, and her eyes were relaxed. She smiled at me and I knew the evil spirit was gone. Saqqara had done its work. The connection between her and the spirit was broken. We walked quietly and finished the Zozer ordeal together.

I didn't realize that this activity would bring anger and accusation from onlookers during the process. The participants were heckled and jeered from the tourist crowd with statements such as "Why are you taking the temple stones?" and "Stop defiling the temples, you pagans!"

This reaction was unexpected. Later, many told me that they were amazed that the comments from the crowds were similar to comments from their parents and friends who had previously judged their beliefs early in life. So, I concluded, it was a success after all. Afterwards, everyone gathered back on the bus to return to the hotel in preparation for the evening entry into the great pyramid at Gizeh. They had to fast and maintain silence from sunset until the sunrise ceremony the next morning.

Just before dark, we returned by bus to the plateau. There was the usual ceremony of complaint and bribery involving the guards and policemen. This time I knew what to expect. The gatekeeper was different this time. I missed Mabrouk.

Once inside, all removed their jackets and put on special robes marked with Egyptian symbols and ancient hieroglyphs made for the occasion. I presented the initiate chosen to anoint the others with a small bottle. It was filled with a mixture of essential oils of frankincense and myrrh. She proceeded to say to each one, as she touched them:

"I anoint your lips, so that you may speak the truth;
I anoint your ears, so that you may hear the truth;
I anoint your throat, so that you may receive the truth;
I anoint your eyes, so that they may not deceive you;
I anoint your brow, that you may have insight;
I anoint your crown, that you may have wisdom."

When she was done, everyone got into line and prepared to ascend the ramp to the Queen's and King's Chambers. Going ahead, I traveled quickly. I received an energy boost from Yokar, who was right behind me. When I arrived at the final set of stairs at the King's entry way, a bright blue star appeared in front of me, throwing a shroud of light blue smoke over the entrance. A deep voice spoke with authority.

"Who goes before the altar?"

"It is I, the high priest. Let me pass. I have business with the spirit."

The smoke suddenly dissolved, removing the barrier from the passage. I then uttered, "Blessed be the maker." I wasted no time in making ready for the ceremony. I placed the special hymns selected by Yokar for the ceremony on the audiotape player positioned just outside the passageway, pointing down into the grand gallery.

I put on the robes of high priest and sat on the altar stone next to the stone cubicle. I entered into trance and Yokar began his chanting right away.

Yokar called all of the spirits of the temple and then addressed the spirits of the four winds. Then he blessed the altar room (the

King's chamber) and called to all of the initiates at the bottom of the grand gallery to begin their ascent. The hymns began setting the tone for the ceremony. Everyone entered the altar room and filed around the chamber walls.

One by one, he called each into the stone cubicle. Then he began a series of intonations that made the entire pyramid come alive. All participants were treated for the particular needs in their energy systems. All had their energy raised to certain octaves. He chanted the sacred Vril that opened the doorway to the future. His chants reverberated into the red granite lintels above, causing harmonic overtones to mix with his incantations. By this process, all initiates had implanted into their bodies higher vibrational octaves of the Life Force from their own future selves. When all this was done, Yokar stood and proclaimed the importance of this ceremony to all present.

Later, many initiates told me they had looked up at the ceiling and found no ceiling, just the shining stars above. Some reported that there were many lights dancing above everyone's head. I knew that when Yokar completed the opening ceremony the altar room no longer existed on this Earth, but had shifted into some other higher dimension.

After a night of total silence and fasting, at five A.M. the next morning, we all returned to the Great Pyramid to complete the final ceremony. This "sunrise sealing" ceremony was also performed within the King's Chamber. It was to seal forever the energy transmission received by the initiates the night before. This ceremony insured access to this experience, whenever they would choose to make use of it. When it was done, everyone hugged and began to sob, laughing and weeping tears of joy.

I returned from the trance state to see a marvelous sight. Everyone was shining with a great light. Young and old alike were beaming with happiness. I knew that this was only the beginning of a long process that would draw many more souls seeking this ancient initiation tradition.

Long Labors End

It was an apocalyptic rain in New York. Don't let the romantics fool you—when it rains here, it's miserable. People hopped around on the street like frogs looking for dry lily pads. It was a bad day; nothing went smoothly. The cold drizzle reached deep into my clothing and down my neck. I looked for the nearest coffee shop and sat in my own puddle.

My favorite book did not escape the wetness of my dripping bag. The bookmark was glued to the binding. Finally, with hot coffee and book in hand, I tried to recover from the water world around me. A familiar presence then surrounded me with warmth.

Hi, Yokar. Must be nice not to deal with water any more.

He ignored my trivial comment and began with some urgency. "There has been a shift, Michael," he said firmly.

The value of my hot coffee and the annoyance of the water faded. "What are you talking about, Yokar?"

"Tellur has gone through another transmutation. The patterns beneath the great temple of Gizeh are dissolving!"

My mind was sluggish, maybe even waterlogged. I couldn't grasp this new information. I pushed at him to explain. "I don't understand. What does this mean?"

"This next solar initiation will be the last in the region of Gizeh," he declared. "You will require additional preparation for this journey."

Yokar sensed my tense feeling with this news.

"Do not worry, my son. It will be fine. We will prepare now for these changes . . . and notify you at the appointed time. When you leave, be sure to go to a crystal shop. Purchase a crystal prism that has an octagonal faceted shape, a size that should fit into your hand." His voice faded as he left me in a hush.

"But wait! Don't go. I have more to ask."

He didn't respond, and sadness filled me.

I loved to work in the temples, especially the Great Pyramid. They were my sanctuary now, comfortable, like old friends. In the past two years I had done five solar initiations. I didn't relish having to Part Company with them. It couldn't end so soon! I wanted to argue about this with Yokar. I imagined that with his power, he could fix it. In the end, however, I knew it was final.

The rain had finally stopped for the moment, presenting a good opportunity to dash for the subway. Preoccupied, I left the restaurant barely remembering to pay the bill. Yokar's message troubled me as I wondered what he meant by additional preparation.

The time passed swiftly, months dwindling into days. It all rushed quickly at me, and I had difficulty adjusting. The plane landed in Cairo with the next group of neophytes. The tenseness gripped me again as I felt my sadness that this would be the last time.

My feeling of tenseness shifted to shock. Conditions in Egypt were very bad, the atmosphere severe! Muslim terrorists had stepped up their campaign against the government. Their goal was to eliminate the flow of tourists and cut the financial base of the government, and their plan was working. In contrast to our experience on the last tour, many hotels were empty and closing. The Mena Oberoi, a popular old-world style hotel in the pyramid area, had always been filled during this time of year. Now, only a third of its capacity was used, and much of the staff was gone. When we arrived, the hotel management was very pleased.

Egypt had always been an unpredictable place. This instability had been underscored by the Iraqi war. Ever since I planned the first trip to Egypt, there had been a threat of terrorism. It was more than any doubt or lack of courage that fueled my fears. The impending violence seemed to be everywhere. I felt that even the Egyptian language sounded harsh and violent.

In Egypt the guides had always assured me that reports of terrorist activity were exaggerated. They said, "They're just trying to sell more newspapers." But there had been incidents, which signalled underlying danger.

For example, one of the participants on an earlier trip had a heart condition and needed help to climb the steps to one of the temples; two Egyptians moved in to assist. They lifted the participant up the stone steps and exposed, beneath their garabias, very large handguns tucked under their belts.

On the same tour, I had decided to take my wife to the Gizeh plateau to show her the Great Pyramid. We hailed a taxi at the hotel and arrived only minutes later. I paid the driver, but then he refused to let us out. I thanked him again, but he insisted we stay in the car. He blocked my hand from opening the door, as he motioned for me to look ahead.

"Not now. There will be a fight!" He said confidently.

And there it was, right in front of us on the plateau, a fight between a camel driver and a trinket salesman. It wasn't long before the trinket salesman screamed obscenities and pulled a knife, killing the camel driver. Before Dianne and I could catch our breath, another camel driver emerged from the raging crowd. The second camel driver approached the trinket salesman while the taxi driver continued to provide some translated commentary for us.

"He is the brother of the driver who was killed."

More yelling and screaming continued from the crowd. Within a flash, the camel driver had drawn from behind him a riding crop. He proceeded to beat upon the trinket salesman's head with the blunt end. I watched, incredulous.

"He will kill him! Watch," our driver continued coldly.

"This can't be true!" I cried. Again and again the camel driver struck the trinket salesman. The trinket salesman staggered backwards. Incredibly, the taxi driver's prediction unfolded; the trinket salesman buckled at the knees and fell to his death. The crowd dispersed quickly.

"We have to go find a policeman now," I declared.

Our driver just shook his head. "Do you see the smiling men on the camels, dressed in the dark blue jackets?"

I nodded.

"Those are the police! You see, they are laughing. They will do nothing because they hate the drivers and the trinket salesmen. They make too much money. They are greedy and deserve to die."

I couldn't believe my ears. I looked out over the plateau. The desert dust brushed over the stones, whisking away any trace of the violence we had just observed. Dianne was visibly shaken. As she struggled to hold back the tears, I squeezed her hand tightly to reassure her.

The Gizeh plateau was nearly empty now. The tragedy was over except for what appeared to be a small funeral procession that had been quickly organized by each of the victims' families and was now moving through the local streets.

We got out and proceeded quickly to the Great Pyramid. As we climbed to the entrance, I looked over my shoulder. I had seen life and death cast down on the stone courtyard like dice. I remember thinking, We don't belong here!

The memory of that day fed some of the awful dread I felt on this sixth tour. I believed this was how it would always be, like an icy narrow cliff road. It would never change here. It would always be a little terrifying!

Yokar has made me realize that almost everything in life has terrified me into paralysis, preventing me from trying anything new. It has prevented me from truly experiencing life to the fullest. With his encouragement, I am beginning to learn that being paralyzed will not diminish any of the terrible things that can happen, but will disable me from engaging in those experiences as they arise and keep me from the possibility of discovering my strengths in the process.

Yokar has provided the impetus for me to invest all of my energy and my enthusiasm in my life. This has been perhaps the single greatest lesson he has taught me so far. I love him for it! With every task he gives me, I have moaned, whined, and kicked almost the whole way. It's a wonder that I've accomplished anything at all with him!

On the second day, we were scheduled to take the group into the Cairo Museum. Dianne and I had recently adopted our son Adam from Poland. He was almost three years old. Because of his history and abandonment, we felt it was important for him to join us on the Egypt trip.

I wondered about this little boy and what strange forces were at work to bring him to this place. As we strolled past the monolithic stone sculptures and reliefs, Adam suddenly tensed in my arms and pointed to a large replica of the pharoah Ahknaton, otherwise known as Amenhotep the 4th.

Wide-eyed, he declared as he pointed, "Me!"

I paused. I ignored his declaration as ridiculous and coincidental. Adam is far too young, I thought, to be so aware of himself to make such an observation. Then after we had walked another eight or nine steps past the huge sculpture, Adam placed his little hand against my cheek and forced my head around, to look at the pharoah's stone likeness again. Once again, with more emphasis, he declared, "Me!" Then he pointed at the stone sculpture. Then a chill went through me. Now I knew why he had come. There was a lot more to this little boy than I was prepared to accept.

"Dianne!" I called out. "Adam is remembering a past existence here!"

Dianne simply shrugged, acting as if she already knew it.

That evening, after the Hotel Oberoi had served a delicious dinner, I sat quietly by myself in the lounge, sipping on some Egyptian coffee. Yokar approached me to reveal his new agenda.

He said telepathically, "Your task this time will be greater. Since the energy is dissolving below the temples, we must insure that the temple spirit guardians are not left stranded with meaningless stones. You will be the instrument to release the spirits after each initiation ceremony is complete!"

I nearly choked on the next gulp of coffee. Dianne approached with some of the others, turned to notice me with some alarm, and said, "Michael, are you okay?"

I struggled to clear my breathing. I nodded and confirmed with a hand gesture. After I recovered, I asked Yokar inwardly about this new development. How am I going to do that? Why didn't you tell me? You should've told me about this long ago!

"If we had informed you then, you would have built up unnecessary fear, as you can see!"

I was in shock and felt weak. The others standing next to Dianne mentioned that I didn't look well. I quickly dismissed my pale appearance as the effects from choking on the coffee.

We all felt tired and agreed to turn in early. Later, I informed Dianne about the true nature of my disturbance. She took the news in stride and was compassionate. I was still trying to cope as she tried to console me. I believed that she didn't grasp the gravity of my new task.

This trip was different in many other ways as well. The group comprised a number of teachers from Mantak Chia's Taoist Yoga system and an equal number of people of various other spiritual backgrounds. There were twenty-two in all, quite an auspicious number! Despite his or her official titles of neophyte on this tour, no one was a beginner in the true sense. Some had returned as veterans from the previous trip. I had the feeling that even the new people had been through this process before, lifetimes before. I felt that many had entered into this journey having already been marked in some strange way.

The next morning just before we were to disembark for the flight to Aswan, Ron Dianna, one of the senior instructors for Mantak Chia, joined me for a second cup of coffee. He had arrived a day before the rest of the group and was eager to share some of his experiences.

He was medium in height and somewhat husky in build. He loved to practice his Tai Chi. You could always find him doing his routines even when he was standing idle. His hairline retreated gradually, and his hair swept into a duck's tail in the back. His forehead sloped into a smooth line above his nose, giving him the appearance of forward movement. Ron's manner was quiet and solemn until he burst into laughter. Then he was radiant and could easily fill a room with his energy.

He explained that he felt very charged upon his arrival in Cairo. He spent the afternoon in the hotel garden, in full view of the Great Pyramid, preparing himself with Tai Chi and meditation for the coming spiritual process. By eleven that night, exhausted and exhilarated from trying to accommodate the pyramid's energy, he decided to go and make direct contact and perhaps make peace with the colossal structure; but the area was closed for the night.

Undaunted, he followed a small path around to the rear of the great temple into the desert behind the plateau. There, he stumbled onto a camel driver's tent and negotiated with the owner for a midnight desert ride.

I expressed my envy at this point. A moonlight ride in the desert by camel sounded so exotic.

Ron went on to carefully describe his ride. As the driver led him through the back streets of Gizeh, he realized that this strange and unknown environment might be hostile. Suddenly, he feared that he might never return. But as they quietly and unannounced passed the sleeping villagers snuggled in for the night, he began to relax. While he stared down into the mud huts, noticing the undefined lumps of bed clothing dimly lit by burning oil lamps, he wondered why he couldn't sleep this night.

The midnight journey ended in a place near the second pyramid. The driver suggested that he could climb to the top for a small fee. Ron was surprised by this offer. After a quick negotiation, he began to make the arduous climb to the peak.

Trying to catch his breath after the climb, he could see the city of Cairo sprawled below him bespeckled with light and the moonlit desert flowing behind. The great black shadow of Cheops shouldered his right. In awe, he sat quietly. What unseen forces had brought him to this place? He relaxed and realized that he belonged here! He decided, at that point, that he would trust these unknown forces to carry him through the mysterious days ahead.

I felt that other participants must have similar personal stories about coming to this place.

After breakfast, we proceeded south to Aswan. Yokar chose this time to continue my training, taking my mind off his new agenda. At the island of Phyllae, I found a comfortable seat at the edge of one of the temple pillars, far away from the group. This temple was very nice and in many ways intact, but it had been moved, like Abu Simbel. We couldn't use this temple site for any ceremonies. The morning sun was rising bright and the sky was clear blue all around. Yokar appeared and approached me quietly.

"Do you have the crystal prism with you, my son?"

"Yes, Yokar."

"Remove it from your pocket. I want to show you how to use it."

As I pulled out the octagonal prism, the sun's rays caught it immediately and dazzled me with many brilliant colors. I was fascinated.

"You have used the sun for heat, light, and to grow food," Yokar said. "You have looked for it to offer you warmth in the pleasure of coloring your skin, and even as a focus of worship in older times. But this orb has many other esoteric purposes."

"Are you referring to the use of the sun in Atlantis?"

"Yes. In many respects, you could say that Atlantis was primarily a solar culture!"

"Yokar, is it possible for you to tell me how you used the sun to power your culture in Atlantis . . . we could use some clean energy for a change! Based on what I've seen here in this culture, we have a long way to go."

"Well, perhaps it is possible that within a few of your years, we will reveal more of this. For now, let us begin your solar spiritual training by increasing your understanding of its power to transform energy . . . your energy!"

"I can use the sun to do that?"

"Oh yes, my son. This is perhaps the most important development in Atlantis," he said. "To begin with, you already know intuitively, that you require the sun's light for your continued subsistence. You know that there is some quality about solar light that is different than the artificial light your scientists have created. Yes?"

"Okay. Go on," I said impatiently.

"The quality you know to exist in the sun's rays is an alive quality. Although you have defined it in terms of magnetic energy, the qualities are cosmic and represent the Life Force in its purest and brightest form available in the physical plane.

"Your scientists discovered one of the special luminary formulas that applies to your sun's illumination. That formulation declares some of the wisdom of the Laws of Octaves."

"You're talking about the seven rays, aren't you?"

"Well, there are actually many more than seven. But your capacity to perceive is very limited, according to your conscious ability. In truth, there are fifty-two rays held within the orb's shining, even though you can recognize only seven of these."

"Wow! Fifty-two rays? So, what are these different rays, Yokar?"

"The names for these are many and you could not pronounce most of them. Besides which, they would have no meaning for you, as you have no knowledge of these color vibrations in your present understanding!"

"I see. So how can I use the light then, to transform my energy?"

"With the right use of the luminary laws, a well-constructed prism of the correct design can direct the sun's energy to pass through such a crystal, compressing the solar energy with its changing angles of density—what you call facets. The sun's energy will decode into the underlying components of the grand ray, or white ray. This process reveals the first luminary law:

He that captures the grand light possesses all there is, but he that possesses the harmonic keys beholds the grand illumination. "

"What does this mean, Yokar?"

"With the right use of knowledge, you can use the rays in their individual qualities to feed your hidden light body, to complete it by giving birth to it and later to give it the energy the light body needs to grow and mature."

"How can I do that?"

"You need to drink from the rays, bring them into your system. By this, we mean for you to bring the sun's light into your organs for sight; use your eyes for this."

"But Yokar, won't I harm my eyes in doing this?"

"Not if you follow these guidelines for your practice. You must observe the rays emitted from the crystal and focus their direction into your eyes. Do not stare directly at them but just off center slightly from the center of your iris. The exposure should only be for two minutes total at one time and divide this exposure time by the use of each eye."

"What do the colors do exactly?"

"Each color represents certain harmonic vibrations that are

attuned to states of conscious activity. As you expose your being to these vibratory states, your being will eventually awaken in response to that particular vibration, in like kind. The light body needs many color vibrations in order to birth, grow, and mature. The manner in which each is administered is important."

"What do you mean by manner, Yokar?"

"All life, at every level of consciousness, is governed by seasons of growth opportunity. Your vegetative growth seasons on the Earth are a perfect example of this. In a similar way, the precise manner which you should expose each color vibration is a sequence that relates to the original relationship of your being and the solar orb at the time of your physicalization, your birth."

"So, what are these patterns, where do they come from?"

"There are two patterns that emerge; the first is a set of three influences that relate to the movement of the cold magnetic force. You are calling these 'spot' activity. The periodicity for these influences is twenty-three years, twenty-eight years, and finally thirty-three years."

"Isn't this the same as what are called biorhythm cycles?"

"Yes, that is correct. Although these should be calculated from the time of conception and not the birthing."

"But no one here knows their time of conception exactly!"

"Well, in terms of accuracy, it is more or less unimportant. The second pattern is a set of dual influences that relate to the male and female force aspects of the solar luminary. The light has male and female qualities. This means you will need to monitor your cycles of biological activity and match those cycles of luminary activity when they are at their opposite peak."

"I'm not sure I understand what you're talking about, Yokar. So, I'm to find out my biorhythms and then determine when I'm positive or negative, and use the sunlight through the prism, in the opposite way?"

"Yes. Essentially. When you are negative in your cycles, the sun's light can be used straight away. It is male in this form. But if you are in your positive cycle, then you will need to draw the feminine portion of the sun's rays for your use."

"So what's feminine sun energy?

"The light is spinning like a spiral in its movement. Do you understand?"

"I think so, but I don't believe there is any previous understanding of masculine and feminine light, nor do we have the ability to acquire it at the present time!"

"Uh hmm," Yokar agreed quietly. "Well, for now, you can at least take advantage of the male side of the light until we can create other ways for you to do it, peacefully."

"How did you do it in Atlantis, Yokar?"

"Though we cannot reveal the precise nature of this technique at this time, we will say for now that it was done by manipulating the lattice structure of the crystal prism by the use of unique sound patterns."

"I see. That's fascinating."

"Now, you should continue with these practices until you reach an exposure time of fifteen minutes per week. No more than this!"

"Yes, as you wish."

I continued to stare at the prism's colored light with wonder as Yokar's energy faded. The ultraviolet color seemed to grow intense with his passing. The consciousness of my physical body returned. I became aware of a hard stone protruding into my backside. Walking around, I discovered that the group was gone. My leisurely stroll went from a jog to a full gallop. I arrived at the dock out of breath. Everyone had already boarded the shuttle boats, getting ready to leave.

The second half of the day ended in dead calm. About twenty of us had taken a felucca sailing boat to the Elephantine Island and were now trying to get back to our cruise boat. The wind had failed. These sailboats had no engine. There was little chance of returning without swimming, and no one wanted that alternative with all of the "liver flukes" reputedly swimming in the water.

The Nubian boat captain was quite young. He was undisturbed by our dilemma. He moved about the boat quietly, tugging at several fishing nets lying at the bottom of the hull. We thought he was going to spend the time in some afternoon fishing while we waited for a rescue. Then he emerged with some oars. Actually, they were two straight boards without paddles! Still, he mounted them onto their stanchions, behaving as though they were real oars.

He began to row very slowly, with great difficulty. The passengers took pity on his situation and offered to help row. Since we were eager to become part of the crew, he began to sing Nubian work songs for us. We joined in at the chorus, laughing the whole time! Our dilemma transformed into another adventure, as we rowed faster and faster. Eventually, we passed all the other stagnated boats on the river. We reached our cruise ship with an enormous appetite, just in time for dinner. With dinner underway, we sailed for Kom Ombo.

Our cruise ship arrived very late in the afternoon. The temple had been alerted to our arrival by ship's radiotelephone. The temple caretakers waited patiently for our tour group to reach the site.

As before, I knew that Yokar would stand erect in my body to perform the ceremony and that I would need someone strong from the group to catch me as Yokar left. I decided that Ron Diana would be a good candidate. Ron took his place on my right. Yokar suggested that the other be Claude Saks.

I didn't know Claude very well. We had met for the first time when he arrived from India to join me on this tour. He was an older-looking man, over six feet tall. His build was slender, but he seemed solid and looked quite fit. His hair was salt-and-pepper gray and pulled back neatly into a ponytail. His eyes were buried under large and bushy eyebrows. His mouth was shrouded by a gray handlebar mustache. He reminded me of an owl, quiet and keenly observing everything!

I soon learned that Claude had been a trader of coffee on Wall Street. He was quite friendly, but I suspected that he harbored a capacity to be ferocious from his days trading in the market. He was honored at the request and smiled softly when I asked him to take a place to my left.

Each neophyte was initiated, as before, in the little antechamber far in the back behind the hypostyle and most holy place. This time, Yokar stayed in my body for a longer time. Ron and Claude waited until after the other neophytes had gone to take their turns in the ceremony. Everyone waited quietly outside for me to emerge.

After Ron and Claude were finished, Yokar began an elaborate series of strange Vril intonations. The wind began to stir wildly. The antechamber suddenly grew colder. He went on and on, making gestures to the Earth and to the Heavens. He offered endless blessings and incantations that sanctified and honored the temple for its service to the light.

Then Yokar offered up to heaven the names of the souls who served namelessly in all the functions of the temple throughout all the eons, as it stood erect in the desert. Then he decreed, by the powers of light and darkness and all creation, that for those who had sworn blood oaths in service to the temple, the binding sacred rites of the temple be broken forevermore.

There was a hush, as though all the spirits took a great breath and held it. When Yokar left my body, I felt much hotter than usual and very dizzy. I emerged from the anteroom blinded by the brightness of the evening sunlight. Ron and Claude supported my weakened body until I could reach a place where I could sit.

Ron and Claude seemed to know intuitively that something very different was happening this time and inquired after my needs. I turned to Ron. I told him that I felt very strange and that a pressure was growing strong between my shoulder blades. The pressure was growing increasingly painful. He helped me to my feet and we all walked around as I tried to regain my strength. Claude was concerned when my breathing became labored. Weakness again overtook me, and they began to carry my weight draped between them.

Yokar descended immediately upon me in telepathic rapport to explain. "Michael, the spirits of the temple have been here a very long time. They do not know how to let go yet! You are going to have to help them."

How do I do that, Yokar? I asked desperately.

"Just open your heart, my son. Let them witness that opening in you. Then they'll come through you. You will become their gateway home. Then the release will begin."

"Jesus!" I blurted out loud. Ron glanced at me and couldn't help but notice my pain.

"Here we go!" I said, trembling with trepidation.

My back burned hot as the pain increased. I vaguely remember someone running up to me to offer smelling salts. But Claude thwarted them; pushing them away and explaining that everything was under control.

Yokar encouraged me. "Just relax and let your heart open. Don't be afraid."

"Okay, okay, " I whispered with a little breath. I relaxed and began to feel my love for all of the temple guards. My admiration poured out to them for their steadfastness and patience. Then I opened my heart.

A rush of fire poured through me like a massive volcano erupting, and then my body turned cold. There were intense feelings of fear and gratitude, sadness and relief all at the same time, all flowing from the fleeing spirits. Their energy rushed up to my face, freezing my muscles. My eyes were forced to close with the accelerated energy. I could feel my legs buckle below me. I began to sob deeply. Then Ron put his hand on my back between my shoulder blades to try to support me. The energy rushed through him too, and he burst into tears. In moments, we three big men were leaning on each other and crying like babies.

Soon it was over. The temple spirits of Kom Ombo were gone, back to heaven, free of their burden once and for all. I sat down on one of the temple stones and lamented. For thousands of years they had guarded this temple, waiting for this moment of release. I came, completed that cycle, and now they were free. I understood. Not telling me ahead of time about what this would be like was very wise. Quietly, I thanked Yokar for his wisdom in holding back.

As we returned to the cruise boat, I began to ponder the task ahead.

I wondered what the other temples would be like. I especially wondered about Karnak with all its dark spirits and history of blood sacrifices.

Yokar folded into my thoughts. "Do not worry. All is well. You performed admirably. We are encouraged that this task will go unimpeded." I sighed in relief. I felt a closeness I never felt before with Yokar. I appreciated his loving kindness and wise guidance more than ever.

The next morning, we arrived at Edfu. The carriages awaited our arrival. The absence of tourists was obvious. There was no endlessly revolving trail of horse buggies and bickering drivers. The streets were virtually empty. Only a few of the trinket salesmen's stalls and storefronts were open. The lull in tourist activity lay over the whole land like a dark cloud, and all seemed to suffer. As we rode along the streets, I wondered if the terrorists really knew what damage they were causing to their country with their fanatical behavior.

As I climbed down from the carriage, a sudden rush of elation struck me right in the chest. I paused to lean against the carriage to catch my breath. I realized that the temple guards knew I was coming. They greeted me before I had even entered the temple. Their energy was different; there was no sadness at this temple. It seems they understood completely what I was doing. They welcomed me as their liberator, with open arms. Like children, the spirits flooded around me, pushing and shoving to touch me, to experience a preview of their impending release.

It was wonderful. My eyes filled with tears. Their freedom was about to unfold. Now, I could have a glimpse of what it must have been like during the Exodus for Moses, when he freed the slaves in Egypt. Truly a time for celebrating. I wanted the others to see what I could see.

The temple ceremony at Edfu went smoothly. Soon after, Yokar uttered once again the sacred intonations of Vril. The spirits lifted from this place without lingering. Their task was done, and they left without sorrow, without remorse, in a great wave. They sailed up and onward. I thought of thousands of sparrows lifting from the trees and spiraling in the sky in a synchronous dance. I wondered for a moment what spiritual "south" would harbor them, for their winter's stay.

We left in complete silence. This time, the experience was totally different. It was actually easy. Except for the ceremony and my trance, it was effortless. Then Yokar added his commentary.

"You see, it can be easy when you surrender to the natural flow of life. They were ready and willing for a long time. They only needed to know that it was finally time to go. And that was transmitted at Kom Ombo."

"You mean they really knew from the release at the first temple?"

"Yes. The vibration of freedom travels easily among those who are burdened."

The Darkness Passes

That night, as the cruise ship readied for the negotiation through the locks at Esna, I felt a grim determination building toward Luxor and Karnak. From my experiences, I perceived them as the Mount Everest of evil places. I was not going to underestimate the forces this time around. I braced myself for a great spiritual battle. Then Yokar confronted me.

"Why do you stiffen yourself for Karnak?"

"Yokar, I think this will not go easy for us. I don't think the spirits are ready or willing to leave these temples. I think this will be a battle or an exorcism at best!"

I could feel Yokar scanning my heart, and then he broke off. There seemed to be a smile turning at the corner of his mouth as he studied me. "You're looking for a fight, aren't you? So, in this case, you think that justice will be served up by force, eh?" "Maybe so, Yokar. I'd like to give that one spirit that tried to curse me a taste of light he'll never forget!"

"Listen, my son. You must realize that your vigor to be the judge and executioner is inappropriate. We have not come to judge them. Even the wisdom that we possess is not sufficient to warrant passing judgment over them. The Most High will serve up the most appropriate measure for their learning in good season.

"You cannot set yourself up as separate from them. Remember, their ignorance could also be yours. You must never use your insight and wisdom to separate yourself from the lowliest of creatures. The opportunity to grow and advance will come as well, even for the truly dark ones."

"Yokar, you mean that even the great dark lord will have an opportunity to experience remorse and transform himself into light again?"

"Yes, Michael. Were it not so, then the laws of compassion would not reflect the infinite capacity for change that extends even to the darkest regions. This suggests that no matter how much darkness exists in any living creature's heart, opportunities have always existed, do exist, and will always exist for change and transformation with the Life Force. Without this grace, there is truly no hope."

I quietly pondered this.

Then Yokar added, "Oh, by the by, we suggest that you consider a ruse to deflect our Egyptian tour guide's attention tomorrow, at the temples of Thebes. We perceive that his zealous nature with regard to these holy artifacts may pose an obstacle to our agenda."

Suddenly I remembered. A psychic prediction was given to me through a friend before we set out this time for Egypt. A crystal would need to be realigned while on this journey. Now, I never pay much attention to psychic predictions. In the overall scheme of things, I have learned from Yokar, the prediction represents only a snapshot of the entire moving picture of life, at any moment. Anyway, it seemed strange that our guide this time might prove to be an obstacle to our purpose here. I wasn't sure, but I had the feeling that the prediction was talking about our guide. In any case, it meant that I would have to remain vigilant.

Although it was nearly two in the morning, I called an emergency meeting of some of the veterans of previous initiations on this journey. I explained to them Yokar's warning about our guide. Everyone agreed that our guide was exhibiting signs of a rigid perspective and some overprotectiveness of his native culture. It was to be expected. After all, he was Egyptian. Removing bound spirits from the temples might be perceived as a kind of defacing. I certainly didn't feel this to be true. If anything, I felt this mission was spiritually humanitarian on all levels. But from the local perspective, you never know! We developed a plan that would keep the guide busy. Meanwhile, some of the key members would assist me in carrying out my hidden agenda.

The next morning, we disembarked the cruise ship at Luxor, known as Thebes in ancient times. The temple of Luxor was located about ten minutes from the docks. The sister temple, the infamous

Karnak, was located a little more than a mile away and required a bus or cab ride from Luxor. Luxor would be our first stop, at my request. This order would set the stage for my ruse to unfold.

Once in Luxor, the group would go through the temple, while the guide would give the archeological details as usual. Then, I would lead everyone into the inner sanctuary, where Yokar would step in and utter the sacred Vril for the ceremony. Shortly afterwards, I would have Sharon, a veteran initiate who often served as my assistant, lead the group in a prayer-meditation in the Holy of Holies inner sanctum while I faked a bad reaction to trancing in the ceremony. My co-conspirators would avail me the necessary fresh air by walking me around outside the temple.

Once outside, the three of us would hail a taxi and rush off to Karnak to perform the necessary release ceremonies required before anyone from the group arrived. It was a bold plan, but would it work?

All good plans have some sort of contingency as back up. I believed I had one too, although I didn't know exactly how it would be played. A black American undercover cop by the name of Charles Leon had joined the group. Charles had come to Yokar after suffering a near-fatal stabbing by an underworld agent.

I agreed that he would record the entire journey, photographically, as part of his payment for the trip. He could speak a little Arabic and fit in well with the colorful native environment. He also believed himself to be from the ancient tribe of Anu. The problem with him was that he wasn't grounded, making him a bit of a wild card. I would use him if and when it was necessary to play out any alternative plans.

Charles became one of my co-conspirators in my plan to escape the attention of our guide. I told him to keep the guide distracted with whatever means he could, should our guide decide to wander from the prayer meditation.

The guide carried out his detailed discussion of the archeological aspects of the Luxor temple and signaled me when he was finished. I brought everyone into the Holy of Holies, and Yokar performed the ritual initiation. Afterwards, I pretended to experience some dizziness and requested Claude and Ron to escort me to the main courtyard outside of the temple hall for some fresh air.

The nearby street was a convenient place to hail a taxi for our jaunt to Karnak. The catch was, Yokar couldn't release the temple guards at Luxor first because we needed them to balance the darkness in the sister temple of Karnak while we were working there.

Sharon carried out her instructions and gathered everyone around to explain the need for group prayer and meditation. No one suspected that this was in any way unusual. A few minutes later, Charles found the guide becoming more than a little curious about my absence. So Charles decided to divert his attention by disappearing on purpose. The plan worked. It drew Sharon's angry attention onto Charles while she was trying to gather the group for meditation. Thus the guide was assigned to the case of finding Charles, the decoy, and not me. I learned later that Charles drew a lot of flack for being irresponsible to the group. But he maintained his role and said nothing.

We arrived in front of Karnak within three minutes. As we entered, I looked at the map of the temple ground plan showing Karnak's three temple complexes. Two older sites sat far in the back, leaving the modern temple near the front. This layout made my task more complicated. The two older sites were being reconstructed and were roped off in the most important places, the holy sanctuaries. There were armed sentries walking along the ropes to prevent anyone from crossing. I turned to Yokar for help.

"Yokar, we really need your help here. We seem to be blocked and cannot reach the older temples."

Moments later, Yokar entered. "We see the problem," he said. "We will handle it soon enough."

We paced along the roped area like three restless cats, waiting for a sign of Yokar's handiwork. Nothing. One of the guards saw us approaching and waved us away with his weapon. I thought to myself, He's carrying an automatic and it looks like an Israeli assault rifle. It was intimidating to look down the wrong end of the barrel. We backed up. But we didn't walk away. I talked about my plan once more, after we were inside the old area, to help pass the time. Ron would act as look-out/observer while Claude stood next to me until I came out of trance. All seemed reasonable, if only we could get past the guards.

I pulled some bakshish from my wallet, hoping that the guard would get the idea. He ignored me. The situation didn't look at all promising. We were about to give up hope when something happened. Another guard entered the area and approached the first guard. They began to talk with each other. Soon the new guard pulled a package of cigarettes from his pouch and offered one to the other guard, who seemed grateful. Then they chuckled together, apparently sharing a joke. The old guard took a sling bag from his shoulder and handed it to the new guard. They were going to change places.

We continued to watch as the old guard walked away. Now our attention was on the new guard. He looked at us as we approached the rope. I pointed to Claude, Ron, and myself and then to the old building area. Then I repeated my attempt to reveal some of my money. The guard stood motionless. I pondered for a moment. Were these guards the only honest guards in Egypt?

Claude began to lament, "Mike, I think Yokar has no effect on these guys!"

"Yeah, I know," I returned. "Maybe their minds are too dense for a Jedi mind trick!"

Just as we were about to give up, the guard pointed to an area further beyond the rope. Repeatedly he pointed to an area of sandy hills and high brush. He tempered his movements with a brief panoramic scan of the area, making sure no one was noticing.

I yelped, "That's it, boys. That's our cue."

We began to make our way along the rope, just on the outside. We were heading for the small hills to the south. I was expecting to see some sort of gate or something. There was just more and more rope and walls blocking our way.

I kept looking at the guard for further clues. I shrugged my shoulders at him indicating our confusion. He pointed again in the same direction with emphasis. The terrain became less civilized. Now the guard moved from his position, tracking our progress. He continued to point toward the hills with more emphasis.

I saw the area more clearly now. It was a good plan. The hills were out of normal view and would provide excellent cover for our entry into the forbidden area. The rope ended just at the foot of the rough. There was a fence, but it was half torn away. The opening was wide enough to permit the three of us to get through.

The guard was waiting at the embankment on the other side. After we joined him, he motioned for us to follow and spoke a little Arabic. Now the guard was in front, leading the way. Frankly, through the entire hide and seek, I lost my bearings. I really didn't know where we were going anymore. My imagination mingled with the sand and dust. I feared that we were being taken to an ambush. He stopped for a few moments in front of an old tree where several workmen were lounging, apparently on a smoke break.

The guard seemed to be well known. He shared some more of his cigarettes with the workmen. Suddenly, I realized that he was well off. There was good reason for all this generosity. He was on the take! I suspected that he was probably wealthy, for a guard. Then I knew that Yokar had chosen him well.

The guard took us a few more steps through some underbrush and there he revealed the temples, as seen from the back. He turned and smiled and pointed proudly at the sanctuary entrance. We smiled and nodded in approval. He tried to speak a little English, asking for his share of bakshish. I stepped forward and handed him some money, speaking in pigeon English, "Here is part now, more later. You watch for us." He smiled and nodded agreeably.

There emerged a new wrinkle we hadn't counted on. As we entered the sanctuary, we found a German archeologist and his wife standing in front of the entrance. He had his camera and notes spread out all over the sacrificial stone like it was his desk. From the look of it, he was planning to be there for another five years! We stood around admiring the Egyptian handiwork, playing like interested professionals. We knew if we appeared to be tourists, our cover would be blown.

We purposely ignored the German and his wife, and they in turn ignored us. We suspected that they believed us to be competitors. Some archeologists practice only a little science and a lot of vanity.

This was not our problem. But their presence was! Again I hailed Yokar internally. "Yokar. We have another problem here. If you could distract them for the needed few moments, we can dispense with this business and get on with the program."

In a flash, Yokar arrived on the scene. "Do not worry, we have created a disturbance in his affairs, sufficient to detain him for awhile."

"Thanks, Yokar. I knew you would help."

Like clockwork, the archeologist was called away, and we entered the sanctuary room of the most holy. There we waited for Yokar to enter. The archeologist returned moments later, however, and continued his paperwork. Claude and Ron were puzzled, and Ron exited the chamber casually to reconnoiter the situation. Soon the archeologist's wife returned, and an argument ensued between the archeologist and his wife. After some harsh words, they were both gone.

Ron returned. He smiled and offered a thumbs-up signal to Claude. Claude relayed the news to Yokar, who was now in my body and waiting to proceed. Yokar quickly entered into a long and complicated set of intonations that were very different than the usual sounds of an initiation rite. The tones carried a distinctly serious and ominous quality appropriate to an exorcism. Repeatedly, Yokar directed his intonation toward the altar and the surrounding stones as well as the chamber itself. Then he offered blessings into the air and into the Earth.

When it was over, Yokar simply declared in his usual manner, "It is finished."

He left quickly, leaving my limp body to fall into the capable hands of my friends. I returned to consciousness moments later. I looked up into their faces, bright and smiling. Then I inquired as to the outcome. I could feel a real difference in the chamber. The atmosphere wasn't as heavy as before. All seemed quiet and peaceful now. But we were not finished yet. There were still two more temples to clean.

We paid the guard the rest of his hard-earned bakshish. He

nodded with a smiling face and said, "Masalam, Doctor." Once again, I had that eerie feeling that he understood what I was doing there. We bid him a fond farewell as we made our way back to the other temple site. The second of the two older temples lay ahead. This one was the entire too familiar, infamous place where I had lost an initiate to the forces of darkness. I felt a twinge of fear mixed with a desire for revenge as we approached.

Yokar halted me in my tracks. "Michael, mind your dark feelings here," he warned. "You're not innocent and they know you well. And you are not welcome. These negative feelings can betray you and our purpose. Go with love, not vengeance."

"I understand, Yokar. I'll be careful. I'll begin to transmute my feelings right away."

"Good," he said.

I found a stone nearby to sit on. I began my meditation practice to find my point of origin. Suddenly, I was surrounded by many beings. It was very difficult to continue my practice with their snarling and chiding at me. They tried to engage me by picking on my weaknesses. They tried to humiliate me by reminding me that I failed to prevent the Japanese woman's alignment to the darkness. I thought, Interesting. They knew that I felt responsible for her temptation. They really do know me . . . even my unconscious feelings! Boy, were they tricky. I really did have to be careful.

Then I resolved to love myself and started my practice again. I went on to conjure my feelings of hatred and vengeance, the children of my fear. Each one of my feelings was like an egg that hadn't hatched. On the surface they were one thing, but broken, they became elements of my insecurity. I was alone with my weaknesses, and alone with my fear. Then, with a final breath, with total allowance, I consumed them, all of them, so that I could feel them, in my belly. I became the essence of my fear, personified. I continued this until there was nothing left outside of me. I possessed and digested it all. There was nothing left outside but strength, warmth, and confidence.

I had completed this practice from Yokar's teachings. I stood up and turned to face that hideous strength surrounding me. Armed with only compassion in my heart, I knew that my weakness was their weakness. With my love and understanding of my own weaknesses, I knew that I could embrace these pathetic creatures of the night. I extended myself to them unafraid. Again, I defined the nature of their impending release through my own path of self-acceptance.

I gave a brief tour to Claude and Ron, commenting on this vile place of treachery, deceit, and debauchery. As I entered the hall of the holies, the air was icy. The spirits were motionless and silent.

Without hesitation, I yielded my body once again to Yokar, who entered and began his solemn utterances. The intonations were strong and penetrating. Ron's body began to tremble uncontrollably. Claude began to feel queasy and braced himself against one of the pillars, believing that he was about to pass out.

The emotional and spiritual blood pacts to this place were finally broken by Yokar's calling in of higher forces. These slaves of darkness were finally free. Yokar had freed not only the spirits of their bondage but also the Earth of its complicity in the housing of it. There remained only one more temple.

This task was in some ways more difficult. This part of the temple had the easiest access to all traffic. The most important area, the Holy of Holies, was a virtual thoroughfare, with people pouring in like a river every few minutes. Within the Holy of Holies was a huge stone block, which had been used as a sacrificial stone. In here, as in the other temples of Karnak, human blood had been spilled. It was as though the dark spirits were using this place as their final stronghold with the flow of innocent people to defend them!

Yokar stood in my body for several minutes, quietly. Time passed like an eternity, as he waited for the right moment. When there were lulls in the crowds, individuals would linger, knowing intuitively that something was about to happen. Yokar waited even for those to leave.

Then, in one final act of force, he uttered the sacred expressions that split the energy and separated the darkness from Karnak forever. He left my body without fanfare. I returned to find Claude standing next to me, looking relieved. Ron seemed noticeably younger and walked around like he had an itch he couldn't scratch. Our job was done in Karnak.

As we exited the temple and proceeded along the avenue of sphinxes, our guide was just entering Karnak with the rest of the group from Luxor. He approached with an obvious disgruntled look. "So this is where you've been hiding. You will pay me many bottles of champagne for your absence!"

"No problem," I said softly to him with an easy smile.

I could tell that he was upset. Even though he was smiling, he wasn't happy about it. Charles approached me from the side and spoke with a Cheshire's grin. "So, how did it go?"

I looked at him, my lips twisted into a wry smile. I cocked one eyebrow and declared. "It's clean, Charles! You can photograph to your heart's content. You don't have to worry."

I sat down near one of the sphinxes just outside of the temple gates. The tiredness and strain finally hit my body. I knew that the worst was over.

My wife Dianne approached and hugged me. Her relief was apparent. She offered me water from her bag. It seemed that I had been sucking on the Sahara for the last few hours. I think I drank most of her supply in one gulp. I looked back on the hypostyle, the entrance chamber filled with the massive columns, and the main courtyard beyond. I felt like a runner after he's crossed the finish line.

I suddenly felt the need for a trophy. I turned to Dianne and asked her for my camera. I re-entered the hypostyle and courtyard clicking away with delight. After I had snapped thirty or more shots, I felt complete. I returned and began to unload the camera with some satisfaction. But when I opened the case, it was empty. I had been had! I was shooting away without any film. Outraged, I demanded another roll of film from Dianne and quickly loaded the camera with a measure of determination. Turning to face the temple once more, I stated with a defiant tone, "I'll be right back!"

I re-entered the hypostyle swiftly. Immediately, I started snapping away. When I reached the center pin, the point defining the center of the axis of the temple, I pointed my camera to the obelisk framing it with the greatest care. My camera suddenly sounded with a loud kerchunk! I looked down to examine the source of the unusual noise. The readout defining my shutter speed and f-stop were absolutely crazy. The outside limit of my camera's shutter was 1/2000th of a second. The reading was 45,000! This is not possible, I thought. Then I murmured under my breath, "What the hell is going on?"

I was utterly frustrated. But I knew in my heart it was hopeless. And I needed to let go of this. So, I yielded openly. "Okay guys, if you don't want me to shoot the place, I won't shoot the place!"

I strolled casually toward the hypostyle gate and my camera went kerchunk again. I looked down and the reading was now normal.

Yokar entered briefly to add his commentary. "Michael, you must understand. I have torn the darkness from this place and I have blessed the stones so that it may not re-enter. But it has not gone away. It lingers above, confused and anxious. The darkness will demand your respect and refuse to accept the mockery of your desire for a 'trophy'!"

"I got it, Yokar. Believe me, I got it! I have learned this lesson today very well."

Our boat was readying to sail in the afternoon for Dendera and Abydos, our last temples in this region. We had returned to the boat just in time for a late lunch. I took a body count and realized that we were missing one passenger, Charles. I knew that in his desire to photographically capture the heart of Karnak, he had forgotten the boat schedule. Ordinarily, I wouldn't be concerned. But I knew that Charles didn't have excess cash and would be stranded here were we to sail without him.

I grew worried for him. Then Sharon yelled out, "Oh, here he comes!" He was running frantically to the gangplank; his sweat was pouring like rain. I sighed. Now we were complete.

I retired to my cabin to rest for a while. But it didn't last long. There was a frantic knock on my door. It was Sharon. She was out of breath and obviously upset.

"Michael," she gasped. "You had better come quick. I think Charles is possessed!"

"What are you talking about, Sharon?"

I pulled my jacket from behind the door and closed it behind me, thinking to myself, Jesus what now? She continued her report as we entered the stateroom promenade.

"Well, he seemed okay at first," she went on. "And we were all sitting around having a good time talking. Then Bianca bought Charles a beer. Well, he just started to laugh and wouldn't stop. Now he mumbles to himself continuously."

I groaned. "Oh, lord. What next? Where is he now?"

"I left him talking with Howard on the lounge deck," she said.

When I entered the lounge deck, I found Charles sitting erect in his chair. Howard was giving him the third degree. Howard was a middle-aged, paunchy-looking man who had been studying the pyramid in Gizeh for many years, trying to unveil its secrets. I suspected it was one of the main reasons he agreed to go on this trip. As I approached, I could hear Howard's favorite subject being discussed—the great pyramid. Howard had seen his chance to probe the spirits for more information. I stopped dead between them.

Turning to Howard, I silently commanded in Vril, "Howard! Stop!"

He stopped short in his questioning and looked startled. Once I had his attention, I continued to chastise him. "What are you doing Howard? Damn it, man! Go somewhere and chill out."

Howard smiled sheepishly at me. Then he lumbered off to another part of the lounge. I directed all my attention to Charles Leon, ignoring the rest of the group. If he was possessed, like the Japanese woman, then I knew I had to get him away from the others quickly. Charles' body turned and looked in my direction. His eyes were blank, hollow, and glowing, and his face pale and pasty, like old chocolate. Charles was clearly not at home! Again, I used Vril to command the spirits in him.

"Charles, you come with me right now."

He stood up and followed me obediently. Fortunately, his room was on the lower deck, far away from the others. On our way past the purser's desk, I stopped to check the manifest, to see who was rooming with him. "Alan, huh. Well, this ought to be interesting!"

We went into his room and closed the door behind us. I commanded him to sit down on his bed. I sat next to him. He was drooling and still grinning. I continued strongly, knowing that I was not speaking directly to him. "This will not do!" I said. "I cannot allow you to do this."

I stared into the face of the darkness as it grimaced and altered his face into a range of grotesque shapes, while still smiling at me. His voice gurgled and seemed to echo through the room. Then he spoke. "Please don't make us leave. We are not wanting the body. We are above the body. We just need to be near this body for now."

I stared at the spirits with a firm resolve of a disapproving parent. "Charles must be in the body now. It is not good for him to be away. I demand that he be returned to his body this instant."

"We assure you that he will come to no harm. We just need to be near this body for now."

"Then return him at once!" I demanded.

Charles returned. He looked very strung-out. Then he spoke. "Michael, what happened? I was running to make the boat. My God, I forgot! I was so busy taking the pictures, I completely forgot. I'm sorry. I'm sorry."

"Relax, Charles. You're gonna need some rest, a lot of it. Now, I want you to stay in your room. Okay? You're not alone! I need you to stay here until I can figure something out, all right? You must stay here for the night, until I come for you. Do you understand?"

He looked at me with a hurt expression and reluctantly agreed. "Okay, if you insist."

"Yes, I insist. It's very important, Charles. You're in a very delicate position right now. I'll come for you." Then I left, easing the door closed, without further comment. As I returned to the lower promenade, I turned to Yokar. "We have to talk!" I demanded. "I need to understand what's going on here! I am a little more than confused."

Yokar responded quickly. "I realize you're wondering how this could happen since the work today. But I assure you all is going according to plan."

"How do you figure that?"

"You'll remember, I told you that I broke the bonds that bound the spirit to these temples. I told you that the darkness was not gone, just separated. Once the energy became separated, it was confused and anxious and hovered above the temples. But the energy could not descend because I blessed the stones so that they could not re-enter."

"Yes. I understand. But what has that got to do with Charles' body being taken?"

"When Charles realized that he was going to miss the passage on the cruise ship, he became panicky. Anxiety and fear filled his heart."

"Yeah, so?" I asked impatiently.

"The darkness and Charles' feelings matched, so they were attracted to him. He brought them to the boat."

"So Charles brought all the darkness from Karnak onto the boat and that's good?"

"Yes. This is good. The darkness doesn't understand about leaving. We wanted the spirits to get the idea of leaving Karnak. A cruise ship is a perfect metaphor for them to understand. But we had to lure them to come aboard. To accomplish this, we needed a vessel that would duplicate, in most respects, their feeling shape: confusion, anxiety, and fear. Charles became that host. It wasn't a problem until Charles imbibed some fermented liquid. This lowered his vibration sufficiently to let them enter and take over the body."

"I see."

"But we believe that you handled the situation very well. Now they are above the body once again. They respect you. That is good!"

I suddenly felt insecure. "You really think so?"

"Yes," Yokar confirmed.

My body shuddered uncontrollably. Reality was truly awesome! My mind was a tumble. It tried over and over to grasp what was happening. I fought like hell to stay on the ground. I decided suddenly to go onto the top deck for a bit of night air. I really wanted a stiff drink, but after what I just heard, I settled for a Coca-Cola.

I didn't sleep much through the night. When morning finally came, I was defending against the dawn. I was not always courageous in the face of the onslaught of the day.

My window offered a fine view of the Nile. A gentle cyan and white sky and a warm breeze brought a welcome softness to my tired soul. I felt weary. The water below rhythmically swelled into a thousand deep blue mounds moving swiftly away. If only I could lie upon it, I thought. What a wonderful massage it would give!

I caught sight of a great white bird afloat on a cluster of old straw, weeds, and junk. As he drifted by, he struggled to stay balanced on the slowly sinking mass. Suddenly, I could identify with his precarious choice of perches. I too was balanced precariously, looking for firmer ground on which to stand. Strange, how I perceived myself mostly as a coward. Yet I found myself in some of the most outrageously demanding situations.

This day was to be no easier than the last. I took a deep breath of Nile-drenched air and braced myself for another round of terrifying adventure.

With one quick glance at my watch—Hmm . . . seven thirty—I quickly got dressed and made my way to the purser's daily roster. I wanted to see if anything significant had changed in the captain's schedule. Hmm . . . looks okay. Breakfast at 8:30 . . . good.

Then I made my way to Charles' room and gently tapped on his door. "Good morning, is anybody up? It's Michael. Can I come in?"

A voice answered but I couldn't tell who it was. "Yes. Come on in. The door is open."

As I entered the room, I found Alan sitting up in his bed. Charles was still asleep. Alan smiled a little.

"How're you doing, Alan?"

Alan looked down for a moment, seemingly to consider his words. "It's okay. Charles talked a lot last night. It was hard to get any sleep."

"I can imagine!" I said supportively. "How is he doing?"

"He complained of being locked in his room, mostly."

"Yeah, I know." Then I hastened to add, "But it was necessary, you know. Even though the confinement was only figurative. I had to keep him away from people like Howard and Ken. And then there were the others to consider. It's going to be hard to keep the rumors down to a small roar!"

Alan nodded affirmatively. "I understand."

"Do you think he's gonna want to eat?" I asked.

"I don't know," Alan went on. "Maybe you should ask him."

I gripped Charles' shoulder gently and offered a soft jiggle. "Charles. Charles . . . are you hungry?" He groaned. His eyes opened quickly. He looked back over his shoulder and stared at me.

"Huh?" He said, appearing startled. "Oh. No . . . no, not really. I'll wait till later."

"Are you sure?"

"Yeah. I'm sure. My stomach is a little upset."

"Okay. I'll be back shortly after breakfast. We'll talk then."

"Yeah, sure," he acknowledged, as he turned over.

Later, at breakfast, I made the rounds of all the tables to see how everyone was feeling. They all had the same look, washed out like they had been drinking all night. Apparently no one slept. The lack of sleep didn't affect anyone's appetite, however. Everyone was going for seconds and thirds. I figured it was an emotional reaction.

We weren't due to arrive at Dendera for a few hours. I would have time to work with Charles. I found that Alan's meal consisted of honey scraped from the assortment of little condiment tubs on the table. Alan was a soft-spoken young man from France who had become interested in Yokar's lectures after he came to live in New York. He and Charles had become friends and roomed together during the trip.

"I want to work with Charles in your room for a little while. Is that okay with you?"

He smiled. "Sure, no problem."

I wasn't sure how I was going to deal with Charles. I figured I would play it by ear, as usual. When I came to his room, he was sitting on his bed reading.

"Hi, Charles," I said casually. "How're you feeling?"

"Okay, I guess." He looked troubled.

I tried to press him further. "Anything wrong?"

"Well, I wasn't wild about being confined to my quarters, you know!"

"I know. I'm sorry for that. But I thought it was best. You understand?" He didn't respond.

Once again something popped out that I wasn't prepared for. I realized then that Yokar must have been prompting my unconscious. "I have something planned for you that will help." I stayed open and relaxed. I waited patiently for more unconscious prompting from Yokar. "I want you to lie on your bed with your head at the foot. Okay? Then just close your eyes. Yokar and I are going to work energetically on you for a bit. So just relax."

I took a deep breath and prepared myself as though I were about to begin a healing. I shook out my hands and pressed my palms together, calling up the neutral component of the Life Force. Then I placed my hands around his head, cupping them as a cradle on both sides. I could feel Yokar's energy begin to stream into my body.

Suddenly, I couldn't help but stare at Charles' belly. There, just above his abdomen, began to form a ball of light. It was growing. Charles opened his eyes and glanced down along his body. He saw it too.

"Oh, God!" He cried. "What is that?"

I didn't understand what Yokar was doing, but I tried to reassure Charles. "Just relax, Charles. It's going to be good. Just let it happen."

Meanwhile, the ball of light continued to grow larger and illuminate the room with a soft glow. It was dazzling. The light didn't stream outwards. It seemed to fold in on itself like some kind of spherical container.

Then it opened up like a giant camera iris and revealed brilliant colors inside. I was spellbound and couldn't take my eyes off of it. Yokar interrupted this captivating moment with instructions.

"This will be the vessel that will carry the dark ones home. You must extend your inner will fibers into the vessel and encourage them to enter."

"Yes, Yokar."

Charles began to sob. "It's beautiful. It's so beautiful. I can see them leaving. They're going into the ball aren't they?"

"Yes, Charles. They're going home. Just relax and don't fight it. Just let them go."

I continued to extend my will into the ball until all of the spirits had entered. It was very difficult. I felt sick to my stomach. The connection to the ball left a peculiar sensation in my belly. It felt like an itch combined with queasiness. I tried to keep myself stable so that I didn't throw up. Just when I thought I couldn't hold out any longer, the iris closed. Instantly, I felt better. My body and Charles' body slumped in relief simultaneously. We both watched as the ball started to get smaller. I realized it wasn't shrinking, but going away. Charles continued to weep after it.

"It's so wonderful."

Then it was over. I knew that Charles was out of danger and my job was done. "Whew! I'm glad that's over," I said with relief.

"Am I free?"

"Yes, Charles, you're free now."

Even though we still had more temples to release, I felt encouraged that the worst of it was over. It would be easy now to do the rest. Sadness entered me once again—I knew we were nearing the close.

We went on to complete the initiations at Dendera and Abydos. The spirits behaved very much as they did at Edfu. They were joyously relieved and anxious to leave.

Back in Cairo, the group prepared for the final ceremony and release of the great pyramid temple of Gizeh. Feelings were high. By now, everyone except for our guide knew what I was doing in the temples. I still thought it wise that he did not know. The preparations to enter the great pyramid carried on as usual. All of the pomp and circumstance of difficulty and squabble from the guards and soldiers became like a vaudeville routine. I was removed from it now. My focus centered on the spirit temple guards and their welfare.

This would be the last initiation rite I would ever perform in this temple. It was a solemn occasion. I could feel the extra effort being made by all the spirits in attendance. Yokar made his final utterances for all those present. His tone in the sacred Vril was special. He seemed to speak to all initiates throughout all existence, completing their fire rite. He spent extra time addressing the spirits of the great temple that night, thanking them for their untiring effort and diligence.

The next morning, we entered for the last time, just before dawn, for the sealing ceremony. Yokar began as usual and blessed the four directions and the Heaven and Earth. Then he began the sealing. The excitement swelled up within the initiates. Their ordeal was over. They were acolytes now and feeling their joy and gratefulness. Everyone hugged and cried, laughing. All wanted to be present when Yokar released the temple guards. He agreed.

He began by calling out the record of the work and praising the spirits for their unfailing duty. He praised the Heavens and the Earth for their grace in providing the opportunity to serve the Most High and the unfolding consciousness of mankind. He praised the elementals for their assistance in the healing of human spirit. Then he uttered the final sacred tones to release them all.

There was a kind of reluctance. It was not fear that prevented them from leaving, but a sense of deep and abiding admiration for the initiates turned acolytes. It rained down from above the chamber and filled the room with a soft golden glow. It was a gentle kiss farewell and a fond wish for goodwill in their continued duties on the Earth. Then they left, all save one.

Everyone began to exit the chamber chattering with excitement. Claude, Ron, and I remained until the last. I looked up to see a shadowy white figure wearing a turban, with arms outstretched across the ceiling of the chamber. He seemed to embrace us with great smiling love and admiration.

I kneeled to give honor to this last spirit. Then I broke into uncontrolled sobs. One hand covered my face and tears while I extended the other hand above me, bidding the spirit a fond farewell. Claude and Ron stood near the chamber door, holding each other with arms locked together, bursting into tears. We all watched as the last spirit faded from view.

The three of us descended to the grand gallery in silence. Each one of my steps said goodbye to the Great Pyramid. When we reached the entrance cave, we found everyone else waiting, with his or her robes off. Together we exited to the early morning sunlight.

To our surprise, more than a hundred Japanese dressed in special robes, kneeling on pillows before us on the plateau below, greeted us. They were going through some special ceremony honoring the pyramid. We all knew that this was no accident. How fitting! The unconscious acknowledgment of spirit was happening on the outer level, too. It was a great celebration. When they were finished, we descended the stones onto the plateau to enjoy our celebration breakfast.

PILGRIMAGE TO THE MOON

"There is a need to deal with the night side of being," Yokar said with finality.

His presence introduced strong pain along my neck. Flashes of cool white light like giant strobes went off inside my head. Then the experience began to shift, alternating between electrical surges down my spine and the friendly sound of his voice creating fuzzy warmth in my belly. I felt very dizzy. I wanted to ask what he was doing, but I was afraid to interrupt.

"The solar experience develops only the light force in the body. The night force must also be developed, for the sake of balance."

Before I could declare my discomfort with the internal fireworks, it all ended. The ringing in my ears trailed off into silence. The pain, lights, and electricity were gone. Silence was all around me although I could still feel Yokar's presence. My alarm about the apparent internal short circuit generated many questions, but I could ask only one. "What do you have in mind, Yokar?"

His energy withdrew, just as though he were taking a deep breath. I was suspended in a kind of electric silence. I barely allowed my heart to beat, waiting for an answer. Several moments passed. I knew, when he hesitated this way, that he was going to introduce something new. A warm rush swept over me. Then my spirit teacher returned with his usual enthusiasm.

"You will go to Greece. There you will re-enact the ancient ritual of Orpheus, at Delphi."

An anxiety overwhelmed me, and that familiar knot started to grow in the pit of my stomach. Yokar wanted me for another mission, another quest filled with unknowns, ripping away my sense of comfort.

Since the very first initiations, I had experienced some continuous anxiety. Now, after many journeys, I was only slightly more comfortable. More than a hundred people had been taken through the first threshold of spiritual awakening. Watching Yokar evoke the energy of ancient rites, in temples 3000 years old, was mind-boggling. The experience helped to keep me humble, but I could feel the responsibility growing.

After receiving Yokar's news about the Greek journey, I contacted a good friend who knew about Greece. His name was Manos. When I called, his wife Barbara answered.

"Hi," she greeted warmly. "Manos is really busy. Can you hold on for just a few moments?"

"Sure," I answered.

Manos was a large Greek man, sporting a silver-white goatee and a black ponytail. He had a sense of humor and a good heart. One could say he was even generous to a fault. I found him easy to know. There was a special quality about him, of having known life fully. His knowledge about most things seemed endless. When I realized that he was only a few years older than I, I felt I had been asleep my whole life. I always liked to think of him as Alexis Zorba.

Manos owned a small video facility, where he produced industrial video pieces. His system had developed some trouble, and my engineering services had been needed. Months later, we collaborated on a new design for a larger system to accommodate his growing business.

While working closely, we had many talks, and Manos eventually learned of my activities with Yokar. Being a practical man, he was reluctant to accept what I was doing. Yokar had been speaking through me in public for almost five years, and the information was astounding. I explained that I provided private counseling sessions, and each month Yokar spoke about a particular subject that followed a theme. Other nights, he would answer questions.

Manos seemed interested and eventually attended Yokar's bi-monthly group sessions while retaining some skepticism. One night after group, I became curious about his reactions.

"So, Manos, what did you think?"

"Well . . . ," he began slowly, appearing hesitant about showing enthusiasm for Yokar, "I don't know." He shrugged.

Suddenly, there was a voice at the other end of the line. "Mr. Michael, how're you doing?"

It was Manos. I told him what Yokar said about the Orphic initiation.

Manos responded, "Hmm . . . that's interesting."

I went on say that it was certain that I could use his help to research some aspects of the ancient rites. Yokar promised to clarify any ambiguities.

Not much was known about the ancient rituals of Orpheus. There were only a few obscure references in the writings of Greek philosophers. Scholars have speculated on certain details, based on engraved or painted urns found in caves.

We agreed to have several meetings to iron out any details and to discuss Manos' involvement in the journey. His family lived in Greece. Although he had had a falling out with them, he felt confident that he could be helpful.

Visions were pouring in from Yokar constantly, building a patchwork blueprint of our task ahead. It was not complete, but with the research Manos added, the picture rapidly became clear. It was very exciting.

We began with a map of mainland Greece. Following the path of the sacred numbers, spelled out in the ancient writings, we could see the "golden section" appearing everywhere. These proportions defined the mathematical value of phi, in which the ratio of the whole to the larger part was the same as the ratio of the larger part to the smaller. The critical path we needed to take on the journey was confirmed. The sites marked a pattern that described the way psychic energy would flow if certain organs of the body were stimulated. The rituals would then represent a sequence of stimulating those organs and opening the psychic channels.

Now that we knew where to go and roughly what to do, we had to deal with practicalities. Manos set out to find travel and lodging arrangements through his friends and contacts in Greece. It was time to inform all of the Egyptian initiates that the lunar cycle of their spiritual work was about to unfold.

Having just returned from Egypt a short time before, many of the participants had exhausted their financial resources. Dianne phoned everyone. The time would be in September, a time of the Autumnal Equinox the ancient Greeks called "Boedromin."

The excitement was contagious. Calls began to pour in from all the initiates. My fears of the unknown gave way as I became immersed in the details of preparation.

The Japanese initiates needed to know about this new opportunity, too. I scheduled a visit to Japan in the months that followed. I found the Japanese economy entering a serious recession and the atmosphere in Japan more conservative than ever. Jobs were scarce, and few wanted to risk their income, even for a special journey. But I knew that a small band of dedicated and enthusiastic souls would be determined to continue the work in Greece.

After I returned to New York, Yokar surprised me with another announcement. "The time of integration is over for the initiates!" He declared. "The initiates must begin their deeper training and learn the use of Vril."

"How will I do that, Yokar? I can hardly do it myself!"

"This will accelerate your own work, too," he declared. "In the teaching, there will arise a mastery for you. Besides, the need is great to begin attuning their energy. Their energy is going to have to work smoothly together, and they will need to know how to work with the harmonies of the Earth. We will give you special patterns that will guide each student. You must schedule the training immediately."

During the months that followed, regularly scheduled classes in New York were set up for the initiates. To begin, I was teaching how to activate the unnamed organ. It wasn't like any normal way of speaking! Feelings, visual patterns in the form of shapes and colors need to be expressed with rhythms of sound simultaneously. The sound of the rhythm wasn't as important as the effect that the rhythm had on the student's breath. Everyone was surprised at the difficulty of the techniques. I encouraged them to form small practice groups and meet more often.

I wanted Yokar to reveal the entire system of temple training originally offered in Atlantis. He was reluctant. The attitude with regard to commitment and force of will was weaker in this culture, he said, making the study much more difficult. I told him that he should reconsider, since there had been some progress among the initiates. He told me that he would think about it.

Yokar addressed the initiates in their first class.

"Vril is the mother tongue of all living beings in the universe, all life," he said. "The Life Force responds best to it. So now, it is time for all initiates to learn the language of the Life Force. To accomplish this, it will be necessary to align the subtle bodies. This way, the energy flows properly. Without this flow, nothing can be done!"

One night, Yokar came to me as I was taking a shower. He dropped a picture into my head and asked me to record it.

"Could I finish my shower first?" I protested.

But he insisted, "Record it now while the energy is best."

Yokar referred to any kind of drawing or writing as recording something. I surmised this must've been from his early experience in Atlantis. The scribes had to literally carve, chisel, or draw things upon wood, stone, or skins in the tribal days before tec logii or technology (tec logii is pronounced teck-low-gee). In Atlantean, tec means "fierce" and logii means "knowledge."

Yokar explained that in the later periods of advanced tec logii, the Atlanteans learned to store their information directly into the Akasha via crystal gates. The Akasha was a sticky quality of the astral field of consciousness and was accessible only by intonation. The crystal gates were called Ruune stones or library crystals.

I sat dripping as he went on.

"To help align the subtle bodies, you will need an elemental pattern. This pattern that you see now organizes the energy to flow through the body. It will channel the various vibrations in the right sequence."

I responded rather disrespectfully. "That all sounds great, but I'm tired and it is running in one ear and out the other, if you know what I mean."

At that moment, I began to feel a peculiar sensation traveling down my spine. It was a mixture of tingling and a distinct icy quality.

Before I could grasp what was going on, I was suddenly wide-awake. The tiredness was gone! Now I was ready to record the Library of Congress if he had wanted it!

"Okay. You win, Yokar. Let me get some drawing paper and we'll get this thing you call an elemental pattern recorded."

When it was done, I stared at it for a few moments and wondered. My eyes went blurry. I rubbed them to re-adjust my focus. Again I stared at the drawing and again my vision went soft. Then I shook my head. I must still be tired, I thought.

I shoved the paper aside and stretched my arms above my head. Once I hit the pillow, sleep washed over me.

The next day, Yokar returned. "The pattern you have recorded must be formed on a nonconductive plate," he said. "The pattern must be formed with metal, preferably gold. The initiates need to wear this pattern over their hearts when they meditate. It will coordinate their energy and assist them in joining their energy together with the others and their energy with the Earth."

"Yokar that will be expensive. Gold is not cheap here!"

He continued, "A coating of this metal will be sufficient over another metal, like copper. This pattern must not be shown to any noninitiate. You understand? It has the ability to influence consciousness and will attract attention."

"I understand. Consider it done, Yokar."

The knowledge of electronic manufacturing helped with this new task. I called several circuit board companies to have it made by an etching process. Only one would agree to make the pattern without a lot of questions being asked. Weeks went by, and the first batch was delivered to the initiates in New York. The instructions for its use became the basis for some additional training.

Preparations for Greece continued to proceed smoothly. One day, I sat with Dianne, staring out the window. The Round Valley Reservoir stretched out in the distance. Its watery blue reflection sat surreal in the green hills of Hunterdon County, rolling away from my view. Dianne softly caressed my shoulders as she asked, "What're you looking at?"

I sighed. "It's so peaceful here. I'm glad we're here."

My body shuddered for a moment. She reached around me, surrounding me with her attention. I felt so important when she did that.

"What's wrong?" she whispered.

"I don't know. Its only days before we leave for Greece. I guess I feel those pre-trip jitters again."

She leaned over me, whispering into my ear, "It'll be okay."

She punctuated her solace with a gentle kiss. Somehow, I believed her. I think she could've said anything then and I would have believed it.

The momentous day finally arrived. Manos and Barbara were already at the airport, checking arrivals in. They looked harried. Soon everyone arrived and we boarded our flight. As I strapped myself in, a throbbing pain jolted me at the base of my spine. Dianne glanced over toward me. She had seen that look before. She leaned over, gripping my arm softly.

"Are you okay?"

"I can't move," I reported. "Yokar is pumping me with new energy again and it's really painful."

She shifted her grip from my arm to my hand and squeezed tightly. There was little else she could do.

The flight was nine hours. My hopes for writing were curtailed by my seating arrangement. The bulkhead was immediately in back, preventing my seat from reclining. There was no room for my portable computer to sit in front comfortably. I decided to join our party, already taking a good stretch in the aisles.

As I approached, Claude interrupted his conversation with the others. He took me aside and said, "I would like to talk to you about one of Yokar's spiritual practices from his recent lectures."

"Which one?" I asked.

"Would you tell me about the meditation to manifest any reality?"

"Yeah. Sure, no problem. What part don't you understand?"

"Well," he went on, "maybe you could explain from the beginning."

I prefaced the explanation with some important ideas Yokar had taught me.

"Claude, there have been many things said about creating your own reality as you desire it. Some of it is truthful, but, by and large, it is full of half-truths too."

I spoke to Claude about the concept of "creative visualization." This is a very popular idea and seems to make a lot of sense. It works with the problem of self-esteem and negative habitual thinking. This is a very important part of the process of creation because if you don't feel good about yourself, you can't ask for anything. But this concept is still incomplete and only half truthful. There are many people trying it and few enjoy any real success with it. It leaves them frustrated and thinking incorrectly. When there is failure, the belief is that they don't deserve the bounty promised them! This technique does not take into account the true mechanics of creation!

"The ignorance about how we can manifest what we want is astounding. I really believe that the truth of our ability has been known for a long time, but those who fear and want to control things covered up the knowledge!

"It's really simple once you get the hang of it! But there are some important things you need to know that Yokar taught me." I repeated what Yokar had told me about the Life Force. It is an energy that supports all living things. It surrounds us, penetrates us, and provides our every sustenance. It is literally the driving force of life. It is intelligent and sensitive to our every whim. Additionally, it scans us like radar and determines what we are feeling and thinking. From what it picks up, it can determine what we want and need. The Life Force is the great provider. It does not judge or discriminate about what we desire. It will manifest both positive and negative experience, depending on what we ask for. It is at the heart of all manifestation.

"Yokar told me that the ancient Atlanteans discovered the Life Force after many thousands of years of observing life unfolding before them. They determined that the energy of Life flows in a balanced way, that is, a neutral quality. They realized that the Life Force is made up of three parts: a male or positive propulsive part, a female or negative attractive part, and a neutral part. As it flows, it responds to the energetic consciousness of all living beings and becomes divided into varying degrees of polarized potential, male and female. The precise way in which the energy comes together manifests all reality according to what is required."

"I see," Claude said. "This meditation can access those polarities?"

"Exactly! By comparison, creative visualization is only part of the process. It's accurate in that the Life Force will follow consciousness. But in that technique, the person visualizes what he wants and will see himself already obtaining it without any other consideration. So doing that will short circuit the potential energy that might have been created by the visualization. Do you know what I mean?"

"Well . . . I don't know. Why don't you go on—it's getting clearer for me."

"Okay. You see, Yokar said that real manifestation must follow the 'law of cooperation.' That means that no single conscious being can control everything. That would be dangerous! Instead, everything really cooperates with everything else. When you ask for something, you have to be willing that it will also be in harmony with what everything else needs.

"So, for example, you might not want it to rain. If you demand that to be so, then you might be violating the needs of a lot of plant life that would need the water. You see what I mean? That doesn't mean what you want will take away from what someone else wants. That idea is a lie, propagated by those who want you to believe there isn't enough to go around. In that way, they control the will of the consumer! But it's possible to obtain anything if you can be patient. This way, it fits in with the natural scheme of things."

"Okay, Michael. So, how do I start the process and raise the potential?"

"This meditation does not require any physical preparation to begin. For example, you don't need to sit down in a quiet place and assume specific postures unless this is preferred. I've actually done it while walking down the street!

"Next you will need to disrupt the balance of the Life Force. In truth, it won't be your energy that will actually accomplish the manifestation. You'll be mobilizing the Life Force to act for you. To do that, you need to be very clear about what you want! I don't mean just clear in your head, but clear in your heart, too! Before you ask for what you want, you need to determine if you are in total agreement about having what you want."

I said that most people want money when they think about manifesting something. That's not a problem, but, very often, they haven't thought through all their feelings about having money to spare! When I ask people to examine their deeper feelings, they sometimes discover a fear that having abundance means losing their friends. In this case, the fear is that their friends may be enjoying only a moderate income and associated life style. They would no longer be comfortable associating with someone who is abundant and living a style of life that is commensurate with the abundance! There is an unconscious desire to block wealth, in order to prevent the loss of friendship.

"The next step is the conjuring of the potential for creation. The Life Force naturally seeks to balance everything. You could say it's so busy it constantly looks to rest. When the polarities of energy are balanced, in the quiescent state, then it has inertia to move. That's why it takes more than visualization to get the Life Force moving!

"When the Life Force is balanced, it has no actual ability to do anything, but the potential to do something is infinite. So when people say 'The possibilities are endless,' they're absolutely right! To create something, you have to unbalance the Life Force and awaken the energy potential of each component, the male and female forces. Once released, the potential energy becomes actual energy released to do work, manifesting your desire!

"This is where your consciousness plays an important role: to direct the male and female potential energy to manifest. When the energy is released, it is formless, waiting to be formed into your desire. Your visualization must be used to 'mold' the energy into the 'desire form.' The individual parts of the Life Force do this automatically, because they follow consciousness. If you make desire molds, the male and female energies of the Life Force will surround the molds and adhere to them, copying the desire mold shape."

Claude's brow wrinkled at this point, indicating some confusion. "It sounds like you are making more than one mold. Is that so?"

"Yes! Picture this. When you visualize your desire, you need to see and understand what is male and female about your desire. You see, all manifested things have male and female dualistic properties hidden within their nature."

"What do you mean by that?" Claude asked.

"Well, for example, you want your book to sell, right?"

"Certainly!" Claude confirmed.

"Okay," I said. "There is a male and female part to that reality. So you need to break it down and see those parts to assure that creation. The male component of your desire is to see all those people looking to buy a book that would be just like yours. It's the expansiveness of buying energy spreading everywhere, or positive propulsive energy. But I hasten to add, it must not, in fact, be your book they're buying."

"Why not?" Claude asked.

"Because then you would be robbing the Life Force potential of its ability to manifest your desire. If you see your book being bought, then you gave it to yourself mentally and short-circuited the desire. By making a homogenous mental mold, you already got what you want, in your fantasy!"

"Hmm . . . I see. So what is the female mold made of?"

"The female component is the negative attractive. The energy is like a pulling or suction feeling. That means it must be a need, your need, the need to sell your book to a lot of people! When you feel your need on the one hand, you must hold it out, mentally separate from the vision of people looking for a book like yours, on the other hand. In fact, the meditation is centered around suspending the extension of these two separate ideas in your mind at the same time—that is, simultaneously!"

Claude added, "Most people have trouble thinking of two things at once, you know!"

"Well, in that case, I always suggest they swing from one idea to the other like a slow mental pendulum. You charge and extend into the universe each idea separately without ever combining the two. This disrupts the balance of the Life Force."

"So how do you know if you have disrupted the Life Force?"

"Yokar said, a good clue is that you suddenly feel sexually excited during the meditation! It will feel like a tickling in the genitals. At this point, Yokar said, you should release the mental projections. As the desire you mentally projected is withdrawn, the action to keep the molds separate also vanishes.

"When you withdraw, the separate molds collapse and the polarized male and female energies come together. Their sudden collapse generates neutral force in the form of your completed and manifested desire.

"Claude, Yokar stressed one point: if your desire mold is homogenous and not a separate male and female mold, your desire will be neutral and have no effect on the potential energy of the Life Force. No manifestation will occur."

"Okay . . . I think I understand now. Thanks, Michael."

"You're welcome, Claude."

We all returned to our seats to receive the next scheduled meal. Before long, the announcement came that we were on final approach. I sat up, feeling a little disoriented. I realized we would be on the ground soon and a thrill raced up my spine. A glow of orange haze hovered ominously over the city of Athens. Ugh! I thought. It must be the Benzena.

The Greek term for Benzene gas is Benzena, the automobile fuel used in most foreign countries. It's effective and cheap but hell on air quality. After the plane parked, we emerged from the cabin into dry, warm air, a bright white and sunny day. We transferred to the hotel without a hitch.

At the hotel, we met Leftaris, our guide. He wore a full beard, roughly trimmed. His dark hair and beard contrasted with his deep blue eyes and warm smile. Speaking softly, he was immediately apologetic for his poor English. His accent sounded slightly Italian.

"My second language is Spanish. Please forgive me. Usually, I devote my efforts to only Spanish tours," he said. He held up our brochure, waving it in his hand, smiling broadly. "After having read the brochure, I was compelled to cancel all of my Spanish tours to make room for this adventure."

Struck by this statement, I surmised that Yokar had been hard at work here in Greece. Afterwards, Leftaris pulled me aside.

"Ah . . . I have taken the liberty to suggest a few things that are not on the itinerary, but I really believe with all my heart, ah . . . that you will feel these are important."

There was a look of concern on his face as if he expected my disapproval. I felt confident that his intuition was fully synchronous with Yokar and our needs. I quickly assured him that he had my complete support. His face relaxed and his smile returned. His head lifted, tilting back slightly as he lingered. His gaze narrowed in my direction. There was a slight twinkle of light in his eyes.

Everyone gathered in front of the hotel. Vasilios, our ground operator, greeted us and welcomed us to Greece. Then he announced he would be joining us on the trip, to insure every possible amenity.

The next morning, we were underway. Leftaris introduced Demetri, who would be our driver throughout the trip. Leftaris went on to say, "You have only to discover the natural grace of this man and his driving skill. We affectionately call him The Master of the Wheel."

Later, as we passed oncoming buses on the road, other bus drivers yelled out to Demetri in Greek. I asked Leftaris about this.

"You see," he explained as he gestured toward the other buses, "even the other drivers call for his blessings!"

I marveled that they all respected Demetri and expressed their deepest affection for him. There was a kind of awe, or reverence that flowed toward him. I decided to observe Demetri more closely. I realized this was no ordinary man; he had also been chosen for this task.

As the bus proceeded toward Elefsis, Leftaris began his discussion of the path of the ancient initiates. He surprised me by proclaiming with a charming smile, "Here we are proceeding along the very same route as did the initiates of ancient times."

He glanced at me to see my reaction. I simply smiled and gave him a "thumbs up" sign. He told Demetri to pull over for a moment. He had something special to show us. Leftaris pointed over to the left side of the road. Almost invisible to the eye were some outcroppings of limestone. The stone had been carved out, revealing several tiny alcoves forming devotional sites, made by initiates in the past, dating back to A.D. 600. They had placed votives inside to honor what they were doing and to ask for favor from the gods. This information would not have impressed the average tourist, but then, we were not tourists!

"According to the ancient ways," Leftaris told us, "it was said that the initiate's path involved things spoken, things revealed, and things done."

At this point, Manos stood up. He turned to the group. "According to ancient accounts and tradition," he said, "the initiates passed an old bridge on the way we are now approaching. Passersby would mock the initiates as they proceeded along their sacred way. In response, the initiates were expected to make obscene gestures back to the passersby. So, in honor of this, I say take this!"

He made ugly faces.

"And this!"

He gestured with his middle finger several times. Everyone laughed out loud.

Moments later, the bus pulled into the ancient site of Elefsis. We emerged from the bus very slowly, like crabs from the shell; with long stretches and yawns we greeted the early morning sun at this first site. The bus ride was only an hour from Athens, but everyone was still jet-lagged from the plane ride. Manos stepped down from the bus, his eyes fixed on the entrance.

"This is the first gate of the Elefsinian Mysteries," he said with quiet reverence and authority.

We were early and all was quiet. Since our group was the first to arrive, we wouldn't have other tourists to contend with. The entrance appeared to begin at the main road. The modern road was built for expediency during a time when the desire for progress overshadowed care of the sites. I believed it diminished the site's importance. Once again, for the sake of progress, something old and sacred had been contaminated by something profane! I was sad about this.

Only a few yards away, ancient stones defined an edge between the old world and the new. Every bit of landscape was littered randomly with various stone artifacts. Some stones were plain, some were fluted; some were standing, and some were lying on their sides. With closer observation, I saw that the rubble was actually organized and tagged with coded numbers. The site was being restored.

The terrain from the road gently inclined. Before me, a layer of stone began a path, which led to a large plateau. The path continued past the plateau, rising to a ridge. At the rim stood the remains of a stone gate, which entered onto another plateau beyond. In the center of the site was a giant rock that jutted up and outwards like a giant clamshell, supporting a little Greek church perched on top. Later, I realized that churches were built on all of the ancient sites as if to usurp the energy and Christianize these powerful places once used by the ancient pagans.

Leftaris continued as if to complete my thoughts.

"Some might think, when coming to Greece, that the temples are laid to waste, only rubble, which the tourists can peruse casually. I tell you, do not underestimate what you see. The temples are very much alive!"

I narrowed my vision to focus upon Leftaris' face, scanning to see the deeper man. It was an intense face, burning with passion. He had set his mind upon a mission, to reveal his heart's true love of the ancient and living mystical Greece.

As Leftaris discussed Elefsis, my attention was drawn like a magnet deep into the site of the rock face above the first plateau. The clam-shaped stone seemed to hover over something. I was astonished at the energy pouring out of it. The sun had grown white-hot against the rock face, reflecting directly into my eyes. I squinted and tried to get a better view, but the light was too bright.

I thought it rude to leave Leftaris in the middle of his talk, but my body carried me compulsively toward the rock. I could not keep myself from it. Minutes passed, and the group was far behind me. As

I climbed, the stone path suddenly opened and I was upon that place. The energy buzzed all around me as if I had disturbed a nest of hornets. My body began to tremble with a strange cold.

"Wow! This is amazing." Yokar, what is this place?

"This is the cave of Pluton, the Navel, one of the gates into the Earth. We are going to open it for you!" Yokar said telepathically.

"Oh, my God!" I blurted.

There was a large rounded stone deeply buried in the ground, in front of the limestone hollow. It seemed to be the only logical place to sit. I closed my eyes to rest. Then, I awakened to the sound of scuffling feet and whispered voices gathering around me. I opened my eyes to find Leftaris grinning proudly at me.

I looked back into his face quietly. "I love this place. Yokar said this is the spot where we need to meet the spirit of the Earth."

Leftaris was quiet for a moment and then he spoke. "Unbelievable!" His eyes widened and his smile broadened. "Things have been said, and now things are shown. Unbelievable! Michael, how did you know that this is the Navel of the Earth?"

"I don't know," I said. "I was drawn to it and Yokar confirmed it for me."

Leftaris dropped his head and stared at the Earth beneath his feet. Slowly he shook his head side to side. I could tell he was stunned.

I stood up and placed my hand on his shoulder, to gesture reassurance. "You had better get used to this, Leftaris. This tour is not about tourism, you know!"

He stared intensely into my eyes. I thought for a moment that he was going to cry. Then he spoke again. "I have dreamed that one day someone would come to share my vision."

I was silent and smiled at him.

"Okay, everyone. Gather round while I go into trance and give Yokar a chance to introduce you to the Earth in this place."

At this point, Leftaris quickly pointed out that we needed to be careful that the caretakers did not see what we were doing. He explained that they were very religious and might cause trouble if they thought we were using the site for something other than sightseeing.

"Leftaris, what else would we use it for?" I asked.

"The Greek Orthodox Church is up in arms about watching all the sites more closely now because a little girl was found dead near one of the temples, apparently killed ritual style, in a black magic ceremony!"

"My God! That's terrible," I said.

Once Yokar had entered, he wasted little time. Immediately he began a blessing in Vril. Everyone pulled closer to cloak our ceremony in secret. As Yokar began a special Vril incantation, Leftaris descended the slope and began to chat with the guards, distracting them.

Meanwhile, Yokar waved his hand in subtle gestures toward the Navel, calling up the Earth force out of the stone cavity. The wind began to blow around us strangely, as if to announce the coming event. After he uttered the final intonations, Yokar instructed the neophytes to go to the wall of the cave and make contact with the awakened force now pouring out. Upon contact, the initiates began to swoon. Many described to me later that the energy felt cool to the touch and the flow of energy tingled through their bodies like electricity.

For this ceremony, Yokar stood in my body. Beforehand, I had asked for someone to catch me when the trance was completed. Claude and John had agreed. As Yokar left my body, everyone gasped. Yokar left so suddenly that Claude and John almost dropped me! Claude confided to me later on the bus, as we were leaving, "Listen, you should tell Yokar to give better notice when he's leaving your body." He was obviously distressed, so I told him that I would mention it.

After the first ceremony at the Navel was completed, we proceeded upwards along the stone path to an amphitheater carved out of solid rock deep into the hillside. This was the Telestrion. More than a thousand years ago, neophytes had come to see the unseen in the Telestrion. Everyone took a seat conveniently provided by the stone mantles. Manos stood before us silently.

Then he began, "According to the ancient rites of the Elefsinian mysteries, the neophytes were brought into this place and given their first glimpse of understanding. It was said that a box was taken out of a basket and then something was taken from the box. Each neophyte was shown something from the box.

"Although it is not known for sure what was shown because each initiate was sworn to secrecy, we believe the original ceremony was similar to the 'sacred seed' ceremony."

Then Manos pulled from a bag an ear of corn. As he broke off the kernels, he passed them around. After the ceremony was completed, no one spoke. As we quietly began to leave, I contemplated the ancient meaning of the seed: We had bonded with the unseen. The seed was a symbol of the rebirth of life into spirit, rising from death, symbolized by our descent into the Navel of the Earth.

The experience returned quietly with us to the bus. Demetri turned the bus with little effort. My mind was turning as well. There were other matters still pressing. I was concerned about the water, the special water of the Styxx, which we would need to perform the final ceremony at Delphi.

Manos had informed me before we left New York that the Greek Orthodox Church had capped the sacred well at Delphi. In so doing, the Church hoped to prevent the continuation of any pagan rituals. How were we to get this water? Delphi was the only true source of the River Styxx.

I leaned back and let my mind go blank. Yokar surrounded me with his usual warmth. "What's the problem?"

I knew that he knew what was troubling me. "What are we going to do, Yokar? How can we complete this task without the Styxx water?"

He radiated a strong feeling of confidence. "Relax," he said quietly. "All will be handled in its own time."

I did not reply. Obviously, his intention was to persuade me by experience rather than logic. I had to yield to his experience. The mounting tension collapsed, and I fell into a deep sleep.

When the bus stopped, I lifted my head to get my bearings. I could see Demetri nodding his head in a staccato fashion while Leftaris gave directions. Demetri immediately headed for a small group of tables in the nearby taverna, for his next cup of coffee.

Leftaris had already gone some distance from the bus.

I called out, "Hey Leftaris!"

He stopped, waiting for me to catch up.

"What is this place?" I inquired.

We had stopped at a small village halfway to Epidaurus. Before me the street opened into a common square. The small taverna nestled beneath a jagged rock face, rising quickly into a set of high cliffs. To the right of the taverna a spiral staircase carved out of the rock climbed gently halfway around to a terrace overlooking the square. Just to the right of the staircase was an enclosed natural area containing huge boulders and small outcroppings. The whole area was sprinkled with various flowers and plant life, with a variety of textures that would make a Japanese garden proud!

Leftaris leaned on a metal railing. One foot was propped lazily on one of the lower rungs. He seemed preoccupied by what he was seeing. As I approached, I could hear a roaring sound rising in intensity with every step. When I reached the edge, where the railing began, I was struck with awe.

A raging river poured through some old wooden gates into the bottom of the natural area. The water carried itself around various stone obstructions as if in a graceful ballet. My eyes lifted slowly to view the scene above. I could see a myriad of canes and broken crutches strewn about the area. It was a grotto and sacred shrine. It was easy to see that many weary believers had honored it for a very long time.

Leftaris finally broke his meditative gaze to answer my question. "Ah, well . . . as you can see . . . this place is where the sacred cave is divided. One cave is dedicated to Pan and the other to St. Anthony."

"Did you say Pan?"

His words caught me off guard. I almost choked on my own saliva. We walked as he explained that this place was special and to be included in our itinerary.

I noticed a different sound as we approached a small precipice. It was the sound of rushing water racing into the Earth below. I could hardly believe it. The water poured violently into the Earth through a series of huge stones placed together, suggesting a mystical entrance! I stared spellbound into the water, which folded into the Earth.

I had seen this before! The vegetation was all too familiar. The Devic (elemental) energy was very strong here. The blue lights, characteristic of Devas, skimmed above the water and raced down between the stones as if in some wild water sport. They invited me to follow them. I sent a silent feeling of appreciation and bid them a fond hello. Sadly, I declined their offer.

"Leftaris . . . what is this river?" I asked.

I held my breath, waiting for him to answer. I already knew what he was going to say.

"Ah, well . . . you know it is the Styxx."

His eyes twinkled. I could see that he was in league with the Devas here. The blue light danced in his eyes reflecting the very same light twinkling above the water. Who is this man? I thought. I just looked at his gaping smile. We both leaned over the edge to share quietly in this wondrous sight.

By now, the rest of the group had awakened. Leftaris went back to join them while I waited at the steps of the shrine. I felt a great weight had been lifted from my shoulders. We had the water we needed. The group climbed the steps to the shrine together. We were unaware of the surprise that waited for us at the top!

At the terrace level, a giant vine tree greeted us. It was the biggest vine tree I had ever seen! Its base was five feet in diameter. The vine trunk was made up of thirty or more individual limbs all wrapped around each other like a gigantic rope. More amazingly, it divided into two sections. One vine sprawled off to the left, masking one cave entrance, while the other draped over the entrance to another cave.

Broad velvet green leaves and pink flowers wove deep into the vines and appeared neatly kept. The shrine attendant said that no pruning or caretaking had ever been done to it. It was all natural.

It was truly magical. Even to the unbeliever, it would've been convincing. Its task was unmistakable. The vine protected the entrance to the inner Earth here. While I gaped in awe at the two caves and their guardian, I could hear a low humming sound emerging from behind. An incredible presence was all around me, but I couldn't figure it out. I squinted for a better view. Thousands of flowers were weaving back and forth amid the thick foliage of the great vine. Then I saw them, millions of them. Bees everywhere.

This phenomenal guardian plant had attracted more bees than one could imagine. They were busy gathering the flower's nectar. I suspected, however, that people who were not in the right frame of mind could easily distract them. If one attracted the bees' fury, it would surely demonstrate an unworthiness to enter this sacred place!

We entered the Pan side of the great cave first. As in all caves, coolness permeated the chamber. This cave was also filled with exciting electricity. Along one of the rising walls was a religious shrine placed in a stone alcove. Deep inside was a small metal pipe from which water trickled. Beside the shrine was an elongated bed of sand for devotional candles. Some of the group made special offerings and prayed for family members and their own initiation. Then I collected the amount of Styxx water I thought would be needed for the final ceremony in Delphi. Everyone gathered for some of the water also.

Vasilios motioned to me. "Michael, we have to get moving now."

Soon we were off to Olympia.

Then Leftaris said, "Ah . . . we have one more place nearby that should probably be seen. Ah . . . for you, the most significant, I think. The only existing pyramid in Greece."

I was surprised and looked forward to this "new" discovery. The pyramid didn't have the elegance of its obvious model, the Great Pyramid of Egypt, but the energy of the place was very strong and unique. Officially, not much was known about the pyramid. It was considered a curiosity and never mentioned in the tour guide as having archeological significance.

Everyone in the group wondered who had built this place and why. Before I could form any questions, Yokar was already providing the answers. I repeated Yokar's words as he spoke telepathically. "Yokar says, it was built around 3000 B.C. and later used by the

Pythagorean followers in approximately A.D. 650. The Pythagoreans were a radical mystical group that had formed around a rogue mathematician and philosopher called Pythagoras."

Then Yokar confirmed that Pythagoras was an Egyptian initiate. "The Pythagoreans' interest was in the mathematics of harmony, tone, and sacred geometry demonstrated by the ancient Gizeh temple of Egypt. They were well aware of the energy of the structure in Egypt and its spiritual significance as a temple."

As I continued with Yokar's explanation, initiates Elaine and Claude pointed at the sky. There, flying above us, swallows began to gather. Their activity was strange. In only moments, a few birds turned into a swarm. Hundreds upon hundreds of birds were all over us. Some darted right at us then returned to join the others flying in a circular pattern.

We had to stop. I closed my eyes to Vril them. Thought shapes of gratitude and love went out to them for their auspicious gestures. From my studies of the Qabbala mysteries, I knew that when swallows gathered, it was a sure sign of spiritual awakening!

Leftaris lowered his head. "More things shown, I just can't believe this!"

As we were getting ready to leave, I noticed Claude examining a plant growing nearby. "Michael, look at this plant. This looks like cannabis."

I leaned over his shoulder to get a better view. The leaves had the characteristic appearance, but the flowers were strange. "I don't know about this plant, but you're right, it sure looks like marijuana." I turned to walk away but my body stopped.

"You need me . . . you need me!" a foreign thought shape said to me, as it penetrated my mind. I looked back over my shoulder at the plant.

"Are you talking to me?" I asked in Vril.

"You need me for the libation," the plant whispered again.

I wasn't accustomed to receiving messages from plant life, especially when I hadn't been properly introduced. I was startled. Yokar hadn't said anything one way or the other. I took a moment to consider this request. The decision seemed to be up to me. Then a warm tingling sensation massaged my belly.

"Okay, you're in," I offered in Vril.

Then I asked Leftaris for a knife. Before I began to cut the plant's limbs, I entered into prayer. I offered my body as soil to all plant life in exchange for their generous offers.

"Make sure you take plenty of flowers, these are our essence, you need them the most," the plant told me.

I yielded with silent confirmation that I understood.

We moved on. The rise to Arcadia came quickly. The climb became steep and the road narrow, with steep cliffs and hairpin turns. Since my seat was immediately behind Demetri, I felt like a co-pilot. The bus had many windows, especially from the driver's perspective. Unconsciously, my hands gripped the armrests to brace myself. I asked Barbara, who sat across the aisle, "Hey, Barb, how bad is this going to get?"

"Honey," she chortled, "you ain't seen nothin' yet!" She laughed out loud. Her eyes sparkled, as she grinned from ear to ear, definitely enjoying herself. She had been through these mountains before. It didn't seem to bother her at all. In fact, I think she thrived on the threat of danger.

Everyone avoided looking down. I estimated the altitude to be 3500 feet straight into the gorge below. The road width was five feet too narrow, as far as I was concerned! Demetri approached every sharp turn with a beep of his horn.

Sometimes, I would venture to look out. From time to time, little wooden boxes appeared along the side of the road, usually at the turns overlooking the steep cliffs. Barbara explained, "They were for people who didn't make it! Usually, the accidents happen at night here."

I gritted my teeth and grumbled, Oh God, what on Earth am I doing here?

I watched Demetri in amazement as he approached the turns, each more difficult than the last. He would swing the front of the bus over the edge of the cliff. I would hold my breath, convinced it was my last. Like a compass turning, the bus would swing back onto the road. I stared wild-eyed at Leftaris. He turned, saw my distress, and smiled calmly. With his full attention on Demetri, he said, "As you can see . . . ahh . . . he is a genius!"

"Does he have no fear at all?" I asked rhetorically.

It was late in the afternoon when we arrived in the seaside village of Galaxidi. Yokar explained that we needed to contemplate the final ascent of Delphi here. We meditated together near the shore, lined up along an old stonewall. This spot offered a perfect view of the slopes of Parnassus and the city of Delphi. It was beautiful.

Before trance, I climbed down to the water's edge, making my way along some miniature archipelagoes. I wanted to make contact with the water spirits. My hand entered the warm saltwater while I Vriled hello. They greeted me quickly and welcomed me with warmth and deep appreciation. All of my concerns melted into their gentle caress.

The water Devas reminded me that we weren't alone on this journey, that we had many friends. While my hand joined theirs, my line of vision reached across the peaceful bay and followed the rise to Parnassus. There, perched among the peaks, sat the city of Delphi. It was like a small pastel jewel nestled in the mountains.

Ascent on Delphi

We scrambled back to the bus and made our way to the initiation site before sundown. The evening ceremony had to be completed at dusk. Tension mounted as we climbed onto Parnassus. As we climbed ever more steeply, the bay fell away and revealed a breathtaking view of the mountains surrounding the sea inlet of Galaxidi. The journey seemed surreal. Demetri was driving more slowly. We finally stopped in front of the hotel after the last few compass turns were completed. After our bags were off-loaded, the bus headed straight for the temple of Apollo. The sun was speeding toward the horizon, and there wasn't a moment to lose.

After we descended from the bus, there was a sharp descent along some stone steps into the temple courtyard. As at many of the other sites, not much of the temple was standing. The circular pedestal called the Tholes, which had been built to honor the goddess Hera, dominated the entire area. Partial reconstruction offered three standing pillars. The architecture was profound and graceful. Although only three of the Doric pillars were standing, I could easily imagine the completed pavillion, composed of a giant circle, pillars capped with an elegant and gently sloping dome.

I began to scan the area energetically to get a feel of the place. We were not alone. Although it was close to closing time, some onlookers were having a smoke and chatting nonchalantly.

I kept talking to Yokar about where would be the best place to begin. He was oddly preoccupied. He kept giving me a warning. "Focus on the ancient part of the temple; you may not be able to stay here!"

We had bribed the guards to allow us late entry beyond closing time, so I wasn't worried. Following Yokar's suggestion, I went to Leftaris and asked him about the oldest part of the temple. He pointed to a small area north of the Tholes courtyard, near the entrance steps.

There, set slightly obscured, were the remains of some pillar fragments, still standing, forming what looked like the lower corner of a building. These stones were very different, not the pale yellow-white marble variety found in the rest of the temple sites. These stones were obviously older and had greater patina.

As I approached the dark red pillars, I sensed an energy spewing from them. There was also an electrical potential surrounding the area. It was so strong I imagined that the authorities had electrified the place! Cautiously, I moved closer. The heat radiating from the stones was immense. It could be felt more than two feet away. My logic tried to explain that the sun had done its work through the day and now it acted like a solar radiator. My reasoning could not explain the heat radiating from behind, where the sun had not contacted the stones. These stones were three feet thick and hot to the touch, all around!

Yokar repeated his warning to me. Then I approached Manos. "I want you to go with the others to that place of older stones," I said. I assured him, "This is the place we need to do our anointing ceremony, but there is a problem."

"What's the problem?" Manos asked with some surprise.

"I don't know, exactly. Yokar keeps telling me there's a problem here. Are you sure we have everything arranged with the authorities?"

Before Manos could answer, the guard swooped down on us and told us firmly that we had to leave at once. By this time, we had prepared everything for the ceremony. Manos began to argue in Greek with the guard. I waited quietly to see the outcome. Manos tramped heavily toward me. I could tell he was not happy.

"What's up?" I asked.

"This is not the guy we made the deal with!" He proclaimed. "I don't know what the hell is going on! It looks as though we have to leave."

I sat down on one of the stones nearby, quietly hoping for some improvement in the situation. The guard grew more impatient. Yokar's ominous tone changed. "Make sure that everyone makes contact with the stones of the old temple before they leave."

I told Leftaris to spread the word about making contact. I told everyone to be nonchalant about his or her approach to old stones, lest we draw attention even to this activity.

Manos was terribly disappointed. He felt he had failed with the most important part of the trip. I quickly assured him that it was okay. I explained that Yokar confirmed it was only the old stones that were significant, to make contact was enough, that we ought to do the ceremony nearby.

The sun was almost down, and Manos rushed ahead to seek another site down the road. Meanwhile, all made the rounds, touching the ancient temple stones a few at a time. Like small mice, we scurried out of the temple site, secretly preparing for the next rendezvous.

We ended up in a small olive grove just a few hundred feet beyond the temple site. The sun was now in its final descent below the horizon. We prepared once again for our sacred activities as I went into a trance. Manos prepared the special anointing libation. The woman chosen as high priestess began a special liturgy to the ancient gods of the lunar cycle.

Under Yokar's guidance, I had made special fabric headbands for everyone. They were marked with the symbol of the feminine night force and the alchemical expression of human psychic energy under the autumnal lunar cycle. Everyone placed the bands about their foreheads, making sure that the symbol was positioned over the third eye.

Yokar blessed and opened everyone's third eye with a sacred Vril intonation under the pale light of the rising moon. The olive branches added to the ceremony by providing a magical light of their own. They waved gently in the night wind. Then the libation was shared all around.

I emerged from trance, bathed in the brightest moonlight I think I have ever seen. Just a few feet below me, everyone stood smiling contentedly. I was the last to partake of the libation. We had now entered into our vows of silence for the night. The only sound was of our feet scuffling along the trail, marking the end of this part of our journey. We boarded the bus and returned to our hotel rooms.

That night, I did not fall into ordinary sleep. I drifted into an altered state of mind. At first my mind waded through jumbled dreams. Then I was standing in the middle of a New York street! I tried to get my bearings. There was no one around to ask any questions. I thought, That's odd for New York. Then I realized it was very late at night.

The night air was October crisp. The odor of freshly cooked Chinese food mingled with the sound of traffic in the background. Everything seemed stark, vivid, and somehow surreal. I felt wide-awake, but I wasn't sure. There was a gnawing feeling in the pit of my stomach. I couldn't tell whether I was hungry or just plain scared. It seemed like I was waiting for something or someone. My feelings shifted to dread. I began to consider ways to avoid this unknown confrontation.

An old bus lumbered slowly down the street toward me. My mind went on pause for a moment. I was puzzled. What was a 1940-ish bus doing around here this late at night? Something in my mind pushed that question aside. Automatically, I began to flail my arms around. I knew I had to flag this old crate down. I was willing to accept anything on wheels to escape the terrible thing that was coming.

It passed me by! The driver had ignored me. Then the bus slowed, brakes screeching, and finally came to a halt. I cautiously approached. The door swung out to allow me to board. I looked up at the driver and called out, "Thanks for the lift."

The driver said nothing. He didn't even look at me. I was grateful and asked how much the fare would be. He ignored my question and waved me silently to the rear.

There was something else odd. His face was mostly covered with a black cloth. The cloth appeared rotten at first glance. He smelled of urine, too, and old body odor. I thought of telling him about his bad manners and his poor personal hygiene. This isn't good for his passengers! I thought. Then I reconsidered. The bus started up again, very slowly. The engine struggled to cope with the next set of gears. I wondered if we would even make the next intersection!

I was just beginning to relax in my seat when another startling idea occurred to me. I was the only one on board! How strange. An old bus is running around town after midnight, with only one passenger. Then I realized that I hadn't told the driver where I was going. On the other hand, I thought, he hasn't said where he is going, either. Perhaps the next stop is the Twilight Zone! I concluded that I really didn't care now. I believed I had escaped, by a narrow margin, a fate worse than death. I closed my eyes for a moment and tried to steal one minute's peace. The bus was suddenly attacked.

Someone was throwing huge stones. Several bashed against the sides. One crashed through the window right next to me! I jumped into the isle to protect myself. Whatever or whoever had come after me was now trying to stop the bus. The driver began to slow down. I yelled after him, "You must keep going, for God's sake! Don't stop now—they're after me!"

But the driver ignored my ranting and raving and brought the old carriage to a halt. I backed up toward the rear of the aisle, looking around desperately. There was no way out. I was trapped like a rat in a hole! I just stood there shaking, waiting for the awfulness to climb on board.

Then, the bus rocked a little. My hour was nigh; something had stepped onto the platform. My body tensed into stone. I could feel my nostrils heaving with the icy air. The darkness blinded me. I strained to see, but my adversary remained in the shadows. To my horror, there was more than one! Clearly, I thought, this means the end.

The bus had stopped near an intersection with a flashing yellow light. The intermittent light partially illuminated the middle of the carriage for fractions of a second, leaving eternal moments of darkness in between. Then I saw them. There were at least three of them, but I couldn't be sure. They ranged in size, but the poor light obscured their features. In an instant, I saw that one was covered with hair—bright orange hair. I grew weak all over. Emotionally, I caved in. I was desperately trying to deny this was happening. I didn't want to be there, to watch my undoing. As they approached me, I could hear myself screaming, "No! No! Please no . . ."

I was helpless to defend against them. My body fell into their grasp and my agony stopped. My body became warm and moist. All my fear melted away instantly! Their arms cradled me, supporting my whole body. I couldn't explain it, but I felt completely safe. Somehow I knew they hadn't come to destroy but to reconstruct me. I was becoming whole again. I began to weep and sob deeply. They looked and smiled benevolently. I felt ashamed of running away from them. They were actually my best and only friends. I still couldn't understand completely who they were. But I knew without a doubt that they really loved me.

Then my lucid vision changed suddenly. I was thousands of fathoms below the ocean riding in a submarine, traveling along a deep trench. I was vaguely aware that no one was at the helm. In fact, the submarine veered off course from time to time, glancing from one rock face to the other, jarring the insides terribly.

I was standing amidships, holding on for dear life. The beings from the bus appeared in front of me, all standing in a row. The inside of the submarine was well lighted and now I could see them clearly. There were five altogether. They ranged in size from what appeared to be a small boy to an adult-sized creature. I say creature here because the largest one was covered with bright orange hair! And one seemed to be female.

The middle one stepped forward and called out for my hand. I extended it to him without hesitation. With quiet pomp and ceremony, he pulled from his utility belt a small ring. It was smooth and shiny and radiated a delightful emerald-green color. He took my finger and shoved it on while he smiled at me! I looked up at him and felt the importance of this action. I was being honored for my ability, my capacity to give, they said. I began to feel an energy pouring from the ring as this being stepped back into the line. The energy filled my body with a sense of incredible knowledge, a growing sense of well being, of joy, hope, and wisdom.

The impact of this awareness, of this sudden rush of available knowledge and wisdom, made me begin to cry and laugh at the same time. With this ring, I was wed to something much greater and older, something that involved the Earth. This storehouse of knowledge was ancient, and I was somehow the keeper now.

I could feel my soul wafting under its influence. I felt the burden of responsibility. I continued to cry and laugh hysterically. Then I blurted out, "The responsibility doesn't matter!"

But inside, at that moment, I knew it did matter. Then I cried harder. Then, in the next moment, strangely, I let go of my fear and it really didn't matter. Then, I laughed again at myself. I emerged from this experience right into full awakeness, sitting up in my room, in Delphi. I was still laughing and crying!

I got up and looked out over my balcony. My eyes followed the descending slope of Parnassus down to the bay of Galaxidi. The landscape appeared magical, illuminated by the moon. I was still shaking from the ring ceremony.

Yokar suddenly appeared and approached me to explain. "Congratulations go with you on this night. You have experienced and completed a rite in an ancient line of spiritual overseers. You are the bearer of the Ring of Tahaar! This signifies that you are worthy to carry the standard of the keepers. You are now the keeper of the gate of Tahaar."

Still sobbing a little, I inquired, "What does all this mean, Yokar? What is this gate . . . I am a keeper of, exactly?"

"Well," he started slowly, "if you'll remember, I told you about the great temple of Gizeh, that Thoth had constructed a great Ruune stone, a capstone for the temple. He programmed it with all the knowledge and wisdom gathered from the Atlantean golden era, the Shoad. The time of the capstone's existence was limited at the great temple of Gizeh. Thoth designed the crystal to self-destruct if it was left unused for a certain period."

"Yes, Yokar. I remember."

"What we really mean by this is the capstone was not destroyed! Thoth had no intention of giving up that easily. He created this Ruune stone as a gate to the great library or "record keeper," the Akasha. This Ruune gate is called Tahaar. If his plan did not succeed with the Egyptian culture, he intended that the Ruune crystal offer its wealth to another culture that might develop later."

"Yokar, will this gate ever be found?"

Yokar seemed to ignore my question as he went on.

"After long searching, we have found one who possesses the potential for spiritual awakening and the right qualities for overseeing the re-opening of the gate of Tahaar. Opening this gate would serve as a great spiritual resource for the souls in the next millennium of Earth's development. That one is to be you."

"This can't be! You've made a mistake. I don't know anything!"

"Michael, you have been specially aligned this hour, this night. The one who bears of the Ring of Tahaar will become the record keeper. The great Ruune of Tahaar will acknowledge you when you call upon it one day. The gate will be at your beck and call after you have awakened and are made ready. Your world will have access to a resource of light, a library of knowledge and wisdom that will help you bring forth what is required for your time and your culture.

"It is true that you know nothing of this now. But with training and practice you have the potential to awaken."

"Yokar, are you sure I am the one for such a responsibility? It feels like a terrible burden because I feel inadequate for the task."

"We have not defined you as being ready! You, by your own actions and willingness to undertake the tasks of spirit on this Earth have defined your readiness. The ring comes to the one who radiates the energy of readiness."

"I feel a terrible fear about this. What should I do?"

"Consume your fear and do not let it paralyze you. The fear will pass. You have felt fear before and you still fulfilled the tasks despite it. It has passed before . . . it shall pass again."

"But Yokar, how will I call on the record keeper?"

"Do not worry about this now. It will come with your training. Does the farmer worry about a seed of corn not becoming an ear of corn bearing many more corn seeds? It will become quite clear to you in time! Do not worry. All things unfold properly with harmony and cooperation."

I could feel his energy leave me. I was still inwardly stuttering. I wanted to relax, but I was at a loss to deal with my utter confusion and shock. I lay back upon my bed and stared at the ceiling.

At 4 A.M. in the morning, another adventure awaited our courageous troop. This time we continued further up the slope of Parnassus, traveling to an isolated area high on the mountain. The road changed from pavement to gravel, and the bus could not continue any further.

We rendezvoused with two taxis at the edge of the tree line. The stars hovered closely over us like a blanket of sapphires. The landscape was dimly lit. The cypress and uneven terrain cast eerie shadows in the moon's silvery light. My fear of heights drove my imagination wild with terrible visions of crashing violently against the rocky slopes below. The headlights from the taxis sliced into the night with narrow wedges of yellow light, barely illuminating their way up the mountain.

The taxis transported us three at a time. It was finally my turn to make the ascent. I wanted to walk, but I knew it would take too long. As we sped away, I was immediately thrown back in my seat. The sounds of rocks spit out from beneath the wheels as the driver tried to obtain greater momentum. The road inclined by 10 more degrees and narrowed further. It was no surprise that the driver was anxious to bring us to our destination. He was as anxious as I to get this dangerous ride over with. So he took every opportunity to accelerate beyond the limits of good sense. The taxi was a Mercedes, providing me with some trust that the car could manage the steep road.

The road grew less passable. I watched out of the corner of my eye as the driver skillfully negotiated boulders and fallen tree limbs. At one point, I glanced briefly to the left as the driver swung wildly to avoid a large stone. The road's edge fell away, revealing a treacherous cliff with only black void beyond. I closed my eyes. If this is my last moment on Earth, I thought, I hope it will end quickly and painlessly.

The driver swerved suddenly from the edge to avoid another stone, and then the taxi slid to a halt. Relieved, I stepped out of the taxi and into the crisp night air. I shivered, bracing myself for the cold. Small flashlights waved me onto a rocky goat path that offered an almost vertical climb. Manos called to me from above, "Well, we'll have to add mountain goat to your long list of talents!"

I wanted to laugh, but I was out of breath!

Past the rocky crevices, a hand reached out of the darkness to assist my last step onto a small plateau. The moonlit rock face jutted straight above me into the starry night sky. The stars twinkled so brightly that I wanted to reach out and touch them. The smell of smoke began to tickle my nostrils. There was cleavage in the stone ahead. The folding rock revealed a cave entrance. The ground sloped gently into a large cavernous chamber. Far below me, the silhouettes of several people stood against a small fire. The view was magical. Manos and Vasilios had placed lanterns in the center of the cave upon some small stalagmites growing on the cave's floor. The small lantern beams found their way through the rising smoke and illuminated the ceiling, while the flickering fire created large dancing shadows on the walls from nearby stalactites. The sound of murmuring voices echoed unintelligibly all around me. The others were already captivated by the hypnotic quality of the firelight. I descended unnoticed.

Quietly, I began to set up the audio tape player with the recordings of ancient Greek ceremonial music. Then I prepared the spot for trance. I removed the urn I had chosen for the final libation ceremony and added the herbs and broken wine, wine that had been mixed with water, a common practice for ancient ceremonial libations. Everything was ready.

I sat staring into the firelight. I wondered how it must have been, thousands of years ago. There was a lot of history inside this cave, violent history. Yokar had gathered men and women here this night, but the gatherings weren't always like this.

The original Orphic ceremony was strictly for women. It was forbidden for uninvited men to come within miles of this place, especially on the eve of the solstice. The rites would last three days and nights then. According to the records, it was death for a man to attempt any approach to this cave. Even on those ceremonial nights, many invited men died sacrificing their male energy for the sake of the female power gathered.

Many have come here with judgments about feminine energy, that it is weak compared to the male force. But I can feel the power that has been generated in this cave by women with the help of Pan. Pan rules here. He controls the Earth current and rules the night. Fortunately now, Yokar has modified this process to enable men to take part. They will invoke their feminine side tonight through Yokar's help. The time of extreme polarity is over. We are headed toward a joining, we are coming home.

I approached the center, near where everyone stood, and began to instruct everyone as to what was going to happen. "We will need to perform a dance celebrating our coming together with nature and our recognition of the feminine force in our lives."

I began to instruct everyone in the steps of a dance that Yokar had shown me. I had known that we were going to dance, but I hadn't known just how until a few days before this night.

I began to replay sounds of ancient Greek music based upon Pythagoras' theory of diatonic scales and spiritual work. Pythagoras realized that Nature revealed its many secrets through harmony and synchrony. The musical tones he developed were based upon the natural rhythms expressed throughout all existence.

The Pythagorean tones differ from modern musical tones in that they are untempered or unmodified. Modern musicologists have known of this difference and realize that compositions using these ancient tones sound harsh or shrill and sometimes discordant. Pythagoras believed that these harsh combinations embodied the very heart of Nature's power to bring about evolutionary changes. He composed his music utilizing these powerful sounds to help accomplish spiritual evolution.

Everyone joined hands and began to move.

The dance began with two rings of people joining hands, one encircling the other. We moved with the cadence of the music, the circles moving in opposite directions. It was a simple set of movements. First we moved to the right three steps, ending with a small dip, then repeated to the left. The movement reversed again and again. From time to time, we stopped to raise our arms high in the air, gesturing thanks to all living things, as the music briefly paused with a singular tone. As we resumed the dance, the movements of the inner ring continued to counter the outer ring's movements.

I lifted my consciousness high above the cave floor. The combined movements of both rings suggested the appearance of churning. Our bodies seemed to screw deeper into the Earth with each rotation. It suddenly dawned on me that the purpose of the dance was to conjure up the Earth's energy currents. And it was working! My body tingled with each rotation.

Then, spontaneously, both circles began to move in unison. I knew it was important, a sign it was time to stop. We had gathered sufficient energy for our passage out of the world of time and space. The physical cave was transcended. We were floating above the normal world in the timeless void. Everyone formed a greater circle for the final libation. The appointed high priestess gathered my urn from the lower rocks and moved from one initiate to the next. As the elixir was consumed, each initiate's soul leaped toward the nether world of the elementals. When all had taken their fill, the group formed into the last important shape, a triangle. Yokar said that the triangle was an ancient power shape that would contain the fire of awareness.

I sat in my chosen place and entered into trance. When Yokar entered, he immediately began to utter blessings to the elementals of the Earth and sky above. He called upon the grace of the Most High to sanctify our work. As Yokar used the sacred Vril, the pops, clicks, grunts, and hisses combined with melodious tones shifted throughout the chamber, carving out of the rock another world, another reality. Openings appeared in several places, revealing magnificent pearlescent corridors between realities. Yokar's final intonations tied the individual initiate's soul to the flow of the Life Force, merging the soul with future experience, imprinting their alternate future selves into the present conscious ego-self.

When he was finished, he went on to admonish the initiates to continue the work of the path and praised all those who had chosen once again to merge with the night forces for a greater purpose. Then he blessed everyone again and encouraged him or her to greet the dawning of the new light of day.

I returned from trance and stared into all the shining, smiling faces. Everyone stood quietly. There was only the sound of crackling fire echoing in the background.

"It's time for a celebration," I declared. "Let's greet the rising sun and share our growing light together."

There was a burst of joy and laughter. We spent the next ten minutes hugging, crying, and laughing. The silence and fasting was over. Two by two, we ascended the rise toward the entrance. The amber light of dawn broke into the cave and diminished the light of the last embers of our fire.

We emerged onto the plateau, gasping at the breathtaking view stretched out before us. Arm in arm, we stood on top of the world. Far below lay vast pastures winding through the great gorge that reached out to the sea. The other mountains stood majestically before us, partially covered by the clouds. A golden pink light spread through them.

Someone called out to look up. I turned around to see what was attracting attention. There stood a totally black goat, perched on top of the cliff far above, looking down at us. We all laughed at the significance of the presence of a goat. Pan had chosen to honor us with his presence through this symbolic animal. Then there emerged another goat. He was all white. He stood beside the first goat and shared the view of us. Curiously, they seemed pleased with us.

Claude and his wife Bette called out to everyone, "Wait! Listen, everybody."

Pausing in our excitement, we began to hear the faint sound of flute pipes, soft bells, and tambourines. My eyes filled with tears. We could hardly believe our ears. We were being acknowledged by all the Devas at this most sacred spot. Pan's pipes were playing again. The sounds were particularly significant because this area of the mountain was deserted and left no logical way for these sounds to come from any ordinary source.

It had been so long since anyone had recognized and honored the

Devas in a celebration of Nature on the Earth. They offered thanks to us and wanted to let us know they were pleased. Everyone began to weep with joy.

Leftaris, still beaming from the ceremony, began to explain that this cave had been used for several millennia by female peasant oracles, long before the temples at Delphi were built.

I realized this experience of coming together and honoring life and each other was not going to end here. Our task was just beginning. Like the sun that was beginning to illuminate the landscape, our new-found love and understanding would serve to illuminate a darker world, now very much in need!

We stayed at Delphi another day to relax. Lynne and her good friend Polly had decided to take a few more photos at the archeological sites. Later, they went shopping and found Barbara browsing in one of the shoppes. Polly suddenly realized that she had misplaced her camera along the way and became upset.

Yokar had taught that the lunar initiations would enhance the psychic aspects of being, but that the energy would remain only potential unless it was used. Initiates needed to practice calling the night force for help in order to develop it.

Barbara recalled Yokar's teachings about the use of the night force. She explained to Polly Yokar's example of conjuring the night force to create what you want. Barbara told Polly that Yokar suggested a woman's handbag was not very different than the void or reservoir of the night force—both were bottomless.

Barbara then suggested that perhaps she could reach into her handbag and call forth Polly's missing camera. Polly became nervous as she watched Barbara reaching slowly into her bag. Barbara smiled at Polly while her ability to summon the night force creative energy was being tested. No sooner had Barbara begun to pull her hand from her bag than a man approached Polly from behind. He handed the camera to Polly, exclaiming, "Is this your camera?" They all enjoyed a hearty laugh.

Some of the people took the opportunity to have private sessions with Yokar. In one such session with a woman named Jackie, an amazing discovery was revealed.

Jackie asked Yokar about the significance of a small disc attached to a key ring she had purchased from the plaka market of Athens. The disc contained a set of spiral lines and strange symbols engraved on both sides.

"Where on Earth did you find this?" Yokar asked.

"I picked it up at the marketplace in Athens," she said. "Actually, I felt compelled to buy it for some reason. What do you think?"

"This is most curious," Yokar continued. "You have here the record of an Atlantean shipping manifest engraved upon this coin! It's partially garbled or distorted. Perhaps it does not reflect the original artifact accurately."

After Jackie recounted this part of her session to me, I asked Manos about acquiring another of these discs. Manos acted quite nonchalant about the disc and began to explain its origin. "The disc is a copy. There are thousands of these copies everywhere in the plaka. The original is on display in the museum on the island of Crete. They found the original disc lying in some old ruins of a Minoan archeological site. They think the site was an ancient shipping yard where they kept sailing ships docked. Actually, the damn thing is made of fired clay, so they can't determine its precise age and they still haven't been able to decipher the writing on it, either."

"Well, that makes sense," I said, "Since Yokar seems to think that it is some sort of Atlantean shipping manifest."

Back in Athens, it was early evening and everyone was preparing to go to the pre-arranged celebration dinner in the plaka. Yokar interrupted my shaving with a telepathic message. "We understand your excitement about the manifest and have decided to translate it for you. You can expect this within the next few days."

"That's great, Yokar. Thanks."

Beyond the Ring of Fire

It was the middle of the night. There I sat, coffee in hand, staring into my computer screen as if it were a stone tablet. My mind began to turn slowly. It reluctantly gripped the continuing task of writing down the details of my journey. Then it occurred to me that maybe this image of a stone tablet was past memory. How many lives with chisel and stone? Was it the same way then, always against my will?

Then Yokar's energy and thought bore down on me like a heavy rain. "It is time to talk of changes."

I would always rant and rave when I was disturbed by anyone else during my writing, but I never minded Yokar.

Some months had passed since we returned from Greece. The immense task of coordinating the activities and handling emotional reactions of participants had caused great physical stress. My recovery was almost complete. Old friends had dropped over earlier for dinner. After cleanup, I had come to my computer to catch up on some long-overdue writing. The night had been long with talk of Yokar and the work in Egypt and Greece. When the house was finally quiet, Yokar brought me some news. Recently there had been an earthquake directly below the great pyramid at Gizeh, and I wondered what Yokar would have to say about that.

"We have mentioned many times that the Earth is shifting. Its nervous system is accommodating altered patterns of vibrations from the Most High, constantly."

"Yes, I remember, Yokar. Would this happen to have anything to do with Egypt?"

"Yes, my son. The shift in the Earth below the great temple has sounded the end of its usefulness for this work. We will now need a new initiation site to provide the necessary changes in the light side of being."

I waited. "Where do you have in mind?"

"There are many places that can define a new vortex, but we must choose one that not only is strong and complete but also may survive the physical changes that are occurring in your near future. One such place exists and is now forming in the land above the Ring of Fire!"

"What is the Ring of Fire, Yokar?"

"It exists at the edge of the frozen male force, what was once called the Agogil Tavarak in Atlantis, at the top of the world."

"You mean the polar ice cap?"

"Yes, my son!"

My body began to shake uncontrollably. Once again the feeling of safety in which I had nestled vanished. With the passage of time, Egypt's terrifying effects no longer threatened me. My body had finally relaxed. But deep inside, I knew somehow that safety was only temporary. My bones had told me that someday Yokar would find a new and creative way to scare the hell out of me.

"We must begin to make preparations for this," he continued. "You must contact the men of wisdom there. You must cooperate together. It will not be easy."

"No kidding!" I responded spontaneously. "How are you planning to accomplish this? They don't even know me!"

"Be patient. Did they know you in Egypt?"

"No."

"It's true. They will not trust you because you are an outsider. With my help, you will talk of their traditions without knowing it. It will influence them. Do you understand?"

"I think so." I took a breath and sighed. "Where is this place exactly?"

"It is called Lapland," Yokar said. "It's above the Arctic Circle. You must go and seek out the male vortex. The energy lines will point the way to the sacred place."

It was now 2 A.M. I felt exhausted and supercharged at the same time. My imagination danced wildly. Visions of Jules Verne, Arn Sagnussum, and journeys to the center of the Earth rolled through my mind like bulldozers. Chills ran down my back as my heart skipped a handful of beats. I thought, there is just no end to this adventure.

The next morning I told Dianne the outrageous news. "Somehow, we have to go there and set it all up!" I said.

"How are you going to do that?" She countered. "You don't know anybody there!"

"I know. But Yokar is going to help."

Soon plans were made to meet with a Finnair representative in New York, as Finnair was the main airline going to this region. As I drove to the city that day, I entertained myself with visions of sleds weaving and mushing through the white tundra while the dogs that pulled them howled on the hunt for new Ley lines.

It actually took several weeks of meetings with Finnair to discuss all the needs for a survey. Yokar filled me in with the rest of the details on the formation of new Ley lines above the sixty-eighth parallel. It was near a place called Ivalo, a small town in the northern part of Finland known as Lapland. The airport at Ivalo was the northernmost point capable of handling jets from Helsinki.

Gus, the Finnair representative, suggested a week-long trip that would include Barbara, Manos, Dianne, me, and possibly Marieritta, one of their staff.

We were asking Finnair to do something rather unusual and very specialized. Airline companies will arrange surveys for travel agents planning group tour packages. But we were a small tour company needing a special survey of our own. We were not travel agents, and this kind of tour, a mystical journey, was very new for Finnair. An airline is always interested in new business, but Finnair's headquarters was dubious about our tour.

Not even Gus could predict the reaction to our request from headquarters. It was clear that we needed to convince them of our ability to bring people into their country. Through Gus's enthusiasm, they might be willing to explore our needs, if it meant serious new business. It seemed that Yokar would have to take a special hand in influencing the outcome of this resistance.

Gus and two friends from the office came to one of Yokar's

question-and-answer sessions. It was important that Gus meets Yokar and to see the number of people interested in the Yokar phenomenon. The personal contact with Yokar was impressive. Many people were in attendance, and they were enthusiastic. Armed with this new experience, Gus returned to Finnair and successfully encouraged the airline to become our business partner.

The survey began a few weeks later. We entered into Lapland, Finland, not knowing anyone or knowing what to expect. Within a few short days and many adventures, we managed to meet, through Yokar's help, important people including Hannele Vaarama, our northern guide, who introduced us to the Saamis, the local tribal people. As Yokar predicted, they were impressed with my foreknowledge of their innermost secret spiritual traditions. So an agreement was arranged between us for the trip planned for the following year.

A year later . . .

In the back of my mind I wondered about how much I could trust the Saamis to fulfill their end of the bargain after a year had passed. It has been my experience that people very often fail to live up to their agreements, despite good intentions. Perhaps it was my old issues of fear and mistrust that made me suspect that these people would also disappoint me.

One week before we were to leave, Hannele sent a fax informing me that Dahilok, the Saami shaman, and his wife Aitar, a Shamanka were going to honor the full measure of our agreement. The terms shaman and shamanka are Siberian expressions meaning medicine man and woman. In Arctic Finland, the Saamis had other names in their culture for these positions, but they are sacred names and ethically could not be repeated.

Our guide Hannele had introduced Dahilok and Aitar to me during the survey trip the year before. I noticed at the time that their appearance was odd. He was a short, stout man, older in appearance than I expected. His gray hair hung long below a leather cap that resembled a Sherpa's hat from Tibet. His eyes revealed a peaceful blue color, but his face had been weathered tough by the arctic cold. He was wearing a long-sleeved jacket and leather pants with a fleece-lined tunic pulled over, and a wide leather utility belt, which sported two knifes, tied the whole outfit together.

Aitar emerged smiling from a building nearby. She also looked stout and quite fit. Her clothing almost matched his, and she also sported two knives. Her cap rounded in front slightly and was brightly colored with intricate red and blue embroidery. Her eyes were also soft brown like silk ribbon, and her hair was pulled back in a loose ponytail, exposing ruddy, round, apple-like cheeks. They both wore the strangest looking boots, apparently made from some sort of skins.

Dahilok was supplying the equipment to get us to the island and providing a lavo (a temporary teepee) when we arrived. For the icing on the cake, he and Aitar would cook a ceremonial meal inside the lavo for all of us as a rite of passage, in the Saami spiritual tradition. Hannele went on to suggest Aitar might drum for us as well.

Somehow we had achieved higher status with our new northern friends. I wondered if Yokar had influenced Dahilok to take such bold steps to help. It never occurred to me to ask. I began to feel that this trip was not haphazard after all, but very well planned by spirit.

One week later . . .

I looked out of the cabin window after we landed in Ivalo. Conditions had been much the same on our survey trip the year before. It was cold, minus 10 degrees, and the landscape was buried under three feet of snow. Hannele met us at the hotel and quickly informed us that Dahilok wanted to have a meeting in Ivalo. We needed to finalize and determine the rest of the arrangements for the final ceremony at Kilpisjarvi. During the survey trip, I had informed Dahilok that Yokar would perform several initiations with the participants before the final ceremony where he would be involved.

Hannele, Manos, and I grabbed a cab to town. Ivalo was about thirty minutes away. We were to meet in a popular restaurant bar, so we arrived early to be sure of getting good seats for the four of us.

We waited about twenty minutes before Dahilok showed up. The wait was worth it. He arrived in full native Saami regalia. He wore long blue tight-fitting pants with a beautiful embroidered pattern along the seam. The pants ended with elf-like boots handmade from skins (which I learned later from Dahilok were reindeer hide). They were bound to his legs by a swath of brightly colored red cloth. His outfit was topped by a bright red and blue tunic, also heavily embroidered and girded by a tooled leather belt sporting his scabbard and knife and some small leather pouches hung by leather thongs.

I felt honored that he would come dressed in what was clearly his most sophisticated cultural attire. The outfit was finished by a most unusual kind of hat, which bore all the same colors and embroidery as the rest of his clothing. It was something like a court jester's cap. It seemed to fit around his head snugly, but four corners jutted outward and drooped down. It was hard not to stare. My pleasure at seeing him again overcame my gawking behavior. We all shook hands as he joined us at our booth.

Dahilok began to talk casually of many things. Then he spoke about his culture and life as a medicine man in his tribe. As he spoke, three Saami men entered the restaurant noisily and sat adjacent to our booth, behind us and to Dahilok's back. By this time, we were already deep into details about the old shamans who had lived in the area. Dahilok told of the history of the land through the Saami perspective. It was fascinating.

I learned that their lives had been hard and often costly. After the Lutherans came to the North and settled in Finland, Dahilok said, their influence was contrary to native life. There were constant conflicts between them. The shamans in particular became objects of their attacks. The Lutherans instinctively knew that these medicine people would not give way so easily to the ways of Christianity.

Dahilok told of many shamans who were persecuted for their natural ways and often sent to Helsinki for trial and execution. But none of the shamans so charged could ever be actually delivered to Helsinki. On the way, using their magical powers, they would just disappear into the nether world. I thought I saw a small twinkle in Dahilok's eye as he proudly declared this fact.

The men who had sat next to us, who were slightly younger, became quite loud and boisterous. They had ordered some glasses of wine and began to indulge. One of them got up and approached our booth and addressed Dahilok by name in Finnish, totally ignoring the rest of us. Dahilok nodded toward him gracefully but said nothing. As Dahilok continued his story, this man began to sing loudly. It sounded distinctly like a sacred song—one of the songs of the Saamis, I suspected. The man was mocking Dahilok; clearly it was meant as a jibe. I could tell Dahilok was mildly annoyed by their obnoxious behavior.

Dahilok continued to speak quietly, as if to prevent the others from hearing what he was telling us. His voice was so soft sometimes that all of us leaned forward simultaneously to grasp what he was saying. The whole time he spoke, I couldn't help but notice that he was tying a knot in a bit of rope he held in his hands. He would tie it and then untie it, over and over. It was almost hypnotic to watch. I realized it was like a mantra, conjuring the energy.

Another one of the three loud men got up and approached our booth. He also addressed Dahilok by name. It seemed that many people knew Dahilok quite well. This time, the man turned to us and greeted us indifferently, asking in English where we were from. He turned his attention immediately back to Dahilok and began speaking harshly to him in Finnish. My intuition told me that he was scolding Dahilok for talking of such sacred subjects with strangers.

Manos and I noticed after a short time that the three men had begun to slur their words. Yet they had not finished even their first glass of wine. They were all totally drunk—so much so that the restaurant owner asked them to leave! We just looked at each other and smiled. We were sure that somehow Dahilok must have had something to do with it! This obvious display of a shaman's influence was impressive and indicated that even though Dahilok was an elder, he certainly had not lost any ability to take care of himself effectively.

Shortly thereafter, the meeting turned to the details of the final ceremony. When the meeting closed, we were all pleased and confident that everything was well in hand.

Each day, Yokar prepared everyone's system with two initiations, one in the morning and another in the evening. Keep in mind that in Egypt these daily initiations occurred along the Nile at temples specifically designed to evoke the energies of the pukkas in their proper sequence.

As Yokar had explained to me before we came to Lapland, the time of Pisces was nearing to a close, and Aquarius would soon rule the affairs of man. Aquarius is known as the water bearer. The time of water means that, spiritually speaking, the need for hard or solid forms to manage evolutionary spiritual energy and social affairs is declining and the development of spirit can be formless in approach. Hence, the temples were no longer necessary!

As in Egypt, Yokar would utter Vril to stimulate the flow of energy through the various pukkas in the body, preparing for the final experience, when the individual neophyte would be implanted with the future self. Yokar explained that the Atlantean perspective on chakras minimizes the importance of the chakra as a center of energy, as it is described by the Eastern Indians. Instead, these energy zones are identified as windows or pukkas looking upon the light coming from each subtle body realm. For example, it is possible to see how the sunlight coming from an open window might make the window appear to be a source of energy, if the viewer had no experience of the world beyond the window.

Yokar explained that the Atlantean temple training emphasized balancing the disharmony of the subtle bodies that generated the light flowing through each pukka. This was by far the most important aspect of the process, rather than trying to stimulate the flow of energy from them. The quality of the light seen flowing through each window could also help the adept to determine the exact nature of the disharmony. So the adept was first taught how to view the energy of each pukka and then how to transform it and balance it with the rest.

On some evenings, Yokar lectured by the warmth of the inn's fire. He would often draw from the elements around him, such as the fire, as a symbol of the transformation of dense matter into energy, to bolster his lectures on the subject of the subtle bodies, and the completion of the light body and its role in the growth of the Earth.

One night I left the inn to view the Aurora in the nearby forest. As I sat under the stars waiting to catch a glimpse of the special lights, I remembered what Aitar had said about calling the lights by whistling. I whistled once in a while, just to hedge my bets, but I found the concept difficult to believe. Then another special light showed up.

"Hi, Yokar. How're you doing?"

"We are always fine. We thought this would be an excellent time to continue your education."

"What did you have in mind?"

"Now that you have an understanding of the point of origin of all things, it becomes important for you to know the rest of this history. As I have said many times, it furthers you to you know where you are, so you can
choose where to go!"

"I understand."

"With this in mind, we can further describe what has happened here. Your sacred scripture describes how the universe was divided into light and dark. And the world was created. These are simple but coded words.

"The shards or pieces from the first soul crystal (meaning that the first soul had gathered its energy into form as if it were a crystal) are now the 'form' aspect of the Most High God. These fragments of the original crystal remaining after the great expansion, the explosion you are calling the 'big bang,' contained the essence of the original first self. The shards are identical in essence but different by qualities relating to their purpose within the original whole. They are bound together by the flow of Energy between them and the Witness of their higher purpose. They are all acutely aware of the Witness that now resides elevated and beyond their form. These shards are what we call the Stellar Mind. Stellar Mind contains the same properties of the will aspect of the original first self, a free will, with an infinite capacity to expand, grow, and evolve.

"At one point in creation, some aspects of Stellar Mind decided, out of free will, to explore an insatiable curiosity of what it would be like to oppose the urge to grow and expand. So the light was cleaved into two: 'the light and the dark,' or the expanding and the contracting. The light continued to expand, and the 'other light' began to contract, creating a kind of darkness. A split emerged, creating a conscious duality.

"As those aspects of Stellar Mind contracted a little more, they experienced even greater curiosity about the reduction of their form. This curiosity compelled them to contract even further! They continued to reduce and transmute their energy until their vibrations created crude density. It was from this ongoing transmutation that all of the lower denser worlds of the physical plane were created, the worlds of physical matter.

"During this process, a part of Stellar Mind became unconscious and identified with its obsession of physical expression. The experience created a binding quality. The reduction of consciousness brought with it a sense of separation from the whole. Stellar Mind had lost, through its interaction with the reduction of itself, a piece of itself.

"But there was still the Witness aspect. This was the saving grace of the Most High. Through the Witness, the awareness or witnessing of these events maintained the memory of what was the original Stellar Mind before it changed. Through that memory, a sort of hologram of the original Stellar Mind was stored. Even though the Witness remembers all that ever was, there was still one small problem. When a part of the Stellar Mind descended in vibration, creating the lower worlds, it separated from the continuum of higher consciousness and developed a sense of separate space and time in its consciousness.

"Now a real difference existed between the two realms. On the one hand, Heaven is timeless and has no space, and on the other hand, physical existence has space and time. This means that throughout the experience of the descending spiritual energy, Stellar Mind managed to lodge itself in various places throughout time.

"Following the scheme of linear consciousness, parts of Stellar Mind are spread out somewhere in the past, present, and future, scattered all over time-space reality. And there it sits without a way to get back!

"The memory of the Witness of the Most High knew what had been lost, but it knew only approximately when, and approximately where. Much of the solution to this problem was built into this place called Earth." (Here Yokar referred to Earth both as a planet and as a metaphor for the physical plane of consciousness.)

"A deliberation occurred in the realm of the Most High. One being, a Stellar Mind, stepped forward and proclaimed its confidence. "It can be done. There is a solution!"

"Who was this, who was so confident?" I asked.

"One of the brightest spirits in the light realm," Yokar answered. "The name was Lucifer. In the Most High realm, there is no hierarchy. So this great need merged together through the great law of harmonic resonance with the one who had the capacity to fulfill that need. Henceforth, this bright one called Lucifer conceived of the Earth realm. It was a place of spirit and matter where the 'fallen spirits' could learn to return to the whole through awakening experiences.

"To accomplish this feat, a physical planet born of spirit was needed. It would be a living planet. This denser orb would have connections through its being to all the light realm. A great spirit named Tellur sacrificed its formless consciousness to take on the planetary form responsibility.

"Tellur transmuted into the living planet Earth with the help of the Saraphim and Nefilim (angelic elementals of the light realm). During the evolution process, polarized physical life grew upon the surface. Eventually, animal life possessing two brains emerged. The plan was to provide a kind of playground where the spirits could experience their addiction to physical density, but they could understand and recover from the areas of binding influence in their consciousness, all under the supervision of the light worlds.

"Now the stage was set, and the fragments of Stellar Mind that were lost and didn't know how to return were invited to come to the region of the Earth. When the time was propitious, after animal life reached a state of advanced development, it became possible to infuse the consciousness of these Stellar Mind fragments into the physical polarized animal bodies. Thus, the Earth provided hosts for the Stellar Mind consciousness to be in the physical, under supervision in a conscious way, for rehabilitation. These infusions took place on the Earth a very long time ago. In your scheme of time, this is millions and millions of years in your past.

"Three infusions were brought through a neighboring body you call Venus. These spirits were infused into the animal bodies in a great landmass once called Gwandana. A specific region of Gwandana was chosen, a land where the Lemur animal lived, and a land that would later become known as Lemuria.

"The first infusion was a total disaster. The animals died instantly from the shock of greater consciousness. There were a few modifications made at once by the angelic Nefilim. The attempt was made again and they lasted a little longer. But still they died. Then another series of evolutionary changes was brought upon the Lemur nervous system. After this, they could sustain the hosting process. And so it was that Stellar Mind consciousness was brought into the Lemur and it became 'human' consciousness.

"Under the influence of the Stellar Mind, these animals descended from their trees, and began to form into small colonies on the ground. Soon they learned to forage on the ground, a trait quite uncommon for the species. They began to take refuge in caves and ground-like fortifications. Later, portions of the hosting species broke off and entered into the water. Their biology drastically shifted. Most of their hair was lost as they lived around the water. Becoming aquatic, they developed gills and a skin not unlike the salamander. Thus they became the first root race, the Lemurian race.

"There was at this time one rebellious spirit who perceived in this process some simplicity and proclaimed, 'We don't need these limited animal bodies.' Out of his rebellion, many joined in favor of his view. They left this region of Gwandana and went off to a very different region in the Earth, a region that corresponds to what is now called the Indies. (This portion of the Indies is now under water, for the most part.) This region was named the Isle of Pan, after the rebellious spirit.

"Pan and his followers proceeded to create their own forms, for which they were the hosts. Influencing and combining with other polarized life forms on the Earth, they sought to create 'new' unlimited life forms. From this attempt evolved much of your present mythology: the Satyrs, Mermaids and Mermen, Harpies, Centaurs, and Pegasus. All of these creatures actually existed at one time or another and constituted the second root race, or Panic race.

"After many millennia, they grew tired, and requested help from the Most High realm. But despite their plight, they still refused to return to the higher realms. They retreated to the nether world, the astral or Inner Earth, where they exist even today. They represent and are responsible for the elemental kingdoms. They are in charge of maintaining all life on the Earth. They are the Devic spirits. They are sometimes referred to as the ancient ones. Their opportunities to evolve are inextricably entwined with the evolution of the Earth and will now depend largely on Man's progress.

"Meanwhile, back in Lemuria, there was a rising problem. The gender of the Stellar Mind spirit was androgynous, meaning it contained both male and female aspects. But the hosting animal bodies were polarized, having separated male and female counterparts. Something new was discovered. Something called sexual drive, a need for procreation.

"The occupying spirits made a request. 'We want to know more about this energy, this polarized force. We do not understand this. And we want to know more about this joining that occurs.'

"The request was put to the spirit in charge of this region. 'We want to be separated into male and female so that we may infuse into the male and female bodies separately and experience this union. It will teach us about the joining. We believe this will bring greater understanding of meaning of the greater union. It will help us return!'

"That was the seduction. Out of this, the overseeing spirit Lucifer, deluded and desperate to create some positive outcome, finally agreed. The splitting of the androgynous spirits into their male and female components had begun. Afterwards, the individual polarized components were infused again into the polarized animal bodies, and then they procreated.

"During the process of procreation, pieces of the male and female separately went out through the offspring, and that set off a geometric dissolution of the original androgynous spirit. Now, there is little left that is conscious. With the original spirit fractured, its chance of finding itself is infinitely more difficult. Perhaps this will explain why sexuality has become so closely tied to what is called one of the original sins. The original sin comes from this deliberate opposition and defiling of spirit, the splitting of the male and female, the disobedience to God, the Most High.

"In the infinite wisdom of the Most High God, through the process of procreation, conception by Stellar Mind would set in motion the wheel of incarnation. Its purpose was to systematically control the exposure of physical experience to the fractured spirit. It would provide a process of recuperating or regathering all of the individual parts that were lost throughout the chaos.

"In the conception process, the female egg is penetrated by the male sperm. The joining creates a ringing, like a bell. The vibration is felt throughout all reality. All spirits who are involved in this process come to that point of conception. It's again like a window. The spirits look into that window through the light of that experience to determine if that life pattern contains something useful for their growth.

"Stellar Mind, through the memory of the Witness aspect of the Most High God, seeks to find what has been lost. The process of conception and the process of incarnation provide a mechanism to find what has been lost through time and space. Since it is approximate, Stellar Mind will choose multiple experiences simultaneously across all time."

"Yokar, are you saying that there is more than one of me existing across time?"

"Well, let's just say that there are different aspects of your Stellar Mind existing in both the past and the future, as well as here."

"I see. Wow! Now that's a mind-boggling thing to think about!"

"Shall we continue?"

"Yes. Of course."

"To economize and to increase the probability of recapturing its lost pieces, the Stellar Mind projects across your entire band of time many aspects of itself. Through the conception process, all the aspects of Stellar Mind simultaneously seek a particular missing part. It approximates the time and place of the missing part it remembers. Then Stellar Mind creates a mold around the missing part through the physical conception and enters the incarnation. This explains why at birth you are left with a kind of nagging sensation of a hole, a sense of longing or looking for something. You don't know what it is. You don't know where it is. And you don't know if you'll ever find it. But you know the feeling relates to you somehow! And you know you will have a very deep sense of fulfillment, a sense of enlightenment, if you do find it!

"Upon transition, if you have found the missing piece, it will be returned to the Stellar Mind. Only then is that life pattern completed. If you do not find it, the process continues until you do. It's important to note here that when a particular life pattern is chosen, it is not guaranteed that what is sought after is found! Further, karma may also complicate and interfere with matters as well. So, what you are doing now influences both your future and your past! It is not linear, not one-way.

"In the process of descending and manifesting into the lower worlds, you have become responsible for the lower worlds. You are the hope and the extension of the light into the worlds of darkness. As you become aware, you awaken to your true identity, to your true being. You will become aware of your relationship to the worlds around you, to the world that you are creating."

Quiet, I nodded in agreement. This was a lot to digest.

Yokar left me, bidding me a good journey. I was alone again at the edge of the forest, with the quietness and the stars overhead. The Aurora didn't come after all! I was disappointed. I returned to find that almost everyone had gone to bed.

Fire And Ice

On the morning of the final ceremony, we were to go through the "trial of Argna, " a trial of the will. In Egypt, this took place in Saqqara, a hike in the sand, almost thirty miles into the desert. Here it was a snowshoe walk less than five hundred meters from the hotel. When the trial was over, many who had been through Saqqara complained, "Hey, Michael, this is nothing!"

I could feel Yokar's presence buzzing though my body and I called out, "By your own words do you define the nature of this day!"

I knew it was Yokar's words. Everyone was silent as we returned. Later in the afternoon, the bus arrived to take us to our rendezvous point with the Saami near Kilpisjarvi.

We found Dahilok and his wife Aitar waiting for us in the parking area. Aitar took Adam, our son, into their house to wait for our return from the ice.

Aitar's car was full of Arctic clothing. Each participant began to pick and choose the garments and boots that fit the best. Dahilok was busy readying the sleds that would carry the people and their gear out across the ice. There were five snowmobiles. Each snowmobile would pull two sleds.

Many of the men began to help Dahilok place the deerskins on the sleds and tie the goods aboard. Groups were beginning to form, and everyone began choosing which sled to ride in. Dahilok stopped this process and re-organized them by weight.

There was one snowmobile that looked very appealing; I climbed aboard to get the feel of it. Noticing me, Dahilok came to me and showed me the controls. I was designated as one of the drivers. I was pleased that another fantasy would be fulfilled.

Dahilok started the snowmobiles, one by one. The last one, however, wouldn't start. The sun was lowering, and the temperature began to drop rapidly. Several minutes passed without success. I thought to myself, well, you can't expect much from oversized lawnmower engines!

These machines were considerably larger than normal snowmobiles. These were not pleasure cruisers. They were workhorses designed to handle the daily tasks required of trucks in heavy snow country where there weren't any roads. The twin skis in front connected to handle bars jutting out at a slant gave the vehicle the appearance of a truncated motorcycle. Sitting on one felt like straddling a horse.

This dilemma weighed on Dahilok. He was troubled by this failure. Dahilok, a natural man, was uncomfortable with these machines. He preferred a good reindeer-pulled sled any day to a snowmobile!

The failure of the snowmobile meant repacking and reorganizing both gear and people. More precious time would be lost. Worst of all, it meant that four snowmobiles would have to carry the weight slated for five!

We were perched upon a cliff overlooking the lake. Bitter cold temperatures added to the wind cutting across the lake. The view was stark and beautiful and yet ominous. The cliff was very high above the lake. It offered the impression that we were at the edge of another world.

The trails headed down a sharp declining slope onto the icy surface below. There was some last-minute discussion about who was going to drive the snowmobiles. It was decided that Dahilok was to lead the way, with Ron Diana right behind him. I was third in line, with Michael Winn behind me.

Dahilok felt that the slope was too steep for passengers in the sleds. He instructed the participants to climb down to the ice and await our arrival.

Once we were on the ice, the pace set by Dahilok was fierce. One of the initiates named Kim was pregnant, so she rode behind me like a motorcycle companion. We believed this would keep the bouncing to a minimum. The breeze was stiff on the icy lake. The cold cut against exposed skin like a knife. Kim's warm body was very welcome against my backside. A small sign appeared in the wake of snowy dust flying into my face. As the sign grew larger, I could just make it out. An arrow was drawn next to the letters, pointing straight ahead. The sign said, "NORTH!"

I chuckled, thinking to myself, North! This is almost as far North as you can get. We're already on the top of the world!

While we traveled on the lake surface, I kept having a vision of people in the water. It was a ridiculous idea, and I dismissed it quickly as being totally illogical. We had traveled this tundra before, and the ice was ten feet thick, solid as a rock. There was no possibility of breaking through the ice.

Dahilok slowed and then came to a full stop. The lake was fifteen miles across, and we were sitting in the middle of nowhere. Dahilok's snowmobile had overheated. He wanted to let it cool down. He dismounted and made the rounds, tugging on ropes and checking gear, insuring that everything was okay. When he remounted the snowmobile, he couldn't start the engine; it had seized. Now we were down to three snowmobiles.

It was obvious that we couldn't go on with everybody on board as planned. One load of people would need to be left behind while we moved to the base site. We would have to return for them. At once, almost everyone's fears of abandonment started surfacing, but eight people reluctantly got off their sleds and volunteered to stay behind.

As we prepared to go, Hannele turned to me and quietly gripped my arm, saying, "Don't forget me, okay?"

I returned a warm and comforting smile, conjuring as much confidence as I could under the circumstances. "Don't worry, we'll be back real soon . . . Just try to relax."

Moments later, we were off again.

Later, at the base camp, Elaine filled me in about what had occurred among the isolated group of eight left on the ice. She was the mother of three young girls and had been developing herself in the Native American tradition. This was not her first initiation with Yokar, and I doubt her last. Elaine had assessed the distance from shore and considered finding her way back in the dark, but it was miles and miles in all directions of nothing but snow and ice. She knew she would be lost.

She calmed her panic by reassuring herself that Yokar had not dragged her this far only to let her freeze to death on the ice. Her feet were turning cold as the light began to fade. Anxiety was definitely on the rise in the rest of the group, also.

"Bird Man" Sam, as he was called, came with Palma to Elaine's rescue with some extra hand-warmer chemical packets. Sam was a quiet man who had spent much of his energy, in later years, trying to be peaceful and loving. Palma had come to Lapland in hopes of healing her fear of abandonment and assault; she had been mugged and never fully recovered from the trauma. They removed Elaine's boots and began to massage her feet vigorously.

Meanwhile, trouble was brewing with Palma. Once the dilemma with Elaine had ended, Palma realized that more than two hours had passed since the sled train left. She began to panic as suspicions developed about a second ski-doo failure. She wandered from one person to the next, trying to get confirmation that the relief team was going to return.

Hannele suggested that everyone keep moving to keep the circulation going. So Palma and Elaine jumped onto the sled and began to hop around. Palma even started to sing a little.

Joanie had withdrawn from the rest of the group and sat off to the side. She said, "You're not supposed to be talking right now, much less singing and dancing!" Joanie was sincere, and she had come to believe strongly in Yokar's rituals. Dramatic changes were already working in her life from her initiations in Egypt and Greece. She wasn't about to let anyone change that.

Hannele reconfirmed her feeling that everyone should keep moving. Hannele was struggling with her shyness in the group. I surmised that she had played concert piano professionally to overcome her fear of public exposure. She was complex emotionally, openly confident of her knowledge of the Arctic wilderness, and jealously guarded her personal connections to the Saami.

Joanie angrily told Hannele that if Yokar were present she was sure that he would not approve of the breaking of silence. Everyone should be reverent before the initiation.

Sam rushed to Palma's defense, telling Joanie that she had no right to tell Palma what to do under these circumstances. Sam explained to Joanie that perhaps Palma was in a different place and needed something different. Sam argued that Yokar must realize that they were under unusual circumstances and should do whatever they could to get through it. Palma became angry with Sam, declaring that she was perfectly capable of defending herself! Meanwhile, Bonnie had put on a parka belonging to Dahilok to keep warm. She seemed helpless in the wilderness and needed support. Dahilok had recognized this and had responded quickly to her needs. Hannele was unaware that Dahilok had given the parka to Bonnie to wear if she needed. Hannele confronted Bonnie, insisting that she take the parka off, that she should not touch any of Dahilok's personal things. Bonnie became very angry with Hannele for interfering with a personal arrangement she had with Dahilok.

Meanwhile, back on the icy trail, it was Dahilok leading, with Ron behind him and me pulling up the rear. By now darkness was beginning to close in, and I was very concerned. I consoled myself with the thought that the lavo (teepee) would be up, and Dahilok would have a fire going in no time.

Several minutes passed along the ski-doo trail without incident. The trail was marked along the snow-covered ice by small twig-like trees planted in a row, about thirty feet apart. The surface of the ice was rough. During the season's changes, the surface melted to soft slush. The shifting pressure caused the ice to buckle in various places; then, after refreezing, the buckled spots turned into craggy outcroppings. Sporadic snowfalls then covered these icy crags, making them look like small fluffy tufts and hiding their true nature.

At first, when I approached one of these harmless tufts, I thought nothing about driving right over them with sleds full of people close behind. I soon discovered my error.

Apparently, Ron made the same mistake, as he drove over a bump and the sleds behind him bounced wildly. Over my wind visor, I watched as his passengers held on for dear life. It occurred to me that should a rider fall off, the driver would never know it. Even worse, the ski-doo coming up from behind might run over one of them.

Dahilok's speed had not diminished. We raced after him with the loyalty of little ducklings following their mother without question. It was a furious pace. From time to time, I questioned the wisdom of this speed, given that the volunteer drivers were crossing unfamiliar territory and had no experience with these machines. As we went over the outcroppings, I realized that the drivers didn't feel the jostling as much as the passengers did. With these thoughts, I began to slow my speed, widening my field of view and easing my tension. I was convinced that the slower pace would insure the safe arrival of the passengers. Psychically, I felt the sense of gratitude swell from behind me and I knew my riders were much happier.

The pace began to slow ahead, and I had plenty of time to catch up. Dahilok and Ron came to a stop. Shortly I was upon them. As my ski-doo slowed down, I passed a large gouge in the ice on the left. It was full of water! As I climbed off, I told everyone to stay put while I investigated. It turned out that Dahilok had tried to veer off the path to avoid one of those outcroppings. As he entered into the deep snow and slush, a foot of water emerged underneath, capsizing the ski-doo. The gaping hole I had seen was made by one of his passengers, Jan, who fell off as the ski-doo became unbalanced. Jan was now soaking wet. It was urgent that we reach the campsite quickly and start a fire.

My body began to tremble as I stared at the hole. There it was: water, just as I had envisioned. God damn it! This ice is supposed to be solid! My fear quickly turned to anger, and I wanted to confront Dahilok about the accident. Suddenly, I had second thoughts. In light of the situation, I checked my anger and tried to calm down. It was also important not to frighten the passengers. This situation was tough enough without creating dissension in the leadership.

Dahilok reached me on foot by the time I corralled my fury. He began to speak to me in broken English and looked considerably shaken. "You must stay on path! Do not go off trail!" Seeing the impact of this incident on him changed my perceptions. I realized he was an ordinary, vulnerable man, like me!

Glancing back at the ominous water-filled hole, I nodded quickly, acknowledging his request. The urge to blame him for going too fast still burned inside, but I bit my tongue.

He turned and headed back to his ski-doo. He immediately jumped on and continued along the icy trail. Ron revved his running engine and followed close behind him without asking any questions. Pausing for the moment, I watched calmly as they sped off into the snowy distance.

The people riding my sleds squirmed in their positions. They looked at me anxiously as I remounted my trusty metal steed. Waving my arm, I yelled behind me, "It's okay. We're going on, so hold on!" Gently I asked the young mother-to-be, "You ready, Kim?"

"I'm okay," she whispered softly. As the key turned, I held my breath. My ski-doo started without a hitch. My eyes closed with a silent sigh of relief. A deep feeling of gratitude went forth for my mechanical friend, the ski-doo, beneath me. A fond relationship was forming between us; we were growing more and more interdependent. A name for this friend occurred to me: from now on, I would call it Ned. I knew better than to take Ned for granted and expected nothing extra from him. Every simple thing between us was gratefully appreciated. This relationship might seem irrational to an outside observer, but nothing about this whole situation was rational anymore.

The heat coming from Ned's engine kept my legs warm and cozy, lulling me into a sense of security. The purr of the motor also helped brace me for the bitter cold striking me in the face.

Suddenly, the snowmobiles ahead turned sharply to the left and off the trail. My sense of security vanished! For the moment, everything seemed to stand still. Adjusting my weight, I managed to stand up while driving to get a better view. I saw that Dahilok and Ron Diana were definitely off the trail. My heart grew heavy with dread. What was going on now?

Meanwhile, I imagined icy waters enveloping me, placing a final and firm grip of cold around my body. We were all doomed. My jaw tightened and my teeth creaked under the pressure. My desperate thoughts continued, this is nuts! What am I doing here?

As if my snowmobile were on autopilot, I turned my steering handles to the left, obediently leaving the trail. Within minutes, Ned started rolling and pitching, wildly dipping in and out of the slush and water. I forced the thought of what might be happening to my passengers out of my mind. I had my hands full and couldn't think of anything else! Ned seemed to be struggling to lunge from one water hole to the next. All I could do was encourage him on. Then, without warning, Ned leaned severely to the right and began to make a slow but deliberate roll. I tried desperately to help him keep upright, but it seemed hopeless.

I jumped up onto my seat with both feet, hearing the people screaming behind me. Perhaps they thought I was abandoning their sinking ship. I leaped to the left running board as a trick horseman would leap in a sidesaddle stunt. My weight halted Ned's momentum and slammed the metal caterpillar tread underneath to dig harder. Ned began to respond, rolling out to the left. With a final boost to the throttle, Ned rose out of the icy grave in one final thrust. In a flash, we were level again.

For a split second I glanced to the rear, expecting the worst. Broad grins of approval beamed from their harried faces, reassuring me that all my passengers still held on amazingly for their lives.

The worst was over. Ahead lay the Island of Lake Kilpisjarvi. It jutted up from the icy lake like a huge monument. We rounded it to the other side, where the other snowmobiles were stopped. People were standing around watching while Dahilok and Aitar made the camp ready. The lavo was not erected and the food was not prepared!

Everything lay on the ground; all stacked together like a circus not quite ready for the tent raising. Dahilok quickly organized the removal of all the gear and supplies. It was after dusk, and darkness was closing in fast. Looking down at my watch, I said to Yokar, "This is crazy. We should forget the lavo dinner. Quickly set up, and get this initiation over with before it gets any later and really out of hand!"

Yokar quickly replied, "There are still the others to fetch, so be quick about it."

I went to Aitar and told her that I was leaving for the others as soon as my sleds were emptied. She agreed.

I was off to pick up the remaining passengers before anyone could detain me further. On the way, I stopped to find Michael Winn, now a passenger, and Mitchell trying to walk to the camp. Their sled had been overloaded, and they had volunteered to walk the last two miles to the base camp. I told them to hop on, but they declined, saying it was close enough to the base and not to worry. I evaluated their progress and their capacity, and said, "Okay, suit yourselves." I had to be off to fulfill my promise and return for the eight members of the first stranded party.

When I pulled into the area, clearly I was a welcome sight. There was tremendous emotional upheaval going on. Elaine looked at me in desperation. "Thank God! Is it soup yet, Michael?"

I returned with a whisper, "They don't even have the lavo up yet!"

She retorted, "Oh . . . my lord!"

Later some of them told me several had given up hope, readying themselves to die on the open ice. They had been waiting more than three hours. I ushered them quickly aboard the sleds, confirming that hot meals and a warm fire would be waiting for them on arrival. With careful negotiation, I managed to turn Ned and the sleds for a hasty retreat to the base camp.

When we arrived, I was at least partially correct. The lavo was erected and a fire was going. Dinner was in the process of being prepared. Later, Aitar confided to me that they had tried to set up the lavo the day before but the winds were too strong. After several tries that ended in failure, Dahilok and Aitar had decided to wait and hope for the best.

Yokar told me to prepare for the ceremony. I chose a spot not far from the door flap of the lavo, to minimize breathing the smoke during trance. I was later told that Dahilok's dog, who was along for the entire adventure, sat in front of me as soon as Yokar entered my body. Yokar requested those who had chosen to be second-level initiates to come forward first.

Second-level initiates enjoyed greater responsibility and had chosen to enter into a second experience of a ritual—either a solar or lunar initiation. Yokar would align their spirits to the vibration of the Solar Logoi of this solar system directly, using the Vril intonation. The Solar Logoi is the spiritual force and conscious spiritual purpose of this solar system represented by the sun and its radiant energy. This initiation usually brought greater upheaval to the initiates' already turbulent experience. The few that went through it, though, were very happy about their decision afterwards.

While Yokar completed each of the initiations in the final ceremony, Dahilok continued to prepare the sacred dinner inside the lavo. Dahilok and Yokar had apparently worked together many times before; the parallel tasks were accomplished side by side without fanfare. The space was cramped and the air thick with smoke, but the fire felt good. The snowy turf was covered by the deerskins we brought from the sleds. It was a cozy feeling inside. Everyone hugged close to each other and shared body warmth and a growing camaraderie not soon to be forgotten.

As we waited for the Saami's sacred reindeer stew to be completed, all eyes were turned to the fire. Its light threw a mystical play of shadows on the walls of the lavo. How many other nights had been spent, I wondered, with these initiates under the stars in smoked-filled, open-topped tents, reaching for the spirit.

Cups of steaming stew were passed around, and we all savored the tasty brew with enthusiasm. The tension had begun to subside as our bellies found fullness, and the drying warmth of the fire soothed jangled nerves. Even my concern for Jan dwindled as she warmed her wet backside by the burning embers. Strangely, the apparent tightness of the space seemed to ease as we adjusted to our new home in the wilderness.

We were spellbound as Dahilok began to tell adventure stories of the Saami medicine people, while Aitar translated. Near the end, he spoke of the reindeer sacrifice and its importance to the spiritual practices of the Saami people.

Of particular importance was the hind femur of the reindeer. This bone, it was believed, carried the spirit and vitality of the deer itself. The shaman chosen to perform the sacrifice would sever the tendon connecting this bone from the rest of the hind leg at the moment of sacrifice. Dahilok explained that a small rounded bone about the size of a small marble, at the base of the tendon, represented the kernel of energy the deer used for jumping. He went on to say that this bone would help the shaman to make his leaps into the nether world of spirit.

Later, the round bone was hollowed out so that the tendon could be passed through as a beaded string. This was then worn around the wrist as a symbol of status. It displayed the shaman's authority and position in the tribe, and multiple bones worn at the same time defined a shaman's level of experience. Dahilok then looked at me and smiled as he withdrew from his bag a fresh hind bone such as he had just described.

Withdrawing his knife from the scabbard strapped at his side, he said, "It is customary among the Saami that the tribal shaman take the hind bone and perform the ceremony of the splitting of the bone. This is a special ceremony. When it is done correctly in front of the tribe, the tribe is blessed and favored by the deer spirit with a strong and bountiful hunting season. It is done correctly when the bone splits into two equal pieces lengthwise with one even movement."

At this moment, he handed over his cherished knife to me and said, "As leader of your tribe, you must do the splitting and then we will all share the marrow of the bone as acknowledgment of the blessing."

Tears welled in my eyes. I smiled nervously. The honor bestowed upon me was momentous. There was a silent hush around the lavo as I took the knife. Many times certain friends had called me a shaman, but I never really accepted the title officially. This recognition from Dahilok was different. This then became my initiation into the Saami tradition.

I murmured a prayer of gratitude under my breath to God and Yokar for this profound moment in my life. With a deep breath, I placed the blade over the bone, trying several propitious cutting positions and intuitively picking the correct starting line. I lunged suddenly, and the blade plunged through the bone with a resounding crack. The bone marrow lay bare, in two pieces.

The quiet was broken by applause and yelps of joy. "Well, I guess we can all count on abundance in this tribe, eh?" I shouted.

Laughter and cheers joined with the black smoke rising up through the lavo's vent, greeting the night sky. With this event completed, we all shared the marrow, which tasted a little gamey with a slight charcoal flavor.

I had a sudden urge to share something of my sacred space. Around my neck through the whole trip I had carried my own medicine bag. This bag meant a lot to me. My daughter had made it, decorating it with intricate beadwork she learned from a Native American friend. In the fashion of Native American shamans, I had buried within the pouch's folds a claw from a tiger, my power animal, and a talisman from Tibet. My close friend Claude gave both to me, from his spiritual quest there. In addition to these, I also placed in the bag other items and gifts from other important moments in my life.

Without pause, I removed all but the Tibetan talisman and presented the bag to Dahilok.

"To my dear friend and teacher from the North, whose generosity and openness needs further recognition, " I said, "I give you something of my own medicine for your tribe and for yourself."

This time his dark eyes, sparkling by the dance of firelight, became misty. He stared at me for a moment with a sheepish smile and a flash of embarrassment. Placing my hand on his shoulder, I let him know that our relationship was permanent.

Everyone let out a yell of satisfaction, declaring the camp had ended. The snowmobiles were loaded in the dark and the most cautious souls were lined up for the first return trip to the mainland. It was already 10 P.M. Again Ron, Dahilok, and I were the designated drivers. Quickly, I claimed Ned as my trusty traveling companion.

Staring out over the tundra, I wondered about the journey home. No less than two round trips would have to be made to get everyone back to safety. Each leg of the journey at night was an hour at least. My body quaked at the thought of it.

My team was readied as Kim climbed onto the seat behind me.

Soon it was discovered that Ron's ski-doo had no headlight. It seemed this struggle would never end! Dahilok arranged for Ron to be in the middle so that my headlight would give him some visibility.

With farewells and good wishes, we were off like a shot. Leading the train, Dahilok kept the same speed as before. This time, I was in agreement. I tempered my fear and good judgment with the need for expediency. Time was of the essence! The bitter night cold had sheathed the slush into a crunchy surface, so we didn't have to worry about water, at least. Ron's ski-doo weaved back and forth across the trail in front of me like a snake. I watched him with alarm, realizing that there was no way to signal him that he was going off the trail. All I could do was pray that he didn't stray too far.

Our speed was frightening. The average ground speed was about one hundred kilometers per hour (65 miles per hour). By now, my agility with Ned felt natural and his response no longer foreign to me. My fear and awkwardness arising from the lack of experience driving the ski-doo had subsided. The shock of the uneven icy surface rising through the support shaft was now absorbed into my shoulders. This took the pain I had experienced on the outward-bound trip out of my elbows, which ached from the original strain.

Yokar hovered over me to drop some bad news. "Michael, this machine is out of fuel!"

I communed silently with him, yelling, "What are you talking about?"

Yokar continued, "I'm telling you that your fuel is spent. But do not worry for now; we will provide you with the necessary motive power you require to complete this first journey. But you will have to tend to this upon your return."

"Okay. I got it."

Soon after this, Kim picked up on my body energy and leaned forward asking, "What's wrong, Michael?"

"Uh . . . hmm. You picked that up, eh? Yokar says we're out of gas. But he was also quick to say that we don't have to worry. He's going to power us until we get back to civilization."

"Oh . . . really! Well, that's good," she said, not questioning my rather bizarre statement.

We were still more than halfway from the shore of the frozen lake. I prayed that Yokar could pull this off. Yokar, I thought, you're the greatest. What a guy! I really trust you on this one. What other channel could claim this? Yokar made no comment.

By the time we arrived at the shoreline, the other ski-doos were closely following behind Dahilok. Like drivers in some wild ride in Disneyland, we would suddenly rise up over small six-foot-high hills and then take sharp right-hand turns, crossing over small bridges and ducking under roadway overpasses. The passengers began to enjoy themselves at this point since the destination was within easy walking distance.

At first, I thought that our destination was fixed. But after several tries, it became clear that there were three possible hotels that our bus could pick as our rendezvous point. On the third try, Dahilok stopped. Moments later, the bus pulled into the parking lot where we were waiting.

In the front was a small inn with a bar and restaurant. I suggested that everyone hang out in the restaurant while we retrieved the others. Ron ran inside to get a cup of hot chocolate, which we both shared quickly before we dashed off again. Dianne hugged me tightly several times. It reminded me of a scene from a war movie; where the hero goes off on some mission not knowing whether he will ever return. It was difficult to conceive that we still had another round trip to make across the ice. Clearly I was exhausted. I could feel the others wondering and worrying about us.

Dahilok was anxious to get going. I called out to him that gas was a problem. He simply nodded, and we were off again, backtracking over the hills and dales of the back roads of the little village.

We stopped at a gas station, but it was now 11:30 P.M. The lights were out, and it was closed. We whizzed into the back entrance of another gas station, but it also appeared closed. Dahilok pulled up to the pump and stared at it for some moments. Ron and I pulled in after him and waited to see what he was going to do. It was confusing. Dahilok seemed troubled somehow. Ron looked at me and I at him.

Then, without warning, Dahilok jumped back onto his ski-doo. I called out a question about the gas situation. He just waved a small hand gesture to me, and we were off again. I fell silent, hoping he knew what he was doing,

Dahilok and Ron moved too fast away from me and managed to do a turn uphill. In a split second they were gone. The last thing I wanted to do was get lost in Kilpisjarvi. Had I not caught sight of the lights flashing behind a small house on the hill, my ski-doo would still be on the ice today! Soon I caught up with them, but I had taken a different route and ended up facing them both behind what turned out to be Dahilok's brother's house. Dahilok looked very perturbed and mumbled angrily at me for coming in the other way. One of the problems with ski-doos is that there's no reverse gear! There was no place to turn my Ned around easily.

Dahilok was scrounging around for something. His brother's garage was wide open; piles and piles of unnamable garbage were strewn about, and Dahilok was rummaging through all of them. Ron and I looked at each other wondering what the hell was going on. We were both beginning to feel irritated by his antics and apparent disorganization. Confronting him would have been useless since he didn't speak English very well. Out of my frustration, racial judgments began to emerge in my mind. Ah, this is what you get when you deal with natives, I thought.

At that moment, Ned's engine began to accelerate and I knew very well what that meant—my engine was empty. It was Yokar's way of letting me know they were releasing control of the machine. As the engine quit, I looked up at Ron and we both looked at Dahilok. He returned our glare with an equal indignance. He muttered something in broken English about the fact that I should have gassed up at the last station. My arms went into the air in total disbelief.

We finally saw what Dahilok was looking for. He had found one can of gas but we needed a way to get the fuel into the tank. Dahilok was planning to siphon the gas; some sort of tube would be needed. Forty-five minutes into the search, Dahilok located a short piece of plastic hose good enough for siphoning gas. After several tries, however, he couldn't get the fuel to travel the full length of the hose. He was about to quit in total frustration when I stood on the seat, holding the can high above my head. We needed gravity to help. It worked. But to my amazement, Dahilok dumped the entire can of gas into my Ned. I'm sure Ned was very thankful, but what about Dahilok's ski-doo and then Ron's machine? Now we weren't much better off than before: I had gas but no one else did!

Dahilik took on the challenge of turning Ned around in the midst of all the obstacles lying about the snow-covered yard. With some fancy maneuvering, he managed to get Ned facing the right way again. We blasted out of his brother's place like it was a space station, traveling down the lake slope, back to the second gas station.

Parking Ned off to the side, I watched as Dahilok returned to the pump. Again he seemed to suffer from confusion. He looked really stymied. I called out, thinking he might need some cash. The pump at the station was set up to take business after hours with both a credit card and a cash machine controlling the automation. It was the first time that I had seen such an operation. Dahilok waived off my offer by showing me his cash in hand.

Then it hit me. "Oh, my God," I blurted, "maybe he can't read!"

Ron looked at me incredulously as we realized the worst. The pump was arrayed with all kinds of buttons and directions describing how one or more of the pumps could be operated, but all in Finnish.

Dahilok inserted his money cautiously into one of the cash machines and watched as it gobbled the money. Red lights flashed everywhere, but we didn't know what they meant. We tried pressing several buttons randomly, hoping to stumble onto the right combination. The combinations were too complex. Nothing seemed to help. Dahilok was obviously at a loss, as bewildered by the machines as we were. He appeared to appeal to me for help and I realized that, in "civilization," he was out of his element.

Ron said, "Now what are we going to do?"

His nerves and concern for the others sitting out in the middle of the frozen lake with a very small supply of firewood were beginning to show.   I shrugged. I had no idea what to do.

Just when all seemed lost, Yokar said, "Michael, press the following buttons in the order that I tell you. First, press the flashing red button on the pumping device you want to use. Then press the first and third buttons on the currency machine. Finally, press the fourth button under the flashing red button on the pumping device. You understand?"

"Got it."

I followed his instructions, and, as if by magic, the red light went to a steady glow and relays clicked on, releasing the flow of fuel to the handle. We were home free.

"Yes!" I yelled out, gesturing with my clenched fist. Ron was beaming. Dahilok's stress vanished as both tanks filled with the precious fuel. Then mine was filled to the top. All of us took a deep breath. But there was no time to waste. Dahilok's face reflected the urgent need to return for the stranded people.

In a flash, Dahilok was gone. Ron and I looked at each other, completely astonished. Dahilok had grown so accustomed to us that he forgot we had no idea of where we were or where we were going. We had no alternative but to wait for him to come back. It didn't take very long for Dahilok to realize we weren't following him. In three minutes, his ski-doo rounded the corner. He made a full circle, and we followed him down into the winding back paths obviously made only for ski-doos.

Soon we ended up on a precipice overlooking the lake. I slowed to a stop, trying to anticipate the next move. Ron, just ahead of me, had also stopped. Dahilok pulled up to the edge where the cliff and the blackness met. Then he simply disappeared! Ron slowly pulled up to the edge, trying to see where Dahilok might have gone. Ron was having second thoughts—what if Dahilok had crashed somewhere at the bottom and couldn't warn us! From my vantage point, I could do nothing but watch. Then Ron suddenly disappeared!

As I nudged Ned closer to the edge of the cliff, I worried that the edge was somehow treacherous, swallowing my comrades without warning. Peering out over the edge, I strained but could see only blackness hanging above the icy surface. The black void fell far below me, far and away, stretching on endlessly, bottomless. Then dimly, unbelievably, I could see two small sets of red taillights bobbing up and down, one after the other, entering into that ominous darkness far below me. Taking a breath, I pressed hard on Ned's throttle and prayed for dear life that I could cling tight. Down I went, accelerating faster and faster. Only after I reached the bottom could I tell I had been traveling almost straight down. I didn't want to think about what this looked like in the daylight!

"Jesus, Dahilok!" I cried.

My speed was about 75 kilometers an hour (about 50 m.p.h.). As the trail loomed out of the darkness at me, I began to notice markings letting me know I was on the right track. The darkness folded in behind me along with the cold. Were it not for my deep and abiding concern for the people, I don't think I would have had the courage for this adventure. My imagination filled me with visions of the remaining people lined up in body bags on the ice the next morning. Discussions from one policeman to another about the victims and their fate on the ice mingled with the whistling of air past my ears. Gritting my teeth, I murmured, "We'll make it, I know we will!"

At one point, Dahilok stopped his ski-doo and ran back to me, demanding that I press the throttle. "Harder," he screamed, as he demonstrated a deliberate pressing on the throttle switch.

I nodded and complied, although my speed increased only to 95 kilometers per hour (about 60 m.p.h.). We arrived to find everyone inside the lavo more or less asleep. It was two o'clock in the morning. The fire had just about expired, and Aitar was beginning to consider taking down an old rotted tree for more wood. But everyone was happy and eager to get back. Hannele gave me a hug of gratitude, and Manos shared his fear for his life for the first time. As everyone began to pack up their things, Manos shared his vision of doom as we stood outside the lavo.

"For a while there, I really began to think something had happened and you weren't coming back for us. Our firewood was low, and the temperature had dropped. I was really worried because the food was running out as well. We all knew there was an old dead pine tree nearby that we could cut down, but given the trouble with the ski-doos, I wondered if the chain saw we had with us would work!"

I assured Manos he could relax now. A warm bed and a stiff drink were not too far away!

We returned to the parking area where the bus was waiting with the others on board and were greeted with a triumphant cheer. The ordeal was finally over. The restaurant was closed and refused to let Ron enter for a victory drink. As he boarded, we promised each other a good stiff shot upon our return to the hotel in Ivalo. The bus ride was quiet and most found some relief through sleeping. When we arrived, Ron and I separated from the group to seek out the all-night burger joint close by. For the next few hours, we shared our harrowing experiences over a couple of beers and some greasy reindeer burgers.

Yokar has given me another great lesson out of this solar initiation. We had to let go of the structure and guided path of the Nile, the pomp and circumstance of the temples of Egypt. In its place, we had to embrace the icy cold and formless energy of the Arctic void. Together we learned to call up the fire of courage and face our icy fears. Together, we learned to balance the energies of fire and ice.

The Cornerstone Revealed

I began to suspect there was deeper meaning to all this globe-trotting and initiation. We struggled to reach strange and difficult places. We watched Yokar alter time and space at each site and experienced his influence as he altered the nature of our being through the infusion of strange and unknown forces. Yet there seemed to be something else, something missing.

Yokar explained that invoking the ancient rites in Egypt, Greece, and Lapland would successfully awaken people to other realities and therefore strengthen them and the Earth. He explained that the Earth needed help to pass through this transition and that we needed help to pass with it.

He admitted on several occasions that it was an experiment. Changing so deeply and so rapidly was a great shock to our systems. The outcome was not certain. Yokar declared that the time was short and that we had not been properly prepared over time by our previous spiritual leaders. He went on to say that they had chosen to keep us ignorant and dependent, with our attention diffused in order to maintain their own sense of power.

Because it was not transmitted, the truth had been eventually lost, and their heirs were left ignorant save for some fragments that became distorted through myths and legends. It is through no fault of their own that present leaders are incapable of helping the multitudes. So we need to change—fast—if we are to adapt to the changes that lie ahead. Yokar perceived that these initiations would offer a way to accomplish rapid changes but with some psychological risks.

I understood all that and accepted the challenges, but the grand view of the coming changes, the "new" Earth he was talking about, represented something of a mystery to me.

I felt a deep responsibility to all these people wanting to go through these experiences. I loved and respected them for their courage. The people who are drawn to this great experiment are compelled by some personal or impersonal irresistible force, unknown to me or themselves, strong enough to overcome any of their personal fears or resistance.

They're still excited about undergoing these transformations, even though the side effects have turned their lives upside down. Surprisingly, many have repeated the initiations to further enhance and intensify their experiences. In many cases, the resulting emotional upheaval is tremendous and has divided relationships, created havoc with careers, and presented a range of physical disturbances, such as headaches, feverish heat, twitching muscles, and nausea. But they continue, all for the sake of spiritual insight.

Many times I asked Yokar to teach the ancient practices of the great temples in Atlantis, but he had serious misgivings. The modern people of the "sixth root race," as he referred to us, are not impeccable and strong like warriors, but weak in the heart and mind. We are terribly diffused. Having scattered our consciousness, we don't possess the force of inner will or the tenacity needed to command the Life Force properly. He often stated that it was doubtful we would or could learn to change quickly! He consistently refused to talk of the temple training. I argued that the training could increase the skills of initiates to manage the flow of the Life Force. But he wouldn't hear of it.

Even with the information and training so far, many pieces of this amazing puzzle didn't fit completely together. There seemed to be something else implied and not yet revealed. I kept looking for an adequate overview that I could explain to the others and to myself. Often, initiates wanted to understand more about what the initiation process was actually doing to them. Yokar decided to explain a little further.

"The problem," he said, "is always that spirit cannot violate free will. In order to stimulate growth, there must be freedom for the individual spirit to choose; otherwise, the wisdom falls undigested to the side. We therefore seek those places in the Earth where the nervous system of the Earth intersects, presenting feminine and masculine vortexes.

"These sites offer opportunities for your rigid perceptions of time and space to be disrupted. The opportunity exists to offer those who are present a joining. The past and future combine together with the present in an altered state of being. The individual gets a chance to join with his 'future self' experience. That experience is actually merged with the present experience. A learning from this is hoped for, but the shock is great. The free will is not violated because: first, the information offered is from the individual's own experience; and second, this change must still be invited by the individual. This 'short cut,' if you will, has been devised to offset the dismal rift in your development."

Early one evening, while I was sitting on the front steps of my home, Yokar appeared and joined me in my appreciation for the setting sun. We both gazed at the light, waiting for the approach of dusk.

"The luminous orb never ceases to please the eye, eh?" Yokar said.

"You know what I'm looking for, don't you?"

"Perhaps!" he responded.

"So, will I catch the Clear Light today?" I asked.

Yokar turned his gaze back toward the amber-red sky, staring directly at the rays of the sun. "You'll have to be clever and fluid like quicksilver. Then perhaps you will manage it."

Clear Light is something rare, magical. It comes only twice in a day, according to Yokar, once at dawn and once at dusk. Some people have seen a bright green corona or flash, identifying its approach. I knew something about the green flash before Yokar came along. I thought it was a myth until some friends who professionally photograph complained about its effects!

One day, Yokar pointed it out and explained its significance. He told me that the light contains a set of coordinates, or guiding information, sent out to all conscious sentient beings. It is like an invitation from all that is light in the center of the cosmos. The invitation is planted in the pituitary, inside the crystal chamber, allowing the recipient an opportunity to go to that spiritual banquet and learn from all those great beings present. The coordinates will also define the next task on the spiritual level. I have been searching the morning and evening light for it ever since.

"Yokar, I keep getting the feeling there is more to this grand scheme of yours. What is this all about? I mean, where am I headed, leading all these people into these experiences? I feel I am half blind, leading other blind people! I know there are obvious benefits, but to what end?"

"Many times we've heard an outcry that ancient knowledge is all but fantasy from the singers of myth and legend. Even you believe it's gone and forgotten, lost forever to the bogs and quagmires of volcanic ash. It is unfortunate that all of you continue to repeat yourselves!"

"You mean through incarnation, Yokar?"

"Yes, essentially this."

I rose to this challenge and defended efforts to learn from the past. "Yokar, with the exception of what you've given to me, I believe we have no choice but to pick through the bones, relics, and dust of the Earth to piece together a history that was barely recorded."

"Oh, it was recorded!" Yokar said indignantly.

"Forgive me, but even you have said that much of the record has been buried far beyond the reach of our present abilities to recover it."

"That may be true, my son, but I was referring to physical records. Your perception of the concept of recording information is limited to stone or paper and now electrical energy. You cannot conceive that others might've developed other means in which to keep accurate records."

"I'm not sure I understand what you mean. What other means?"

At this point, Yokar stood with his back to me, hands formed into fists upon his hips. As he carried on with me, he gazed steadily at something distant, deep in the astral kingdom. My inner vision fell short of any long view beyond the physical realm. The astral distance looked very much like a dense fog bank.

Yokar's emanations sometimes obscured any other view anyway. It was much like trying to catch sight of a bird as it flies into the sun! I believe it was the effect of his light, stretching and magnifying reality around him. When I asked him once about the ability to see into the astral distance, he said it required painstaking practice to focus the consciousness.

Suddenly, I had the idea he was trying to measure words, weighing how much he wanted to reveal.

"What is it, Yokar? What are you trying to tell me?"

"I told you once of Thoth's attempts to raise the African tribes of stone into conscious awareness, in hopes of recreating or resurrecting the culture of Atlantis."

"Yes, I remember."

"The great capstone, the cornerstone of the great temple at Gizeh was to be the tool for this. But, unlike the Taoi stone, it was not just an instrument used for controlling the weather, to supply the energy and power to run a civilization. This was a great Ruune stone, a library crystal, providing a gate to the Akashic Record. In Atlantis, we used the Akasha (the property of the astral field that records consciousness) as our permanent storehouse of knowledge, a remnant of understanding given to us by our benefactors from the constellation Orion. The written record was simply temporary. Our knowledge and understanding were actually stored with stones like this one, not physically inside the stone, but held within the binding energies of its lattice structure, interdimensionally. In other words, we discovered the way in which the Akasha stores sentient experience. The Ruune then becomes a key to a gate of the Akashic Record. As I mentioned to you before, this particular gate is the gate of Tahaar."

"Yokar, you seem to speak of this in the present tense. Are you speaking metaphorically now?"

Yokar ignored my question. "I said to you that Thoth had set into the great Ruune a limit. This limit protected the uneducated man from himself, should the uninitiated or profane attempt to access the Ruune unwisely. The Ruune was constructed to self-destruct, to vaporize, should any time pass without the proper access."

"Yes, I remember. What a loss! It's too bad that this had to happen."

"I said it vaporized; I didn't say it was gone from existence!"

"What! What do you mean?" I blurted out. "Where is it then? If it's not gone, is it hidden somewhere on the Earth?"

"Not exactly. But it has not left the Earth!" Yokar said mysteriously.

"Is this some sort of riddle that I'm supposed to solve?"

"No, not exactly. You have asked what this is all about. So now the time has come to explain to you what we have in mind.

"What we are attempting to accomplish here with you has been attempted before. During the time of Babylon, in a city called Shinar, a unique tower was constructed to geometrically harness the energy of the gate of Tahaar. The result was a disaster after the gate had opened. Those people were not prepared and were driven from the tower because they were uninitiated to the keys of the gate.

"When the gate opened, it filled them with an infinite flood of information that altered their consciousness and drove them mad. Hence, it was reported that they returned from the great tower babbling nonsense. The others quickly surmised that building the tower had angered their God somehow. A legend emerged from this event describing the Tower of Babel and the divine intervention and punishment of Babylon for its arrogance in attempting to reach God!

"Using knowledge handed down through the Egyptian priesthood, an Ark was constructed by the Israelites to carry the codes of conduct from their leader Moses. This Ark of the Covenant provided a perfect vessel for their most treasured possessions, but it also provided a direct intermediary key to the gate of Tahaar. The downfall of Jerusalem at the hands of Titus signaled the Ark to be carried off to Tannis, and it was lost through many secret exchanges into antiquity.

"Two thousand years before your time now, during the cycle of Pisces, another attempt was made to access the library Ruune. This was the third time in twenty-five millennia since its construction. The attempt was undermined and the secret was hidden amongst a secret sect or remnant from a brotherhood of disciples living deep within the mountains of Gaul, in a place called the Renee Le Chateau. They were given charge of this chalice of knowledge from a man called Jesus of Nazareth."

"But wait, Yokar, I don't get it. Where is the gate of Tahaar now?"

"The gate is no longer physical in terms that you understand. The great Ruune vaporized and transformed into its energetic form and is held suspended in the Earth's atmosphere as an energy matrix. This is the 'cup of grace'!"

"So this 'gate' has been hanging up there in our atmosphere for all these thousands of years and no one knows about it?"

"Many of your religious leaders have known about it over time. Many secret schools have known about its existence too, but no one has been able to access it."

"Why is that, Yokar?"

"The great Ruune has a kind of combination locking mechanism, very much like one of the locking mechanisms that you use now. This crystal needs all of the combinations 'sung' to it at the same time in order for it to open properly. These were called the 'keys to the kingdom' by the Nazarene. Jesus was referring to the combination required to access the great Ruune of Tahaar. He passed those keys over to each of his disciples."

"So, that means there are twelve keys to the Ruune!"

"No. The combination that Thoth programmed into the Ruune is the same as the sacred intonations of Vril; that is, there are seventy-two keys. Contrary to popular opinion, there were a total of seventy-two disciples close to the Nazarene. After the breakup of the followers of the Nazarene, the disciples split up and found refuge in many other parts of the world. Twelve found their way into Gaul and founded the brotherhood of the Templars."

"So, if the disciples of Jesus had the keys, why didn't they access the Ruune when they had the chance?"

"They did, but for only a short time, long enough to determine the most important points on the Earth to position themselves before they separated. They also raised their individual wealth considerably, donated by nobleman and the clergy of the church in exchange for their help. Even the pontiff high priest knew of their knowledge and swore allegiance to support them, knowing full well what they possessed. The church had hopes that the Templars would pass the keys on to the church for safekeeping, at some point. The ability to intonate Vril was eventually lost, and many of the Templars were killed for political reasons. The secret of Renee Le Chateau fell into myth and mystery."

"So, the great Ruune is again lost to mankind!"

"Not exactly."

Yokar's eyes twinkled as he smiled at me.

" What are you saying?"

"You have been chosen as keeper of Tahaar. You bear the emerald ring. It is in your hands now! With our help, you may be able to access the great Ruune, but you will also need the cooperation of others. You will not be able to accomplish this task alone. You are meant to be the guide. You will need others who can master Vril and speak the keys of the great Ruune together to open the gate of Tahaar and to the Akashic records of knowledge and wisdom."

I was speechless. My throat closed and tears welled into my eyes. I felt unworthy and the burden was great. Fear filled me with paralysis.

Yokar tried to console me. "Michael, there is no need to be alarmed. You have much more training to complete here. There are also the others you will have to train as well. We will help you accomplish these things. This is why we are here now, to assist you in your desire to be gate keeper!"

My tears fell in a gushing torrent. "Yokar, I can't believe this is happening."

"It's what you asked for, is it not? Did you not say to the Most High, you wished more than anything to bring your brothers and sisters to awareness, that you would sacrifice everything for the sake of their righteousness? The Most High has seen your compassion and loves you for it. It is also why you were found worthy to be high priest and the bearer of the Ring of Tahaar. Let him who asks, be given unto."

"Yokar, will there be enough people who want to fulfill all of the keys?"

"It's difficult to predict human behavior, my son. First they will need to respond and then they will need to be trained. All we can say to you about it is this: many will be called but few will choose!"

Epilogue

"There is no power; it's an illusion!" Yokar declared.

My mind was so busy trying to assess the problems at hand that I hardly heard Yokar's words. I was in Egypt for the first time. There was a tourist glut and hardly any rooms at any hotels anywhere. My frustration and anger mounted toward the hotel manager, as he told me again there was no room for some of my participants. I felt so powerless. I was in Egypt without any resource of authority. My ground operator wasn't accessible, and his aide was insecure and pretty useless. I just wanted to scream at the top of my lungs.

"That's ridiculous!" I said quietly to Yokar. "There is power everywhere. These people certainly seem to have the power to upset my plans for this tour!"

"Oh, I know you believe deeply in a struggle for power, the wielding of influence, of your will over another. You also think there is apparent power in your machines and also with your third order atomic devices, a terrifying power."

"Yeah, you bet," I returned defiantly. "So you're trying to tell me, this influence I'm experiencing right now, the manager's denial of available rooms, is my imagination?"

"Have you forgotten that you make your own reality?" Yokar chided.

"No. I haven't forgotten. But this is different. His reality is conflicting with mine. It's his creation, not mine!"

"Michael, this man is just doing what you ask him to do."

"What! I don't recall ever having asked him to give me a hard time."

"Just the same," Yokar went on, "your unconscious energy communicates the intention to create conflict. You expect to have trouble here, don't you?"

"Well, yes. But . . . "

"And you prepare yourself for the worst that can happen, right?"

"But Yokar, this is Egypt. You see how they operate."

"So, if you perceive that they are unconscious, then you must be ever so much more clear, so that you can help them to be as clear as you need. You must not blame them for your unconsciousness."

"How do you get that I'm unconscious?"

"Because you do not anticipate their unconsciousness and blunder through, waiting to be undermined by their unconscious activity. So is this not intent to be unconscious on your part? Who is more unconscious, the one who receives the unconscious commands or the one giving them?"

"I don't understand, Yokar."

"Try to see it this way. If there is a wall before you, and you, not noticing that it obstructs your path, run smack into it, do you blame the wall for unconsciousness and accuse it of purposefully obstructing your path? You could, of course, do that. But what purpose would that serve?

"Is it not true that, if you were paying more attention, you could anticipate the presence of the wall, avoiding the impact well in advance? You expect too much from the wall. It's doing what it's supposed to do. The wall creates an obstruction for whoever needs it! You want it to behave unlike a wall, to step out of your way. You make the wall responsible for your lack of preparation and attention. Yes?"

"Yeah. I see your point."

Yokar always made sense. It was terribly irritating sometimes. At times, his advice and insight became sharp nails on which I had to chew. I knew he was right, but I didn't like it. But he never seemed to mind when I got angry at him.

Yokar continued, "The problem of this misconception about power starts early, in childhood really. You are taught from this time on that power is something to be obtained. The parenting structure reaches into the child's mind and wields influence, the kind of influence that sets limits on the expression of the child. This limitation elicits a response from the child to overcome the limiting factor on its experience. The child then launches onto the path for attaining power over the influence."

"Do you really think a child thinks about power that early?"

"Absolutely! Not only in the dwelling place of the parenting structure, but it is propagated throughout the educational programs in all of the institutions all over the globe. Is it not inscribed onto your halls of learning, 'Knowledge is power'? So, it is taught that you should gain as much knowledge as soon as you can. Why, in order to be smarter? No, because you will have power. So, everything is based upon how much power you can accumulate."

"But Yokar, I think that they mean gaining knowledge gives strength to the children and to the country. It is often believed that the children are the country's best resource."

"And for what reason? To add that knowledge to the rest of the resources of the country to make it strong and well defended. And that strength is what you call power, as you understand it!"

"It's not absolutely clear to me that this is true, Yokar. Can you give me another example?"

"Why, yes. We think that in your consciousness you will agree that there is a direct relationship about how much power you have and how much currency is jingling in your pocket. Yes?"

"Perhaps," I said quietly. I still wondered where he was going with this.

"You immediately combine the level of authority and influence together with large amounts of currency. You believe that these go hand in hand. Is it not said amongst your brothers and sisters: 'if only you had enough currency, there would be nothing that you couldn't do.' This translates to power. In your beliefs, you feel that doing or accomplishing something is relative to power and influence. Yes?"

"Yeah, okay."

"In order to attain great wealth, you need to have knowledge. You will use knowledge to acquire wealth and with the wealth acquire influence. To have influence in your life is power. Yes?"

It was clear to me what he was getting at. But I felt a resistance to quickly agreeing.

"You wield influence on your environment. You set the tone for your life by the use of currency. The entire world economic system centers on the use and exchange of currency. This is merely a symbol. The currency represents your energy! Your energy and everyone else's pooled together form a tangled web of trading.

"Much of the delicateness of the Earth, and all those who live upon it, relates to the maintenance of what is called the balance of power. In truth, this term is really meaningless. There is no balance of power. There are only those who wield a lot of power making sure that others do not have enough! In other words, we are talking about supremacy."

"Yokar, how did we get from trying to get ahead in life to controlling the world?"

"Follow me for a moment and you will see. After much of the cultural and institutionalized training is completed, then begins, in a subtle way, the learning of 'the ropes'! This term relates to learning how to play or have influence over others to avoid abuse.

"Much of the trouble with the affairs of human beings arises from the three sources of abuse: helplessness, inadequacy, and insecurity. These feelings come from the belief of not having enough power to avoid the experience of abuse. When you don't have enough power, you fall down the ladder of the pecking order, a barnyard term that defines a hierarchy of negative influence. In other words, the ones who have the power to influence get to abuse the ones who do not. The rate of your grumbling relates to how much abuse you have to experience from others above you."

"Yeah, like this hotel manager!"

"Do you see? You see him above you. It is the case of all forms of abuse. It always comes from those who are above, elevated beyond your sphere of influence, beyond your control. So, they apparently have more power than you.

"You see, it is this sense of elevation that you seek. The attaining of power gives you a sense of elevation over others. It is a sense of importance. Here is the key, my boy. If you wish to obtain lots of power, you are already truly powerless. You are starting with no value, a sense of worthlessness. By obtaining this so-called power to influence, you try to compensate for the worthlessness. If you are feeling adequate, and sensible about your worthiness, there is no desire to wield influence, to reign with power over others."

"So there is no benefit to having any kind of power?"

"You will find that if you lust after power you will suffer."

"Suffer how, Yokar?"

"There is a range of afflictions. One is fear. When you scramble to obtain power, you will always be afraid you're going to lose it. One will come along who is more powerful than you! In Earth's recent history, men of power wielded weapons that projected explosive bolts. They were called slingers of the gun."

Chuckling to myself, I corrected Yokar. "You mean gunslingers, Yokar."

"Well, yes. This was the authority when there was no outer law to prevent negative behavior. The amount of law governing an individual depended on how much the individual enjoyed an expertise in handling this weapon.

"You can see, then, that wielding this sort of influence promotes fear. In the same way, if you have a lot of power, there is a field of fear around you. All those who come in contact with it are affected and run away because the feeling of fear catches them. Perhaps you should extend this concept to the entire Earth. There is an ongoing attempt to gain power, wield influence, and control the environment. This effect generates a field of fear around the entire globe, making the atmosphere precarious and volatile. All this in an attempt to gain a sense of safety!

"If you take a gentle stroll down one of your streets at night, and a thief comes to you, beats you, and steals your money, it could be said that the thief has more power than you because, first, the thief has successfully abused you, and second, the thief has taken your money. So, the thief has robbed you of your power, apparently. The sense of power lost gives rise to its dual complement: a sense of victimization. If you believe in powerfulness, you must also believe in victimness. They are but opposites of the same coin."

"So how does this fit in with creating your own reality?"

"Nothing can come to you, in your experience, that you do not invite. All of your experience is your own creation, even the abuse.

Although many say that they believe in this principle, they will ignore it when it comes to children. Children, it is said, are innocent. They are truly victims of many forms of abuse. But I tell you that this cannot be, if the original principle is true. Applying this truth means that even children are responsible for their experiences that they have chosen their life patterns, whatever they may bring. Nothing occurs that has not been previously structured. There are no accidents! Therefore, whatever occurs is intentional, and whoever is involved belongs there, at the scene of the experience."

"I know—all the things that have happened to me in my life, that I have learned to hate, I invited."

"Yes, my son."

"But it seems to me that this principle suggests that it's all some sort of facade here. Fake. Is this true? Is anybody being really hurt?"

"Good for you! You're beginning to understand. The answer to that is no! Try to imagine for a moment. You purchase tickets for a play. You enter the theater, and it is cut off from the outside world. The characters unfold their story of woe. And if they're good, you will be convinced of their storytelling. You will observe the tragedy, the apparent abuse of one character of the other, and you will be outraged.

"But at the end, you will leave the arena where this play has unfolded. You will exit once again to the outside world and perhaps you will linger over a cup of coffee, talking about the greatness of the performances. But you will not suffer from the tragedy of the characters, for their tragedy is only a myth, a myth for entertainment purposes. You know that the actors are not the real characters. You know that they will depart from this arena stripped of their role as the characters. You know that they will carry on with their real lives between performances.

"But I tell you, you do not see this with your own life! But it is identical in all respects. Every day you get caught up in the roles of the characters and believe that all this is true harm. These experiences are all staged for the purposes of your learning. The real quality of your being goes unharmed. Your true essence continues to evolve as the Stellar Mind, the true actor.

"You are not what you do, not what you think, and not what you feel. There is an intrinsic worth to your being, without any of this. You don't have to do anything for it. The virtue of your presence is significant enough. You are just that. A worthy creature, alive!

"You have managed to learn from a range of difficulties, through the pain, conflict, confusion, and misconceptions that yielded the awful 'truth': you are somehow less! With your insecurity, a doubt has arisen. In time, many fantasies were created about your lack of worth. You have come to believe that you must compensate for this deep-seated 'truth.' This process begins when you are a child. Acts of others, in ignorance, can diminish the innate being. This is the illusion. But as a child, you do not have the acquired experience to refute it."

"Yokar, how do we fight and overcome this devastating illusion?"

"These 'real' wounds define a tragedy about the self. From these brief interludes of 'abuse' you come to derive a mythology about yourself. A ring of fear develops around the mythology. This becomes a ring that you will not cross. You suffer from the effects of the mythology of the 'flaw.' You will not dare to approach and pass through the ring of fear to discover the real truth of yourself. You believe that if the ring of fear is penetrated, then the awful truth will be confirmed. Yet the effects of the endless mythology are just as devastating on your life, operating as though the flaw were real!

"You must consider this. The mythology means to die a thousand deaths. The truth, on the other hand, impacts on you only once. The terrible result of not facing your true self is that it leaves you open to further abuse.

"Believing in the mythology, you never find your true strength or worth. So, when the lie is perpetuated and the power is apparently wielded, it ties perfectly into your belief. You come to accept the idea that one can have power and another one cannot. You lose the sense of equal opportunity. All of your culture is based upon these ideas: your lack of energy; your financial laws of supply and demand; that there is not enough to go around. These concepts contribute to the ascension of power barons. Then you become manipulated as victims. Naturally, you don't want to be in the category of the have-nots, so you struggle for power. This is called the world of affluence."

"Yokar, you're talking about the American dream!"

"Yes. We believe you refer to it as having a chicken in the pot and two travel machines in your dwelling and so on. It is a wonderful dwelling for which you can hide in your fear. This should tell you something. It's a dream!"

"But Yokar, everybody wants to live the good life, everybody wants a slice of the pie."

"That's not the problem. What we question is the sacrificing of the being for the sake of it. You live and struggle for the dream and you forget about the importance of the being. Your teachers don't talk about that. They talk of the importance of knowledge and the acquiring of skill. They continue the sense of unequalness in you. 'Well, Johnny can do it, too bad you can't. You can't do it, you're out!' It means that you will play in the grease, whereas Johnny will have the greaseless opportunities for affluence. He is one of the chosen. So you will develop a sense of unequalness, a sense of inadequacy, and a flaw! You will develop a false sense of influence, of power.

"The false-self or ego starts early. You might say at the beginning, out of the birth canal. The child emerges to find that the parents cannot accept the child as he or she really is. The child would be crushed by this disappointment and not survive even the first few minutes of life. But its amazing power to create its own reality steps up and saves the day. The real self creates instantly an ego-self, that possesses all of the superficial qualities that the parents are looking for in the child. In a brief but unconscious moment, the child transforms and suddenly is everything the parents ever wanted.

"The false-self begins its first task on the Earth, to preserve and protect the undefended spiritual true-self from the original perceived flaw. It will do so by providing the first line of defense, a divided consciousness. One level is conscious and the other is the unconscious. We will refer to this unconscious part of the false self as the babysitter. The task of the babysitter is to protect the spiritual true self or baby at all costs, even if it means opposing the will of the conscious part of the false-self, the ego-self! Meanwhile, the ego-self will continue the facade of acting as the "improved" model of the true self.

"The problem with the unconscious babysitter and the ego-self aspects is that they are both cut off from reality and the natural flow of life. It is because they are distortions of the natural flow of life. A new problem arises from this separation from reality. The ego-self becomes paranoid and begins to believe that it is the true self. A greater importance is attached to its survival, creating a new alliance with the unconscious babysitter to help it prolong its existence. The growth of the spiritual true self becomes a real threat to the false self in its totality. So the ego-self and the unconscious babysitter work discretely to suppress the growth of the spiritual true self. The true-self retreats further into the recesses of oblivion, and its original flaw becomes a legend that forever haunts the ego-self until death occurs.

"There can be an awakening. The dreamer, or the ego-self, realizes that its reality is only a dream, and it begins to suspect the truth about its origin and the reality of the true self. At this point, the ego-self enters onto a spiritual path. And through the spiritual work develops the longing to merge or rejoin the true self. The unconscious portion of the false self, the babysitter, feels betrayed. It begins to resist any growth of the ego-self by secretly undermining any spiritual efforts and by reinforcing the ego-self fear of the alleged true-self 'flaw.' Through negative experience in the physical reality and constant badgering, the unconscious babysitter tries to convince the ego-self that it's hopeless.

"The alleged 'flaw' grows unchallenged by the ego-self and becomes 'real.' The support of that belief in the flaw by the ego-self will eventually affect external physical reality, distorting reality in accordance to nature of the flaw. The ego-self will create and draw to it a similar reality, an illusion of true physical reality. Others of a similar ego-self and alleged true-self flaw mutually support this illusion of physical reality. The ego-self tries to compensate for the flaw by adding superficial qualities and strengths to the ego-self facade and by influencing others to agree to the false values, which attribute a strength and power to the ego-self facade.

"Once again, this is an illusion. Those who wish to control promote this illusion. But this is not power. This is separateness. This is negativity. And, as I have said to you before, negativity is self-limiting by nature. It has to be empowered or fed. It is not self-generating. It cannot survive on its own. It must survive by parasitic action. It thrives on the weakness that presents a lack of positive action."

"I don't understand. What do you mean by that?" I asked.

"Where it is necessary for action, and that action does not occur, then lethargy, apathy, or non-action feeds negativity."

"I see."

"When there is a sense of inadequacy and worthlessness, there is a sense of isolation, of separateness. You feel alone. Cut off. This creates more fear, and hopelessness. The belief is that tyranny shall prevail. Always, when there is an atmosphere of tyranny, there lingers, huddled in the nooks and crannies of life, a glimmer of hope that goodness, pleasure, joy, and light will come to save you.

"Is it not true that, in the hour of need, you ask, 'Where is our savior to take us away from this tyranny?' It is an ancient call. When you believe this way, you create more separateness. You go on to deny the truth of your being.

"The ones who terrorize you, who tyrannize you, do so because you allow it! You throw your sense of power to them, through your acknowledgment that they are greater than you. You subject yourself, prostrate yourself before them saying, 'Do not hurt me. I will do anything you ask. Just be kind to me.'"

It was very hard to accept Yokar's words. I didn't like the idea that I could or would throw away my power. I found myself cringing. I wanted to see myself as strong. Not cowering. Not prostrated before the powerful ones, not in that way. Yet, I could feel my fear of the big men, the boisterous men, and the bullies. And I could feel my fear of the hard women, the ones who could castrate you in the blink of an eye. I began to drop my resistance. I knew he was right.

Sensing my opening, Yokar seemed to offer compassion as he continued. "I say this to you because this belief is still so strong in you. You complain of tyranny and you ask for a savior. But you are unwilling to rise up and claim your own worth. You say, 'How can I do this? I cannot do this! I need a stronger one, stronger than I, who can do it for me. One who can save me from this abuse.'

"Have you not noticed that the ones who do come, the ones answering to the call of savior, are short-lived with their influence? They are made separate because saviors always call on your worth and proclaim your strength. But it is too much for you. You refuse to admit that it could be your strength and your worth that could save you. And you reject and annihilate them so that you can worship them and forget what they have taught you.

"Tyranny has no recourse if you refuse to allow it! It has been proven many times in your own history. When tyranny goes too far, you revolt. The consciousness rises among the masses and becomes strong. The masses rise up in revolt and, in one fleeting moment, they say no! Tyranny whimpers 'oh, okay.' Then it limps off into the darkness. There, it waits. It waits for you to become lethargic and apathetic. Then tyranny sneaks back in, looking for the opportunity to seize another hold when you are weak.

"Tyranny knows that you are inexperienced at ruling yourself. And it knows that you will forget how bad it really was. You are really looking for one who will lead you, one who is stronger and greater. You would prefer to be ruled, benevolently, in the end. Tyranny will come to fill the bill! But you are the only one who can rule your roost. You are the only one who has that capacity and that worth. But this is direct knowledge and no one can give it to you. You must discover it yourself.

"Michael, the secret to true empowerment is in the acknowledgment that all things work together. All things cooperate to exist side by side. The flow of energy is accessible to everyone and everything. There is an abundance of this flow, and all can partake of this to their fill. There is no power. There is only cooperation. The true self and false self must join again in cooperation, if the total being is to prevail and grow.

"When you assert yourself for reasons of power, there is a great terror that enters your heart. In the concept of wielding power, there is the fear of abuse. Do you realize that as you cling to power you put yourself in danger of learning how to abuse? You will become one of the abusers. Is this what you want? Do you want to become one of the thugs here? Do you want to perpetuate the tyranny, to keep the darkness fed and flowing?"

"No, Yokar."

"You must discover the truth about yourself. You must enter the myth of the flaw that you fear will surely destroy you. You must risk looking at yourself honestly, so that you will know the true value of yourself. With this knowledge, you will come to realize the truth about the dream and about the ones who weave it.

"You will come to understand that all reality exists by virtue of cooperation. It is a greater family of life. No one thing possesses any power. The strength is in the union of all. Do not lust after the power; it is only a dream, a great seduction to turn you into a thug, to make you an abuser. There is energy in that for sure. But it makes you more complicated. It complicates your ability to open, to accept yourself and to accept abundance. "Know that what you aspire to be, what you admire and feel envious of in a hero, exists already in your own being. You cannot see the value of a thing without possessing that value in yourself! You cannot embrace that which you do not know! So, do not create a creature of myth that will save you. Reach into yourself; pull yourself up, save yourself. For the sake of the Most High God."

* * *

After many years of study with Yokar, I've come to understand that some people realize that the deal on Earth is to claim the divine heritage, claim the soul, and pick themselves up by the bootstraps and proclaim their divine connection. They realize it is possible to declare the absolute reality of the Most High Realm on Earth through their own divine action.

It is really up to us to manifest God through our behavior. We need to demonstrate the will of God in the physical plane by complete surrender to the flow of divine energy, the Life Force. I believe it is our true mission to accept and merge with the flow of the Life Force, cooperating with all of our being toward the continuation of harmony with all things, all existence. We should not wait for a savior. We have been shown many times that only we can save ourselves from the destructive influence of our illusions and disharmony.

We can begin to trust each other and ourselves so that we can live in love and support of the Life Force streaming toward us from the Most High God, but only if we make fully conscious the betrayer who lives inside. Now I can see the meaning of Judas' role in betraying Jesus. He was a metaphor. The truth is that we live with a part of us, the unconscious false self, the babysitter that works to undermine everything that we want to do. It will betray us even as it smothers us with a kiss of good intention. The babysitter loves you very much and yet it does not want to you grow. In the end, the ego-self and babysitter will have to let go of their illusory sense of power.

*   *   *

"In view of all of this, Yokar, what about the original split in the being? How will this spiritual work and these initiations help the issue of the original separation?"

"There is yet another initiation planned for you, a most holy union that will form the basis for the Congress of Heaven and Earth, a third initiation, that will be used to combine the male and female aspects together again and combine the true-self and false-self. This act of joining the split false self and the male and female energies will create a vibration of androgyny, which will resonate to the higher level of the spirit, the true self.

"This vibration will act on the separated being through the law of harmonic resonance. In accordance with the inverse alchemical law—as it is below, so it shall be above—this congress of individualized consciousness, in its male and female aspects, will help call forth the memory of all of the lost parts and speed your spiritual recovery, that you may finally come home to Stellar Mind and the Most High realm."

Glossary

Acolyte

An individual who has undergone some initiatory practice and rite of passage ceremony that defines the beginning of some spiritual work or purpose.

Adept

An acolyte who has perfected some spiritual training to the level of mastery.

Akasha

[Indo-Aryan] An aspect of the astral kingdom that exhibits a sticky or retentive quality; it is sensitive to all conscious vibrations from sentient beings and stores all experience within its infinite field of influence.

Akashic Record

The total record in the astral kingdom of all sentient experience throughout all time and existence.

Argna

[Atlantean] (As in the trial of argna.) The force of inner will, not to be confused with the concept of ego will.

Astral Projection/Soul Travel

The act of separating or freeing the actual living conscious awareness of the astral subtle body from the physical body.

Atlantis

A lost continent thought to have had its existence in the region of the Atlantic stretching between the Azores and the Bahamas in a time before the flood accounts. Legend suggests that it was destroyed by submersion beneath the sea.

Atlantean

A citizen of the continent of Atlantis; an artifact or some concept relating to the culture of Atlantis.

The Babysitter
The unconscious reactive portion of the false-self that seeks to resist any growth of the conscious false-self, or ego consciousness.

Bioenergetics
An energy arising from the body, consisting of a bio-plasmic field; relating to a system of therapy designed to arouse the biological energy through emotional/body stress positions.

False-Self
The aspect of true-self divided into an ego consciousness, separate from the true-self, made up of two components; an unconscious protector called the babysitter and the conscious ego, the common ordinary consciousness believed to be the actual true self.

Gizeh Capstone/Taoi Crystal Aspect
An object that belonged to the apex or upper portion of the Great Pyramid temple at the Gizeh plateau; of legendary origin, defining the great master crystal, an aspect that was capable of controlling the weather. It was programmed to respond to incantations of the Atlantean sacred Vril and used for early initiatic practice in the temple.

Channel
A psychically gifted person who exhibits the property of communications with elements or beings from dimensions of reality other than the known three dimension of physical existence.

Chakra
[Indo-Aryan] An energetic source of energy shaped like a lotus blossom flower. Seven centers of energy are said to exist within the subtle nature of the human body closely relating to the nerve plexuses.

Chamber of the Greatest Ordeal
The lowest chamber of the Great Pyramid; there, priest candidates were tested through trials of the will and courage.

Diva/Deva
[Sanskrit] A divine energy aspect of God, also relating to ancient elemental energies of Nature.

Elemental

[Norse] An energy spirit, usually found in the three lower realms of Nature: plant, animal, or mineral. Said to be responsible for the care and maintenance of the respective kingdoms.

Golden Ratio

The golden section emerges from a geometrical play of proportions involved in generating the geometry of the pentagon within the geometry of the circle; this property relates to the mathematical value of phi, a proportion that is defined by the ratio of the larger part, as is to the whole, being equal to or similar to the ratio of the smaller part is to the larger part; defines the ratio of 18:19; a quality that symbolizes unremitting activity.

Grand Canal of Light

A path of initiation along the Nile River, set in various temples that relate to various aspects of human spiritual development through the human body.

Gate Keeper

This term defines the role of a spiritually gifted individual or high priest who is responsible for watching over the threshold or gate between two dimensions of existence.

Guide

A spiritual friend or guardian having charge to teach or assist from the realm of spirit, with the contracted embodied spirit on the Earth, not to be confused with angels. (note: Guardian angel—a misnomer—can mean guide .)

I Ching

Also called the Book of Changes, ancient oracle of yarrow sticks developed by several Chinese philosophers to teach the player the way of the Tao or natural order of things.

Initiate

One who has passed the rites of initiation, through some spiritual process of development or arcane school of esoteric training.

Lemur/Lemurian

Of legendary origin, relating to the first animal creatures to host human consciousness involving the first, second, and third root races of Man; Lemurian relates to the fourth and final successful development of bipedal aquatic humanoids existing in a small region of the continent of Gwandana located in what is now the Pacific basin.

Ley Lines

Lines of energy that stretch across the surface of the Earth in a giant web-like pattern or grid, forming the Earth's nervous system. Places where two or more of these lines intersect is considered a power point or sacred place.

Libation

An elixir used during high ritual ceremonies of spiritual initiation and transmutation, usually involving one or more of a number of psychoactive substances in addition to wine and honey, olive oil and milk.

Life Force

A primordial creative conscious and intelligent energy that springs forth from the origin of all things, the elemental building block of all the worlds both visible and invisible. It flows around and permeates and binds all living things together, containing three aspects: male, gemale and neutral components.

Lunar Initiation

A sacred and ancient rite of initiation performed in Greece relating to the night side elemental forces or psychic agents governed by the lunar phases of the Moon.

Medium

[late 19th and 20th centuries] A psychically gifted individual capable of communicating with another dimension of existence beyond the third physical dimension; usually attributed to the belief in spiritism or communicating with the souls of the deceased.

Most High/ Most High God

[antediluvian] The prime creator God, or First Soul, Father of Fathers, the All and Everything, complete and divine origin of existence encompassing ten universes.

Neophyte

An individual who has just begun to enter a spiritual path of personal development; a beginner.

Negative Attractive Force

[Atlantean] The female aspect of the Triune Stream or Life Force, describing a pulling in or vacuum-like action, a sucking force or contraction movement.

Neutral Force

[Atlantean] The neutral energetic element arising out of the combination of the male and female forces of the Life Force, the creative substance from which all things are formed, the mother of all fundamental forces of Nature.

Pan

Mythological creature, part man and part goat, demonstrating strong sexual images in mythology. According to pre-Flood accounts, Pan was the leader of a rebellion during the third infusion of Lemurian root race, and established a separate island colony of half-breeds of all different species. Pan subsequently transformed himself and his followers into the Deva Kingdom of Middle Earth.

Positive Propulsive Force

[Atlantean] The male aspect of the Triune Stream or Life Force, defined by a radiative expanding nature, pushing-out quality, dynamic active principle.

Ruunne Crystal/ Gate of Tahaar

One of several passages or gates designed to provide maximum security to the great library of Atlantis. The Ruune is manufactured as a geometric key; when activated by Vril, it opens the three-dimensional consciousness to the fourth-dimensional holographic record of Atlantean knowledge and wisdom. The records are stored in the medium of the Akasha in the Astral Kingdom.

Ring of Tahaar

A legendary ring made of Emerald which when worn signifies the bearer to be a high priest and gate keeper, in this case the keeper of the Tahaar gate, one of the access points to the Atlantean library.

Solar Initiation

A sacred and ancient rite of initiation performed in Egypt relating to the invocation and awakening of the light forces within the body.

Solar Logoi

[esoteric] A conscious spiritual force or radiant energy believed to represent a pattern of spiritual development involving the transformation of fear, residing in the solar system and specifically located in the body of the sun.

Stellar Mind

[Atlantean] The form aspect of the triple mystery of the Most High realm, defined as energy, form, and witness; essence differing by qualities relating to the original matrix of the first soul.

Subtle Body

[esoteric] The imprint of the structure of consciousness onto the Life Force operating at various vibrational aspects of existence, that relate eventually to a physical incarnation.

Taoi Crystal/Power Crystal

[Atlantean] Fire dwelling, a perfect crystalline matrix manufactured by alien super science, capable of storing sunlight and starlight and converting that energy to a standing neutral wave from which many other forces could be derived, such as heat, light, motive power.

trance

An altered state of consciousness, often characterized by robotic behavior or strange forms of communication; a condition of great mental concentration, resembling sleep, often induced by narcotic substance or otherwise mystical or religious fervor.

Triuune Stream

[Atlantean] The three aspects or triple force of the creative force of Life.

Tellur/Tellus

[Sumerian, Greek der, TELLUS] The spirit that was transformed into the living planet called Earth, for the purposes of transmutation and transformation of stellar minds caught in the physical vibration of contraction.

Unnamed Organ

A secondary expression describing the organ responsible for

original forms of communication before the use of the vocal chords and voice box, unnamed because the original Atlantean term is unreasonable for the average individual to speak.

Vril

[Indo-Aryan] The sacred language of spirit speaking from being, the communicative link to the elements, used by the Atlantean priesthood for all rituals and ceremonies.

www.ingramcontent.com/pod-product-compliance
Lightning Source LLC
Chambersburg PA
CBHW052012070526
44584CB00016B/1717